Palgrave Macmillan Studies in Banking and Financial Institutions
Series Editor: **Professor Philip Molyneux**

The Palgrave Macmillan Studies in Banking and Financial Institutions are international in orientation and include studies of banking within particular countries or regions, and studies of particular themes such as Corporate Banking, Risk Management, Mergers and Acquisitions, etc. The books' focus is on research and practice, and they include up-to-date and innovative studies on contemporary topics in banking that will have global impact and influence.

Titles include:

Kimio Kase and Tanguy Jacopin
CEOs AS LEADERS AND STRATEGY DESIGNERS
Explaining the Success of Spanish Banks

M. Mansoor Khan and M. Ishaq Bhatti
DEVELOPMENTS IN ISLAMIC BANKING
The Case of Pakistan

Mario La Torre and Gianfranco A. Vento
MICROFINANCE

Philip Molyneux and Munawar Iqbal
BANKING AND FINANCIAL SYSTEMS IN THE ARAB WORLD

Philip Molyneux and Eleuterio Vallelado *(editors)*
FRONTIERS OF BANKS IN A GLOBAL WORLD

Anastasia Nesvetailova
FRAGILE FINANCE
Debt, Speculation and Crisis in the Age of Global Credit

Dominique Rambure and Alec Nacamuli
PAYMENT SYSTEMS
From the Salt Mines to the Board Room

Catherine Schenk *(editor)*
HONG KONG SAR's MONETARY AND EXCHANGE RATE CHALLENGES
Historical Perspectives

Andrea Schertler
THE VENTURE CAPITAL INDUSTRY IN EUROPE

Alfred Slager
THE INTERNATIONALIZATION OF BANKS

Noël K. Tshiani
BUILDING CREDIBLE CENTRAL BANKS
Policy Lessons for Emerging Economies

Palgrave Macmillan Studies in Banking and Financial Institutions
Series Standing Order ISBN 978–1–4039–4872–4

You can receive future titles in this series as they are published by placing a standing order. Please contact your bookseller or, in case of difficulty, write to us at the address below with your name and address, the title of the series and the ISBN quoted above.

Customer Services Department, Macmillan Distribution Ltd, Houndmills, Basingstoke, Hampshire RG21 6XS, England

Financial Boom and Gloom

The Credit and Banking Crisis of 2007–2009 and Beyond

Dimitris N. Chorafas
Member of the New York Academy of Sciences

First published 2009 by
PALGRAVE MACMILLAN

Palgrave Macmillan in the UK is an imprint of Macmillan Publishers Limited,
registered in England, company number 785998, of Houndmills, Basingstoke,
Hampshire RG21 6XS.

Palgrave Macmillan in the US is a division of St Martin's Press LLC,
175 Fifth Avenue, New York, NY 10010.

Palgrave Macmillan is the global academic imprint of the above companies
and has companies and representatives throughout the world.

Palgrave® and Macmillan® are registered trademarks in the United States,
the United Kingdom, Europe and other countries.

ISBN-13: 978–0–230–57811–1 hardback
ISBN-10: 0–230–57811–X hardback

This book is printed on paper suitable for recycling and made from fully
managed and sustained forest sources. Logging, pulping and manufacturing
processes are expected to conform to the environmental regulations of the
country of origin.

A catalogue record for this book is available from the British Library.

Library of Congress Cataloging-in-Publication Data

Chorafas, Dimitris N.
    Financial boom and gloom : the credit and banking crisis of
2007–2009 and beyond / Dimitris N. Chorafas.
        p. cm. – (Palgrave Macmillan studies in banking and financial institutions)
    Includes bibliographical references and index.
    ISBN-13: 978–0–230–57811–1 (hardback : alk. paper)
    ISBN-10: 0–230–57811–X (hardback : alk. paper)
        1. Credit – United States – Management. 2. Risk management –
United States. 3. Secondary mortgage market – United States.
    4. Financial crises – United States. I. Title.

HG3751.C462 2009
332.10973—dc22   2008046498

10 9 8 7 6 5 4 3 2 1
18 17 16 15 14 13 12 11 10 09

Printed and bound in Great Britain by
CPI Antony Rowe, Chippenham and Eastbourne

"It got drunk and now it's got a hangover."
The George W. Bush analysis of Wall Street's troubles
(The Economist, 9 August 2008, page 4)

Contents

Part III Bank Supervisors and Their Remit

List of Tables

List of Figures

Preface

If finance and economics were art, then what has happened with the subprimes since July/August 2007 would have been a museum piece for future generations. But this is not the case. John Maynard Keynes once said economics was the *dismal* science, and dismal indeed, thanks to Alan Greenspan, is the aftereffect of the second big bubble in a decade.

Standard & Poor's, the credit rating agency, says that although more people and companies will have to seek refinancing in 2008, the real peak will not occur until 2011 to 2014. By all likelihood, well before that time the Tamerlanic destruction of the Western financial system by *collateralized debt obligations* (CDOs) will be exceeded by an even greater eruption, that of *credit default swaps* (CDSs). Lessons have therefore to be learned from the CDOs and proactively applied to the CDSs and *auction-rate securities* (ARSs), Wall Street's most recent hangover.

* * *

The present credit crisis, banking crisis, and crisis of confidence began with the mid-2007 housing bubble in the United States, punctured by the failure of the subprimes mortgage market. This was serious enough by itself, but it has been exacerbated by the highly geared way mortgage banks, commercial banks, investment banks, and other institutions have securitized and sold shaky home loans.

Mortgages were pooled with other mortgages, the pools were sliced into tranches, and marketed worldwide as bonds to banks, pension funds, insurance companies, hedge funds, and other entities generally known as "investors." No one knew, or cared to know, how much risk was embedded in them and how this exposure could be managed if the worst comes to the worst.

Packaged as *collateralized debt obligations*, which are obscure and complex structured instruments, the senior tranches of pooled subprimes were rated by independent rating agencies as AAAs, the highest credit grade, though everybody knew they were junk bonds. Banks even used them as regulatory capital, while regulators looked the other way till CDOs become the eye of the credit hurricane. In this swindle:

- Low-net-worth families bought houses they could not afford, because of the American dream of house ownership: "Your house is your castle."

- All sorts of bankers exploited these people, not just for the fees but also, and mainly, to create raw stuff for new and highly risky financial products which offered fat bonuses.
- Banks bought other banks' CDOs they poorly understood, overleveraging themselves from thirty times up (the now defunct Bear Stearns) to forty times up (Lehman Brothers).
- Then they restructured and diced the mortgage-based securities, and kept on selling them to still other American and European banks as well as a long list of investors.

Supervisory authorities did not react when the same shaky mortgages were repackaged ten to thirty times over and sold on. These transactions have been even more leveraged than happens in the futures market for energy, where a barrel of oil is bought and sold up to fourteen times before it is even pumped out of the ground. The Federal Reserve, the Securities and Exchange Commission (SEC), and other regulators watched this happening in the false belief that markets correct their own excesses.

Rather than reining in the markets, Greenspan's Federal Reserve welcomed everybody's high gearing because the new homeowners were happy, the Bush Administration looked favorably at the redrawing of the financial map, and the global sale of CDOs brought home pounds, euros, yens, and yuans to fill (at least temporarily) part of the US current-account deficit.

But all pyramiding eventually comes to an end. Everyone profited so long as US house prices rose; when the subprimes bubble burst, homeowners as well as the banking industry were in deep trouble. Subprimes, however, which have been the source of the 2007 crisis, are becoming yesterday's event – even if their fire still burns and its range, depth, and duration are unknown. The International Monetary Fund thinks that their black hole may eventually hit $1 trillion.

No bank's trade or portfolio position could ever have zero risk, because it is on risk that the financial industry builds its fortune. Risk however must be steadily measured, subjected to limits, controlled, and audited.

The problem today is that not only the management but also the supervision of banks, particularly of big banks, is wanting. In a televised interview on 1 April 2008 Dr Henry Kaufman, probably the best living economist, said that:

- *If* some banks are too big to fail,
- *Then* they should be very closely supervised.

Kaufman proposed that for the twenty-five to thirty US banks and other financial institutions too big to fail, there must be a special regulatory authority which steadily watches over them, to assure the stability of the financial system. The same principle should apply to the big banks of Europe, Asia, the Pacific Basin, and the Americas.

Speaking at the Harvard Club on 9 April 2008, Dr Paul Volcker, the respected former Federal Reserve chairman, said that financial crises usually don't happen in the absence of underlying economic problems, adding that the financial system had failed the market test. He also stressed the point that current events had shown available risk management tools don't work. Volcker's thesis is that:

- The world's economy needs a global regulatory solution;
- Regulated institutions are in better position to face crises than unregulated ones;
- A country cannot inflate its way out of current economic problems; and
- Lack of stability in the dollar is likely to hurt the world economy.

"I consider this the biggest financial crisis of my lifetime," George Soros stated during an interview in mid April 2008. The well-known hedge fund investor and philanthropist added that this had been a *superbubble* that had been swelling for a quarter of a century before it finally burst. Subprimes and CDOs, however, are far from being the only issues threatening to tear apart the world's financial fabric.

The origin of the oncoming 2008/2009 crisis, which risks making the subprimes just a rehearsal, is different. It relates to the subprimes bubble only in the sense that mortgages are loans, and banks have been using all sorts of loans – particularly corporate loans – as raw material for *credit default swaps*, a totally unregulated market. This will be the second and bigger credit superbubble.

A CDS enables seller and buyer to separate the risk of default from other features of a loan or bond, like its interest rate. Theoretically, therefore, it looks like an insurance policy protecting against the risk of default. But in practice this is an instrument for speculation on credit quality, which has been inventoried in a big way in the portfolios of banks and plenty of other investors, and is now turning into toxic waste.

Not only are CDSs far from being the perfect hedge, but also $50 trillion of them are outstanding. By comparison, the weight of real loans behind them is tiny. CDOs are highly geared instruments, concentrated among a few big players, and their unravelling has the power to tear apart the global financial system. According to market rumors, Bear Stearns had $10 trillion of CDSs. Had it gone bust the whole US banking industry would have collapsed.

A tandem of big losses involving global banks can also be lethal. With the economy in the downside, experts think that an abundance of financial problems may bring the default rate in the US to 3 percent, which will represent a cool $1.3 trillion in red ink – four times the sub-primes abyss up to the present time. Neither can anybody assure us that the rate of bankruptcies will not be higher (it is already 12 percent for US subprimes), or that losses will not snowball throughout the financial industry because of its high leverage and very thin capital base.

The lagged effects that the credit crisis has had on the overall global economy are just beginning to appear. The news is that American bank regulators are preparing for an increasing number of potential bank failures. Other jurisdictions will follow. What was first seen as a US subprimes problem is slowly being understood to be a global crisis, with big financial entities becoming the spearhead of a Second Great Depression.

* * *

My thanks go to a long list of knowledgeable people who contributed to the research that led to this text. Without their efforts the book the reader has on hand would not have been possible. I am indebted not only for their input but also for their constructive criticism during the preparation of the manuscript.

Let me take this opportunity to thank Lisa von Fircks for suggesting this project, Keith Povey and Mark Hendy for the editing work, and Vidhya Jayaprakash for the production effort. To Eva-Maria Binder goes the credit for compiling the research results, typing the text, and making the camera-ready artwork.

DIMITRIS N. CHORAFAS
VALMER AND VITZNAU
JANUARY 2009

Glossary

Understanding the Jargon Used in Modern Finance

Over the last few years the financial and banking industry has developed not only a bewildering array of sophisticated, esoteric, complex, and risky instruments but also a jargon labeling and describing them.

   The objective of this glossary is to help the reader's understanding by explaining briefly the terms used in this text. The definitions have been deliberately kept simple but accurate. A more detailed explanation, along with examples, is found in each chapter where the term is used. In alphabetic order:

Adjustable-rate mortgage (ARM)   A mortgage with an interest rate at a lower level for an initial fixation period, but thereafter changed by the lender to a higher level.

Alternative-A (Alt-A)   A mortgage risk category considered to fall below prime but above subprime credit rating; Alt-As are done with little or no borrowed documentation.

Arbitrage   Exploiting price differences for identical financial products or other commodities, on different markets.

Asset-backed securities (ABS)   Securities backed by a pool of assets, such as loans, which serve investors claims through payment streams.

Auction-rate securities (ARS)   Debt instruments, typically municipals, other state-sponsored and corporate obligations with a long-term maturity, for which the interest rate is regularly reset through an auction.

Basel II   The new capital adequacy framework for commercial banks established by the Basel Committee on Banking Supervision.

Carry trade   Borrowing funds – or taking positions at a low interest rate – then reinvesting at a higher interest rate, typically in a different currency.

Collateral   Assets pledged or transferred as a guarantee for the repayment of a loan; also assets sold under a repurchase agreement.

Collateralized debt obligation (CDO)   A structured financial product based on a pool of assets (debt instruments) which serves as collateral.

Collateralized loan obligation (CLO)   *See* Collateralized debt obligation.

Commercial mortgage-backed securities (CMBS) *See* Mortgage-backed securities.

Commercial paper (CP) A bearer debt security used for short-term borrowing, typically issued as revolving paper of maturity between 1 and 360 days in Europe, or between 1 and 270 days in the US.

Conduit A special-purpose vehicle purchasing receivables and financing such purchases by issuing commercial paper.

Consolidated balance sheet A balance sheet obtained by netting out positions (loans and deposits) in the aggregated balance sheet of the parent company, its divisions, and its owned subsidiaries.

Credit default swap (CDS) An agreement in which, against a fee, the protection seller agrees to pay the protection buyer a compensation if a specific credit event takes place, such as default or late payment.

Credit derivative An instrument separating a credit risk from an underlying financial transaction, transferring this risk to an investor. The CDS is an example.

Credit enhancement (CE) A contractual agreement aimed at enhancing the credit quality of a securitized portfolio, securitization transaction, tranche, or other position.

Credit rating A scaled classification of the creditworthiness of borrowers, or of the securities they issue.

Credit risk The risk that a counterparty will be unable to fully meet its financial obligations, because of default or unwillingness to pay; counterparty risk is a wider concept of credit risk.

Credit risk transfer (CRT) A technique which theoretically enables banks to reduce their concentration of counterparty risk by passing on unwanted exposures.

Current account (at national level) A balance of payments account covering all transactions in goods and services, income, and current transfers between an economy's residents and non-residents.

Debt security A promise by a borrower, or issuer, to make one or more payments to the lender, or holder, on future dates at a specified interest rate.

Default risk The risk of loss when, because of insolvency, a borrower no more fulfils its obligations to its creditor. Default risk underpins credit risk.

Deflation The decline in the general price level, usually shown in the consumer price index (CPI).

Derivative A financial instrument whose price, directly or indirectly, relates to the market price development of other financial product(s) or commodities.

Equities or **shares**   Securities representing ownership of a stake of a publicly quoted company.

Euroland   The economic area formed by European Union member states in which the euro has been adopted as single currency, in accordance with the Maastricht Treaty.

Financial account   A balance of payments account covering all transactions, portfolio investments, financial derivatives, and reserve assets between an economy's residents and non-residents.

Foreclosure   The legal process through which the lender possesses or repossesses property securing a mortgage, when the borrower defaults.

Gross domestic product (GDP)   The value of an economy's total output of goods and services, minus intermediate consumption and plus net taxes on products and imports.

Household debt service ratio   The ratio of debt payments to disposable personal income – including outstanding mortgages and consumer debt.

Implied volatility   The expected volatility in the rate of change in the price of goods, services, real estate, securities, and other instruments.

Inflation   The increase in the general price level reflected in the consumer price index and other statistical measures.

Interest rate swap (IRS)   A contract whereby two parties agree to exchange interest payment flows on fixed dates in the future, during a specific term.

International Financial Reporting Standards (IFRS)   Standards developed by the International Accounting Standards Board (IASB) to promote the dependability, transparency, and international comparability of financial accounts.

Investment grade securities   Securities with a rating of BBB– or higher. The highest rating is AAA.

Junk bond   A debt security with a credit rating below investment grade; also known as a high-yield bond, or speculative grade bond.

Legal risk   The risk that legal uncertainties, a poor legal framework, or corrupt law enforcement will cause or exacerbate credit or liquidity risk.

Leverage   Typically, borrowing with the aim of increasing return (as well as risk) by means of debt financing; also known as gearing.

Leveraged loan   A loan that has either no investment-grade rating or else an issue premium of at least 150 basis points over LIBOR.

Liquidity facility   A credit line generally granted by banks that has not yet been used; as such it guarantees the borrower future provision of liquidity up to a specified amount.

Liquidity risk The risk that a counterparty will have insufficient funds to meet financial obligations when they come due, though it may be solvent.

London Interbank Offered Rate (LIBOR) A generally accepted interbank rate on the basis of which individual institutions calculate the rate they apply.

London International Financial Futures and Options Exchange (LIFFE) The London-based derivatives market.

M3 A broad monetary aggregate comprising currency in circulation and overnight deposits (M1), deposits redeemable at a period of notice of up to three months (M2, plus marketable instruments – such as repurchase agreements, money market fund shares, and debt securities with a maturity of up to two years issued by banks.

Main refinancing operation A regular central bank's open-market operation in the form of reverse transactions, normally with a maturity of one week (in the euro system).

Marginal lending facility A standing facility that commercial banks may use to receive overnight credit from the central bank, at a specified interest rate, against eligible assets.

Market liquidity A measure of the ease with which a given asset can be traded in a given market.

Market risk The risk of losses from movements in market prices, on-balance-sheet and off-balance-sheet.

Marking-to-market The revaluation of a security, commodity, futures, or option contract, or any other negotiable asset to its current market value, which is the nearest proxy to its fair value.

Monetary financial institution (MFI) A credit institution or money market fund that together with other MFIs forms the money-issuing sector of euroland.

Mortgage-backed securities (MBS) Securities backed by a pool of mortgage loans. They are subdivided into CMBS and RMBS.

Non-investment grade A credit rating below BBB–. Such securities, also known as junk bonds or "high-yield" bonds, are speculative.

Non-performing loans Loans whose full redemption is uncertain.

Operating income The total of a financial institution's interest, commission, and trading results.

Operational risk The risk that poor management, fraud, operational mistakes, technical malfunctions or other reasons will cause or exacerbate credit or liquidity risk.

Option An instrument giving the right but not the obligation to purchase (call option) or sell (put option) the underlying asset from/to a counterparty, some time in the future.

Originate to distribute model A questionable banking model in which debt is originated (at consumer or company level), pooled up, and cut into tranches for sale to investors.

Originator A financial institution that sets up a securitized portfolio for its own account, or owns purchased receivables to be securitized and sold to investors.

Over the counter (OTC) The trading of financial instruments outside established exchanges – usually bank to bank.

Primary market The market in which new issues are placed or sold.

Prime broker A financial institution providing a ranges of services for hedge funds, such as custody, securities lending, collateralized loans, trade settlement, and administration of securities.

Private equity Capital invested by private companies, generally in other companies not listed in exchanges.

Residential mortgage-backed securities (RMBS) *See* Mortgage-backed securities.

Risk premium A premium compensating investors for taking on a higher amount of credit risk, securities of lower liquidity, or other discounts in credit quality.

Risk profile The ratio of a bank's, or investor's, exposure weighting risky assets to total assets.

Risk provisioning The net expenditure on writedowns, credit losses and other reasons executed or set aside following the assessment of exposures.

Risk-weighted assets On-balance-sheet and off-balance-sheet items weighted to assess default risk, in line with creditworthiness classes defined by Basel II.

Secondary market A market in which securities which have already been placed or sold are traded.

Secured debt The debt backed by collateral that can be sold in case of the borrower's default.

Securitization A transaction based on a pool of assets (debt products) whose credit risk is distributed across at least two tranches with different risk profiles.

Senior debt The debt that has precedence over other debt; for instance with respect to repayment if loans made to a company are called in.

Settlement risk A risk that arises from credit risk and liquidity risk. Settlement in a transfer system may not take place as expected because one or more parties default on their obligation(s).

Short position The position of a bank or hedge fund that has sold a security it does not own, in order to speculate on the price falling.

Solvency ratio The ratio of a financial institution's own assets to its liabilities. The higher this ratio is, the sounder is the bank.

Special-purpose vehicles (SPVs) SIVs and conduits established for the purpose of conducting securitization transactions with the intent of isolating the SPVs obligations from those of the originator.

Spike An extremely short-lived price movement in the spot market.

Stress test The simulation of the effects of large deviations from normal market developments, usually at the level of 5, 10, or 15 standard deviations from the mean.

Structured financial instruments Derivatives; usually instruments bundled in such a way that a novel product is created with a higher risk quotient than the original instruments in the pool.

Structured investment vehicle (SIV) A special-purpose financial vehicle, similar to a conduit but also refinanced by issuing medium-term notes and capital notes.

Subordinated debt The debt that can be claimed only by an unsecured creditor in the event of liquidation after the claims of higher-standing creditors have been met.

Subprime borrower A borrower of poor or no credit history who does not qualify for a conventional mortgage or other loan; theoretically, he can borrow only from lenders specialized in dealing with subprimes.

Syndicated loan Granted jointly by several banks, with one or two credit institutions assuming responsibility as originator(s) and/or lead manager(s) of the loan.

Systemic risk The risk that the inability of one or more major financial players to meet their obligations, or serious disruption in the system itself, could tear apart the financial fabric.

Total return The return on investment including appreciation, extraordinary gains, and interest, minus losses being sustained.

Tranches Horizontal parts of a structured financial instrument, like a CDO, with the distinction made between the subordinated first-loss tranche, mezzanine tranche, and senior tranche – which is the last to bear losses.

Underlying The underlying in a derivatives transaction may be a specific commodity price, share price, interest rate, currency exchange rate, index of prices. Or, alternatively, a variable applied to the notional principal amount to determine the cash flows or other exchange of assets required by the derivatives contrat.

Underwriter The originator and/or securities trader who makes a commitment to buy a given securities issue at a certain price, wholly or partly. With this he assumes risks in exchange for a fee.

Value at risk (VAR) An elementary (and obsolete) risk metric indicating maximum expected loss at specified confidence level (probability) in a specified time period.

Volatility The measure of fluctuations in price of a financial instrument, or other commodity, within a specified time period.

Writedown A downward adjustment to the value of loans and other inventoried assets in the balance sheets of a bank when it recognizes (typically by marking-to-market) that their market values have declined.

Writeoff The removal of the value of loans from the balance sheet of a bank, when these loans are considered to be totally unrecoverable; also known as credit loss.

Yield curve The relationship between interest rate and maturity of an investment for issues with the same credit rating.

Abbreviations

ARM	Adjustable-rate mortgage
ARS	Auction-rate security
CDO	Collateralized debt obligation
CDS	Credit default swap
CE	Credit enhancement
CLO	Collateralized loan obligation
CMBI	Commercial mortgage-backed index
CMBS	Commercial mortgage-backed securities
CP	Commercial paper
CRT	Credit risk transfer
forex	foreign currency exchange
GDP	Gross domestic product
IRS	Interest rate swap
IFRS	International Financial Reporting Standards
LIBOR	London Interbank Offered Rate
LIFFE	London International Financial Futures and Options Exchange
MBS	Mortgage-backed securities
MFI	Monetary financial institutions
OTC	Over-the-counter
RMBS	Residential mortgage-backed securities
SIV	Structured investment vehicle
SPV	Special-purpose vehicles
VAR	Value at risk

Part I

Credit Crunch Ashes and Pains

1
The Mismanagement of Credit Risk

1. Are we running out of bubbles?

We are still in the midst of a major financial crisis that hit the western world in a vicious manner, and continues to shake the confidence of businesses and of consumers. For all practical purposes the Federal Reserve has got it wrong (Chapter 2), starting with Alan Greenspan who tried to work out his surroundings by feeling his way by touch in a darkened room. Additionally, an uncontrolled financial globalization has made things worse, not better (Chapter 3).

The turmoil of the subprimes (Chapter 4), fundamentally a deep credit risk crisis, created a tremendous uncertainty in financial markets, and put also in doubt the whole structure of central banking and of regulation. Not just securitized debt (Chapter 5) but also equities and commodities have been affected by what is going on in segments of the financial industry while volatility is on the increase.

Speaking at the Harvard Club on 9 April 2008, Dr Paul Volcker, the respected former Federal Reserve chairman, said that financial crises usually don't happen in the absence of underlying economic problems. The financial system has failed the market test. He also stressed the point that, as current events have shown, the available risk management tools don't work, adding:

- The expanding economy of the world needs a global regulatory solution.
- Regulated institutions are in a better position to face crises than unregulated ones.
- A country cannot inflate its way out of current economic problems, and
- Lack of stability in the dollar's value is likely to hurt not only the United States but also the world economy.

"Unless we learn from this crisis, another one will put the world economy back on to the rocks in the not too distant future," says Martin Wolf, the *Financial Times*'s senior economist and commentator. It takes exceptional individuals to court the hatred of governments, central bankers, and regulators, rather than compromise on issues they believe in.

The fact that monetary policy and bank supervision have failed is nobody's secret, even though not everybody expresses himself as clearly as Volcker and Wolf. According to Citigroup, the sharp rise in oil price has been driven principally by a sharp uptick in funds flows. Lombard Street Research, a consultancy, sees an iron bubble.[1] To others, it looks *as if* we are running out of bubbles, but governments are inventive. According to many economists who don't forget the equity bubble of 2000 and those that preceded it, three more bubbles are waiting in the wings of the credit crunch, the subprimes, and their cohorts:

- Debt bubble,
- Inflation bubble, and
- Moral hazard bubble.

The latter is the mother of all bubbles, which grow and burst based on the dynamics of the financial instruments underpinning them as well as the way in which they are manipulated and marketed. One of the best most recent examples is *auction-rate securities* (ARSs; Chapter 3). For almost 18 years these were generally accepted debt instruments. Then they turned into another case of defrauding investors.

On 7 August 2008, New York Attorney General Andrew Cuomo announced that Citigroup would buy back some $7 billion worth of auction-rate securities it sold to retail clients, charities, and small businesses and had agreed to pay a $100 million penalty. Other Wall Street houses such as Merrill Lynch and UBS had also sold a king-size amount of auction-rate securities to their retail clients. The *Wall Street Journal* reported that Merrill's retail investors held about $7 billion of such securities while UBS clients held a total of roughly $24 billion. (Both figures were later revised, as we will see in Chapter 3, section 4).

A better-known and significantly greater exposure than that from ARSs comes from *credit default swaps* (CDSs; defined in the Appendix to this chapter). As financial instruments, credit default swaps have not been under government supervision, even if banks and insurance companies, which engaged in massive CDS trades, are regulated. The main sore points of CDS exposure are:

- Moral risk,
- Poor pricing,
- No limits,
- No reporting on positions,
- The CDSs' growing mass, and
- The potentially unaffordable cost in case of bankruptcies.

All six bullets describe failures similar to those which characterized sub-primes, and led to the 2007 bubble; only the amounts involved are much larger (section 4 of this chapter) and the positions are more leveraged. As the European Central Bank's Financial Stability Review puts it:

> Losses on leveraged positions do not change the absolute value of debt liabilities, but they increase leverage ratios and therefore may require managers to deleverage in order to comply with leverage limits, by promptly selling some of their investments. If these sales were attempted in markets that were already frail and resulted in a loss compared to previously booked investment values, leverage ratios would rise again.[2]

Some cases of deep red ink involve outright fraud. At the end of January 2008, it was revealed that in the US the FBI is investigating the sub-primes disaster including the part played by complex and opaque Wall Street derivatives, their originators, vendors, bankers, brokers, traders. In fact, not only the FBI but also the Department of Justice, Internal Revenue Service (IRS), and Securities and Exchange Commission (SEC) have been after the wrongdoers (Chapter 2). Investors, too, have brought to justice institutions, which misbehaved, and so have municipalities who lost a packet with the subprimes.

In the last week of January 2008, Britain's Financial Services Authority (FSA) warned that there was probably more fraud on the way, because of misdeeds surfacing from times when regulatory action was lax, and also because different individuals were pressed into dishonest acts by falling markets and adverse financial conditions which they are unavoidably facing. But no action has been taken, or at least reported:

- Eight whole months after the FSA statement, what is left of it is just words, and

- It looks as if the presumed agents of malfeasance are keeping their prosecutors under lock and key.

In an article in the *Financial Times*, Tony Jackson observed that several of the subprimes and other derivatives cases (section 2 of this chapter) involved the imputation of fraud. John Kenneth Galbraith had called this practice *the bezzle*, remarking that it rises and falls with the economic cycle: "In good times, people are relaxed, trusting, and money is plentiful. But there are always many people who want more."[3] Combined with lax supervision, this *"more"* sees to it that in the collapse of one bubble are often found the seeds of the next.

Wise people do appreciate the lessons the market teaches. John Devaney, a hedge-fund manager who had to sell his 142-foot yacht and his Gulfstream IV after making wrong bets on mortgage bonds, told an audience: "I'd like to thank the market for dealing me a direct hit. As a trader if you don't get sucker-punched every once in a while, you don't understand what risk is."[4]

The frequency with which traders and bankers acquire and lose big yachts and personal jets increases in proportion to the loss of authority by central bankers and regulators. This is not just my opinion. A wholesome 59 percent of economists, bankers, and financial experts participating in a special session of the January 2008 World Economic Forum in Davos, Switzerland, voted that central banks lost control of the economy.[5] The cost may be staggering.

A key lesson from financial crises which have happened during the last two decades, from the October 1987 stock market shock, through the American Savings and Loans debacle, the Japanese banking collapse, East Asia's meltdown, Russia's bankruptcy, and the Swedish banking crisis, to the equity bubble of 2000, is that the economy benefits from the main players' rapid acknowledgement of losses and quick recapitalization. A speedy loss absorption:

- Initially accelerates the credit tightening, and
- Causes a greater upfront shortfall of gross domestic product (GDP), and therefore recession.

But this is counterbalanced by positive results. Provided new capital is injected (Chapter 2), the economic recovery tends to be rapid and sustained. Exactly the opposite is obtained by interminable arguments and counterarguments, delays, and indecision. An example of wrong policies is provided by Japan, with its banking system in coma for more than a decade in spite of massive spending by the government. One can only hope the same errors will not be repeated by the American authorities.

2. A quadrillion dollars in derivatives

Innovation in banking has been promoted by *rocket scientists*, also known as "quants." They are physicists, mathematicians, and engineers who formerly worked in missiles, or nuclear or space projects, and now work for big banks.[6] During the last 20 years, they have made significant contributions to the financial industry at large, increasing the sophistication of its instruments. The downside of this uninterrupted innovation in financial products has been that:

- Much more attention is being paid to novelty than to the management of risks it brings along, and
- Monetary policymakers and regulators have been left widely behind, because so many commercial and investment banks are way ahead of the curve in quantitative methods.

One of the results of intensive research and development on new financial products which has involved rocket scientists, bankers, and traders is that year after year the banking system's exposure to complex financial instruments has increased by 30 percent to 35 percent. It grew from practically nothing in the mid 1980s to the astronomical amount of *one quadrillion dollars* (in notional principal)[7] by the time the July/August 2007 subprimes crisis hit.

Even conservative estimates put the global derivatives exposure at more than half a quadrillion. An April 2008 article in *The Economist* had it that at end of 2007 the overall market for over-the-counter (OTC)[8] derivatives had been $455 trillion. Given that OTC roughly represents 80 percent of all derivatives trades, this means a $570 trillion derivatives exposure at end of 2007[9] – or $770 trillion at end of 2008, given that such exposure increases at about 35 percent per year.

- The exact number is an educated estimate, and whether this is 1 quadrillion or ¾ of a quadrillion is unimportant.
- The critical issues are the colossal order of magnitude; the fact that its increase is unstoppable; and that its inescapable ending will be a God-sized bubble.

The fact that the financial industry and those responsible for managing the economy cannot estimate in an accurate manner the *value* of investments and their embedded risks is a great medium-to-longer-term worry. Years ago Bernard Baruch wisely said that *value in an investment* is like *character in an individual*. An economy can stand under adversity and overcome tough times more readily:

- When true values are created, because they help to survive financial panics;[10]
- Whereas, by contrast, fake values crumble and their debris poisons the global financial environment, as the 2007 subprimes crisis has demonstrated.

If worst comes to worst, in connection to the banking and credit crisis of 2007/2009, it is conceivable that the losses of the banking industry might hit several trillions of dollars in real money, an amount which is mind-boggling and, for the layman, difficult to comprehend. It does not take a genius to appreciate that:

- The global banking system is bankrupt, and
- The early twenty-first century's puzzle is how highly paid chief executives and board members let their institutions sink like the *Titanic*.

The fact that models and their underrated risk estimates turned sour is no surprise; if anything, it is surprising that this has not been discovered faster. The way the current criticism goes, "The banks' risk models try to put a value on how much they should realistically expect to lose in the 99 percent of the time that passes for normality, and draw on a mass of historical data which can produce a false sense of security." That's absolutely nonsense:

- The 99 percent level of confidence was established by the Basel Committee, along with the silly and unreliable VAR model extensively used by banks.
- In the majority of cases the "mass of data" is non-existent. If anything, there is scarcity of data.
- Top management has messed up and biased model results. An example is the decision by the board of Dresdner Bank that the correlation coefficient should be equal to 0.25 in all cases.

This does not mean that rocket scientists never make mistakes. Like everybody else they do. It is always difficult to make predictions, particularly about the future, the physicist Niels Bohr once said. Precisely for that reason it is highly unwise to put blind faith in models. Moreover, modeling has been extensively used to design new, complex financial instruments, but only scant attention is paid to analyzing the associated risks.

Beyond these microeconomic considerations, a macroeconomic concern of central bankers and regulators is the impact of rapidly expanding *derivatives* trades on monetary policy. Another is that many of the new financial instruments hide the reasons which have classically triggered bank failures, with the result that several big bankruptcies may hit the financial market at once, as the reader will see in section 4 of this chapter.

To make this issue more comprehensive, let's briefly examine from where this real and present danger comes. The International Financial Reporting Standards (IFRS) applicable in the European Union and in other countries (most particularly IAS 39) define a *derivative* as a financial instrument whose value changes in response to the change in an *underlying*. For instance, an interest rate, equity price, or index. Leveraging comes from the fact that a derivatives transaction usually requires

- Either no initial investment, as the commitment is longer-term; or
- An investment much smaller than would be needed for a more classical contract with a similar response to market changes.

In America, the Financial Accounting Standards Board (FASB), most specifically in its latest Statement of Financial Accounting Standards (SFAS), defines derivatives as financial instruments with the following characteristics:

- They have one or more underlying and one or more notional principal amounts, payment provisions, or both.
- Usually, they call for no initial net investment, and when this is needed it is smaller than that called with other instruments.
- They require or permit net settlements, or provide for delivery of an asset that practically puts the buyer at a net settlement position.

Notice that these characteristics are not negative, *per se*. Derivatives can be useful instruments *if* and *when* used with measure and in connection to a commercial transaction. The danger comes from the huge mass of derivatives, exclusive bank-to-bank transactions, plenty of greed but lack of limits, high gearing, and substandard risk management – which, taken together at the quadrillion dollar level, are dynamite for the global economy.

3. "26-year-olds with computers are creating financial hydrogen bombs"

Regretfully, neither accounting standards nor central bankers and regulators have defined in clear, unambiguous terms the likely disastrous aftereffect of leveraged derivatives, if the bets go wrong. In contrast to this passivity and silent acceptance of overwhelming risk, knowledgeable experts provide lucid descriptions.

26-year-olds with computers are creating financial hydrogen bombs,

said Felix Rohatyn, former senior partner of Lazard Brothers and US ambassador to Paris.

We do not know the web of interconnections between banks established through derivatives,

suggested Dr Alexander Lamfalussy, former general manager Bank for International Settlements (BIS) and first CEO of the European Monetary Institute, the forerunner of the European Central Bank.

Behind the big guns is a growing number of smaller outfits anxious not to miss the boat, who cobble together over the counter (OTC) derivatives in an attempt to keep up with the play and get their share of the market – with limited regard to the dangers,

underlined in one of his lectures V. Fitt, senior executive of the British Securities and Futures Authority (which preceded as regulator the Financial Services Authority (FSA)).

The risk of fraud, too, has increased with rapid financial innovation, for novelty's sake.

In recent years some large scale frauds, and near frauds, have been facilitated by derivatives. We view them (derivatives) as time bombs, both for:

- The parties dealing in them, and
- The economic system.

This has been the opinion of Warren Buffett, the well-known investor, who adds that

> Derivatives contracts are of varying duration (running sometimes to 20 or more years). Their value is often tied to several variables, and their ultimate value also depends on the creditworthiness of the counterparties to them. True, there are methods by which the risk can be laid off with others. But most strategies of that kind leave you with residual liabilities.[11]

(The subprimes debacle proved that Buffett has been absolutely right.)

Derivatives exposure varies by type of financial instrument, amount at stake and economic conditions. Default risk on credit derivatives can occur for the notional principal amount of the trade to the extent of its replacement value. Other examples where the full notional principal is exchanged are currency swaps, and all-or-nothing (binary) derivative contracts. Interest rate derivatives, by contrast, are subject only to a partial loss of notional principal, with this fractional amount varying with interest rates as well as with volatility and market psychology.

Options, futures, forwards, and swaps[12] are the better-known and relatively simpler types of derivatives. Swap agreements and forwards contracts are generally transacted over the counter, bank-to-bank. Futures contracts are like forwards but exchange-traded, and in the case of paper losses they usually require daily cash settlement. Option contracts can be exchange-traded or OTC-transacted.

Options bought have default risk to the extent of their replacement cost, except where the writer is required to post collateral. Options written (sold) represent a potential obligation to counterparties. Therefore, their pricing should always reflect pragmatic estimates of expected volatility – which is rarely, if ever, the case. As the 1997 bankruptcy of NatWest Securities documents showed, the result of underpricing options can be catastrophic to the bank.

Let me repeat the statement I just made. Options, futures, forwards, and swaps are basic derivative instruments which are most helpful in providing hedges, but they can become explosive when used to excess and for speculative rather than true hedge reasons.[13] An easy, but not foolproof, way to detect true hedges is to test whether they are connected to commercial transactions, because in these cases the bank acts as intermediary for the account of a client.

This test, however, becomes much more difficult with complex derivatives designed to satisfy requirements of the moment, particularly so as these are expressed in terms of "Make me an offer," giving free reign to the imagination of rocket scientists. The CDSs of which we talk in this chapter, and collateralized debt obligations (CDOs), covered in Chapter 6, fall in this class.[14] Among them is hidden the financial hydrogen bomb to which Rohatyn made reference. Moreover,

- The global economy cannot absorb these massive amounts of derivatives trades, and
- The *quadrillion dollars* in highly leveraged derivatives is tarnishing the reputation for competence of the Establishment's elite.

Evidence of incompetence is the unprecedented scale of losses in the banking industry resulting from designing, trading, and warehousing highly leveraged, half-baked, structured financial instruments like collateralized debt obligations (CDOs, Chapter 6), as well as from sloppy risk management. The loss to the US and global economy is immense, but the losses suffered by individual banks, too, are eye-popping. Table 1.1 provides the reader with a short list of *loss leaders* – from 1 August 2007, to 31 July 2008 – mainly due to CDOs.

Yet, while collateralized debt obligations are the burning theme of the day as these lines are being written, and the International Monetary Fund (IMF) says that banking industry losses and writedowns will probably reach $1 trillion, that's not the worst news – partly because some of the torrent of red ink has already run its course. By all likelihood the financial hydrogen bomb will be the credit default swaps (CDSs; see section 5 and the appendix to this chapter). That's why they are the theme of Chapter 1.

With corporate defaults on the rise, the Tower of Babel of CDSs may unravel, while the prospect of widespread counterparty woes "overhangs the market like a Damocles sword," George Soros has opined.[15] Adding to the sense of an impeding crisis are the strains felt by bond insurers (sections 6 and 7) that had written CDS contracts for banks in the silly "hope" of hedging their mortgage risks. In short, throughout the financial industry:

- Risk control has taken a holiday, and
- Personal responsibility has gone along with it.

Critics say that not only board members and CEOs of big banks don't give a penny for risk management, but also regulatory authorities and central banks have shown an inordinate amount of laxity over the

Table 1.1 Top ten year-on-year big bank losses and writedowns (L&Ns) due largely to CDOs

Institution	Jurisdiction	L&W ($bn[1])
Citigroup[2]	American	55
Merrill Lynch[3]	American	52
UBS[4]	Swiss	44[5]
HSBC	British	27
Wachovia[6]	American	22[7]
Bank of America[8]	American	21
IKB[9]	German	16
Royal Bank of Scotland[10]	British	15
Washington Mutual[11]	American	15
Morgan Stanley[12]	American	14
Top ten total		281[13]

1. Order of magnitude as of 31 July 2008.
2. In October 2008 to restructure its balance sheet Citigroup received from the US Treasury (read the American taxpayer) $25 billion.
3. In September 2008, to avoid Lehman Brothers's fate Merrill Lynch merged into Bank of America.
4. UBS received from the Swiss government the largest handout of them all: 60 billion Swiss francs.
5. Plus second quarter 2008 losses and writedowns announced after 1 August 2008.
6. Wachovia was going against the wall and in October 2008 was merged into Wells Fargo.
7. Plus second quarter 2008 losses and writedowns announced after 1 August 2008.
8. Bank of America received $25 billion from the US Treasury.
9. The German taxpayer (wrongly) injected euro 10 billion into IKB which was then sold for peanuts by the government to Lone Star, a vulture fund from Texas.
10. Royal Bank of Scotland descended to the abyss and was saved at the twelfth hour through massive injection of British taxpayers' money.
11. Washington Mutual went bankrupt and the remains were purchased by JP Morgan Chase.
12. Morgan Stanley converted its status to bank holding company and received $25 billion from the US Treasury.
13. Out of the banking industry's red ink of over $400 billion year-on-year.

derivatives gambles which have been taking place in the last dozen years. No surprise, therefore, that the moment of truth is coming on the heels of such loose bank regulation, bringing nearer the destruction of the financial system and the Second Great Depression.

4. The visible blight of failed bank management

Financial derivatives, as we know them today, really started in the 1970s, with the regulators suggesting that profits and losses are written off-balance-sheet. Derivatives were small game at the time; since then, however, they have both mushroomed and undergone dramatic changes with:

- The availability and trading of derivative instruments becoming commonplace, and
- Financial products once considered "exotic" morphing into mainstream.

Additionally, booming derivatives trades have seen to it that these instruments are no longer minor off-balance-sheet receivables and payables. They are integral part of balance sheet activities not only for banks, hedge funds, and other financial institutions, but also for a long list of other firms including pension funds, insurance entities, oil firms,[16] manufacturing companies – and for private individuals. Huge losses with derivatives are therefore of great concern, because they affect every sector of the economy in a big way.

After the announcement by the European Central Bank that at the closing of 2007 bank losses from securitized subprime mortgages stood at $320 billion, the newswires advanced the estimate that (excluding exposure to off-balance-sheet vehicles) the remaining bank exposure to subprimes was roughly $380 billion. Some analysts disagreed, suggesting that the $320 billion already lost is no more than a third of total losses. (Hence, the $1 trillion torrent of red ink estimated in section 1 of this chapter.)

One of the big banks, which so far got a relatively small hit from the subprimes debacle of "only" $2 billion, has been JP Morgan Chase. Quite likely, its management acted more carefully given its over $40 trillion exposure to other derivatives. But JP Morgan also has in its books a huge amount of leveraged loans and bonds, many related to buyout of the go-go years, which amount to a cool $250 billion of unsold debt. And, as a leading dealer in credit default swaps (CDSs), the Morgan Bank may find itself in another abyss of losses (section 5 of this chapter).

An interesting hindsight on this CDS business is that its usefulness is much less than what was supposed to be, while its risks are in the upside. Additionally, just like the case of subprimes, the coming credit derivatives debacle is evidence of the mismanagement of credit risk. CDS games started in 1991 because the net interest margin of American commercial banks had been under pressure, with the result that:

- Credit risk standards were bent, and
- New leveraged instruments were invented to fill the gap.

Bankers say that *if* they were to enforce a cautious attitude to lending (which they should have done years ago), *then* their return on equity would fall; hence the laxity which prevailed till July/August 2007. Statistics from the investment banking sector are also eye-opening. In just one instrument, namely *asset-backed securities* (ABS), when the crisis started:

- Lehman Brothers had an exposure equal to 460 percent of its equity;
- Bear Stearns, 400 percent;
- Morgan Stanley, 120 percent;
- Goldman Sachs, 100%; and
- Merrill Lynch 100 percent.[17]

Neither can the argument be accepted that a major crisis in the derivatives market became apparent only in 2007. Back in February 2003, a warning on systemic danger due to happen in the derivatives market was issued by an American regulator, the Office of Federal Housing Enterprise Oversight (OFHEO). A document entitled "Systemic Risk: Fannie Mae, Freddie Mac, and the Role of OFHEO" warned that major problems at either Fannie Mae or Freddie Mac, both huge derivatives contract holders, might lead to default on debt.

To appreciate the size of the disaster, one should remember that in the US market, Freddie Mac and Fannie Mae are household names which, though created by government initiative, were not provided with any explicit government guarantee. The 2003 warning was a danger signal for investors; this did not please the Bush Administration, and the day after the report was released, OFHEO's CEO joined the list of regulators who had been fired. A rolling head should have given the market further evidence of trouble in derivatives markets; it did not.

Curiously, in the much bigger 2007 crisis OFHEO did not make itself heard. Yet, on 20 November 2007 Freddie Mac announced a $2.0 billion loss, while also revealing that the value of its inventory of mortgages was down by $8.1 billion; the two together made a $10.1 billion hole in its finances. In the aftershock, the housing market superpower was scrambling for finding financing.

(It has been a deliberate choice not to include in this book case studies of America's giant government-sponsored enterprises (GSE): the Federal National Mortgage Association (FNMA, Fannie Mae; created in the 1930s) and Federal Loan Mortgage Corporation (FHMC, Freddie Mac; which saw the light in 1970). Fannie and Freddie, which among

themselves recycle and therefore sustain one out of two US house mortgages, were supposed to help American families buy their own homes
by making the mortgage market work better by supporting the secondary mortgage market. In 2008 the result has been a disaster.)

Freddie Mac and Fannie Mae were not alone in their search for fresh
capital. The better-known banks, too, were in the same track. With
moral hazard in full swing, one way some of them found to unload
the toxic waste in their portfolio was to sell it to their clients at stellar
price. This has been done in the form of so-called *alternative investments*
which, to say the least, are a cheat.[18] In their rush for profits to justify
their lavish bonuses senior managers have paid too little attention to
litigation risk. Yet,

- Legal proceedings can adversely affect operating results, and
- They dearly impact on reputation and credit ratings.

Some of the problems shaking Germany in 2008 date back to 2004,
when Deutsche Bank, Commerzbank, HypoVereinsbank (HVB), and
others sold to companies and local government authorities complex
interest-rate swap products. The treasurers of municipalities had no idea
about what derivatives were, but they were reportedly keen to optimize
the interest they paid on their debt.

After the financial instruments bought by German municipalities
proved disastrous, Commerzbank, HVB, and others sought to settle. To
the contrary, Deutsche Bank decided to fight in court allegations that
it had given bad advice on a product that locked its clients into potentially huge losses. In consequence to this decision, by 2008 the largest
German credit institution is faced with:

- Two cases threading through the courts, and
- Up to forty others which are being prepared.

The most interesting case is that of the city of Hagen which sued
Deutsche Bank for losses of $57 million on a nominal investment of
$170 million. Hagen bought "ladder swaps" without appreciating their
exposure. Other German municipalities did the same, because ladder
swaps were quite popular at a time when local governments felt they
were paying too dearly in fixed-interest payments as euro interest rates
were falling. Sensing a market in the making,

- Deutsche Bank offered to swap the fixed rates for floating, and

- It based the instrument's level on the difference between two inter-est rates, the 2-year and 10-year swap rate.

What the Hagen treasurer did not understand, prior to signing the con-tract, was that the interest rate spread was subtracted from an arbitrary figure, then doubled or trebled and added cumulatively to the nominal amount (an often used trick). Also, a clause in the contract specified that in most cases the issuing bank could terminate the instrument every 6 months after the first year, leaving the holder with about 2 per-cent profit under best conditions.

To Hagen's sorrow, the interest rate curve of the euro flattened during 2005, and this meant that by the end of a 5-year deal the client could be paying as much as 25 percent to the bank. It is indeed most curious that so many treasurers were prepared to accept such one-sided "bargains." About 700 are estimated to have done so, with 200 public utilities or municipalities among them.[19]

5. Debt crisis takes center stage: $62 trillion of CDSs[20]

In the aftermath of the crisis which hit the global financial system in July/August 2007, uncertainty about the prospects for economic recov-ery remains high and risks surrounding the outlook for financial activ-ities point to a downside. Included in this outlook have been potentially broader than currently expected banking losses, a more significant impact of the ongoing reappraisal of exposures in financial markets, and a wider spread of negative market sentiment. Other economic risks have come from:

- Additional oil, agricultural produce, and other commodity price rises,
- Concerns about increased protectionist pressures, and
- The likelihood of disorderly developments due to the persistence and increase of global imbalances.

For 2008, and by all likelihood for 2009, an overriding financial expos-ure finds itself in the aftereffects of credit tightening.

There was a time, not so long ago, when the credit risk banks assumed was directly linked to the loans they gave, therefore, to their counter-parties in the lending business. Today this is valid only in part because banks have a double exposure to credit risk:

- One from classical default, and

- The other from credit spread connected to novel financial instruments.

This credit spread of credit default swaps (CDSs, briefly mentioned in section 1 of this chapter and explained in the Appendix) is measured by individual counterparty, as well as by groups of counterparties that share similar attributes. Its widening has negative impact on a firm's perceived creditworthiness, consistent with the fact that credit default swaps are seen as insurance-type instruments intended, or at least attempting, to protect the holder against default by a counterparty.

Rather than fulfilling that premise, CDSs exceed subprimes in potential destruction of financial and economic power. As a Basel Committee study aptly commented:

> [T]he notional growth of credit default swaps (CDSs) more than doubled in both 2005 and 2006, with a significant portion of this growth associated with the creation of complex structured credit instruments, some with highly embedded leverage. As another example, conduit financing (which is not new) became more complex with the growth of certain segments that engaged in more aggressive maturity transformation.[21]

Summing up this statement, CDSs are highly leveraged and very risky. According to some estimates, there are about $5 trillion in actual corporate debt "insured" by $62 trillion (!) in credit default swaps. Several estimates talk of much higher ratios than this 12.4 times average – up to 30 in the case of Delphi, the auto parts maker, which defaulted in 2005. In contrast to this scary figure of $62 trillion in CDS exposure, the US mortgage bubble has been about $20 trillion. Reportedly, of all CDSs in portfolios:

- 50 percent are held by banks,
- 24 percent by hedge funds, and
- 26 percent by other types of entities.[22]

Given the way the banking system works, nearly all of them will all find their way into the banking industry. Banks loaned the hedge funds the money they needed to play the CDS game with them. Because of this, some experts foresee a crisis like the 1933 "bank holiday" followed by bank foreclosures.

Another mischievous and uncontrollable security is the constant-proportion debt obligation (CPDO). Its users are gambling on the fact that, historically, investment-grade bonds have offered returns that more than compensate for the risk of default, and they are taking advantage of this spread using borrowed money. (A similar argument was employed in the 1980s with the so-called "fallen angels," leading to the crisis of junk bonds.)

- The CPDOs' leverage is high, often up to 20 times.
- Yet, they are used to supposedly sell default protection against a basket of bonds.

When spreads widen rapidly, the leverage proves to be their undoing. It is therefore not surprising that by late February 2008 the prices of some CPDOs fell, forcing gamblers to buy insurance against further falls to the tune of $30 billion of protection against an index of credit default swaps. This:

- Pushed up the cost of such insurance, and
- Made it more likely that corporate bonds would default.

An altogether negative characteristic of CDSs and similar geared derivative instruments is that they tend to expand the supply of credit in the upswing, but they have the undeniable effect of choking it in the downturn. One of the negative impacts of CDSs comes from wider spreads which indicate that the cost of credit insurance is increasing, because the perceived risk of default is rising.

In January 2008 there came to the public eye a fairly conservative estimate of the wider economic impact of credit default swaps. This suggested that up to 3 percent of CDSs, which had been outstanding at the end of 2007, hence nearly $2 trillion, was guestimated as being in the frontline. How much of it was ripe to fall into the abyss?

On 2 February 2008, an article in *The Economist* stated that such a serious person as Bill Gross, co-founder of PIMCO, the money-management firm, put the potential losses from such contracts at 1.25 percent of outstanding amount of CDSs. This would mean a cool $715 billion.

- *If*, say, half that money could be recovered (a hopeful estimate),
- *Then* the loss from credit default swaps would stand at roughly $360 billion – but this is a big IF.

Equally troublesome is the fact that the estimated amount of CDSs as of end 2007 keeps on being revised upwards. In January 2008 it was said to be $45 trillion; a month later, in February 2008, the news has been that the amount of outstanding CDSs at end of 2007 was not $45 trillion but $50 trillion, an 11 percent upwards correction. Then on 13 April 2008, *The Economist* stated that (always as of end 2007) the amount of inventoried CDSs stood at $62 trillion, a 24 percent uptick from the previous $50 trillion estimate.

Any exposure, which on a monthly basis is revised upwards, is typically underestimated. A tandem of upward corrections suggests that plenty of things are hidden and the worse keeps on worsening – as with the 1929 Great Depression. Sticking to the Bill Gross estimate of 1.25 percent potential losses of outstanding CDSs, the red ink's reference value has been:

- $562.5 billion in February 2008;
- $625 billion in March 2008;
- $715 billion in April 2008.

Given that the amount of inventoried CDSs has the nasty habit of increasing by about 30 percent per year, even if no new revelations of hidden exposure materialized the American (and by extension the global) economy may well be faced with $80 trillion in CDSs at end of 2008. If so, then

- The reference value of red ink from CDSs will be at the level of $1.0 trillion for "only" 1.25 percent of defaults.

Other, rather pessimistic estimates talk of more than double the aforementioned 1.25 percent of defaults: up to 3 percent and beyond. Moody's Investors Service, the rating agency, suggests that defaults are about to rise sharply, carrying the prospect for big losses for CDS writers which could run into several trillions. That is particularly true of those banks which, for whatever reason, have failed to properly hedge CDS risks.[23]

Belatedly, the market awakes to the fact that exposure associated with insuring financial credit might have been grossly underestimated, and therefore dramatically underpriced. Fingerpointing is not uncommon when things go bad, but in this case the party which messed up its actuarial business is, by all evidence, the protection providers. What particularly unnerves the experts is the very high leverage ratio, which can easily kill some big banks, insurance companies, and other protection sellers. According to well-informed sources:

- The equity available with CDSs is a mere 2 percent of liabilities, and

- This corresponds to an ominous leverage factor of 50, instead of the conservative 20 I assumed – a level the financial industry will find nearly impossible to support.

Experts debate how to assess the risk embedded into these statistics, which is practically synonymous with the product of exposure at default (EAD) times probability of default (PD). While exact figures on default likelihood are not truly available (the previously stated percentages as well as much else that can be found are educated guesses), the most likely aftereffect of a CDS watershed is that the US economy will contract by about 5 percent. If matters get worst it might emulate Japan's economy, which has been contracting by 1 percent to 2 percent per year, on and off, since 1991.

Whose the fault? Miscalculating the looming danger, in May 2006 (a year prior to the subprimes crisis), Alan "Double Bubble" Greenspan[24] noted that the credit default swap is probably the most important instrument in finance. Greenspan also explained that what CDSs truly did was to lay off all the risk of highly leveraged institutions (read banks) on stable American and international institutions (eventually destroying them).

The looming huge CDS crisis, coming on the heels of the subprimes hecatomb, is indisputable proof that in real life the market does not function as a theorist central banker, weak monetary policymaker, and absent-minded regulator had hoped (see Chapter 8). There are many surprises when actual defaults occur because:

- CDS contracts are technically complex in relation to the identity of credit risk being hedged, and
- CDS documentation, which is highly standardized, does not exactly match the terms of the underlying credit risk.

On actively traded names, CDS volumes are substantially greater than outstanding debt, which makes it difficult to calculate exposure, set pricing and settle CDS contracts. When Delphi, the former GM subsidiary and auto parts supplier defaulted, the volume of CDSs outstanding was $28 billion against $5.2 billion of bonds and loans. And as an added flavor, the use of credit derivatives can dearly affect the central banks' monetary policy.

6. Wrong-way risk: the downgrading of monolines

In April 2005, the Basel Committee on Banking Supervision published a Consultative Document, "The Application of Basel II to Trading Activities and the Treatment of Double Default Effects." Since a year later this became one of Basel II's pillars, one would be excused for assuming that compliance to prudential supervision would have required that the new regulation is thoroughly observed. This has not however been the case.

A most important subject elaborated by the aforementioned document is found in the document's Part 2, "The Treatment of Double Default," which addresses recognition of the particular protection afforded by having credit insurance, as well as the aftereffect of cases where the guarantor itself is over-leveraged. Defined as *wrong-way risk*, this process involves:

- The existence of high correlation in creditworthiness of protection provider *and* obligor of underlying exposure, and
- The fact that such risk correlation is due to the performance of the subject entities, related to economic factors which are accentuated in case of crisis.

Already in March 2007, a quarter prior to the widespread subprime casualties, Standard & Poor's, the credit rating agency, said average credit ratings are in decline because companies are generally taking on more debt. With this, the cost of buying protection against a default rose, accompanied by growing nervousness about opaque risks in some big financial groups.

The more the market sensed danger, the more debt derivatives have been trading at positions normally associated with companies holding credit ratings close to junk. Not only in America and Europe but also in Asia, between mid July 2007 and mid January 2008 the spreads of credit default swaps significantly widened. South Korean default credit swaps, for instance, went from about 10 basis points to 60, as shown in Figure 1.1. This happened in the west as well, in spite of the fact that:

- Some banks' ratings were more secure than generally thought, and
- A big chunk of the investment banking sector was still enjoying strong earnings, in spite of the subprimes crisis.

One of the prevailing opinions has been that the deterioration in sentiment in the market, particularly in credit derivatives, had partly arisen because market players thought that the surfacing problems in subprime mortgages, in America, would have a long-lasting effect. An additional concern was that some investment banks had taken big proprietary risks, a policy that could well backfire if markets remained turbulent.

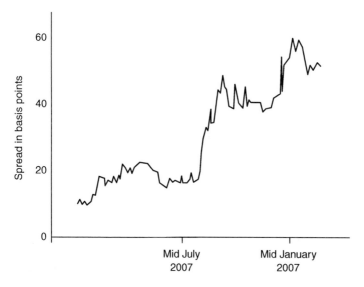

Figure 1.1   Widening spreads of Korean credit default swaps, July 2007 to January 2008

An even more potent factor, in my judgment, has been the downgrading of bonds by independent credit rating agencies. Moving slowly, too slowly according to many critics, on 30 January 2008, Standard & Poor's downgraded or threatened to downgrade more than 8,000 bonds and collateralized bond obligations (CDOs), noting that losses by financial institutions tied to them could rise to more than double what had been originally thought – to the level of $265 billion.

According to some opinions, this has been nothing less than a prelude to the downgrade of monoline insurers – companies like MBIA and Ambac (section 6 of this chapter) – which went out of their charter of insuring municipal bonds and acted as guarantors of subprimes. With limited financial resources for the risks which they assumed, the monolines have guaranteed an estimated $2.4 trillion of outstanding debt.

Their fault, experts suggest, was that of breaking the narrow confines of protection to municipal bonds, moving into uncharted territory. In fact, they did worse than that by renting their AAA rating to dubious securities, for a fee. As competition for municipals grew, they were seduced by the higher returns of structured finance, particularly what seemed to them to be the infinite market of subprimes.

In mid January 2008, Ambac Financial reported a $3.3 billion quarterly net loss after it recorded $5.2 billion in writedowns[25] from its credit-derivatives portfolio, which includes the subprimes. Subsequently, on 18 January, Fitch cut its AAA credit rating for Ambac, suggesting the monolines may not be reliable counterparties for the states and cities that work with them – and by extension for banks and investors who:

- Accumulated pseudo-AAA securities in their portfolio, and
- As the crisis gains steam see their investments turn into ashes.

Credit rating downgrades of troubled monoline insurers could trigger a potential financial tsunami as far-reaching as the subprime mortgage crisis itself, said Josef Ackermann, chief executive officer of Deutsche Bank, on 7 February 2008.[26] The alert came as the banking sector continued to suffer from fears that rating downgrades to bond insurers could lead to another round of writedowns of investments and renewed capital constraints.

- *If* the monolines are downgraded,
- *Then* the bonds they insure will not only fall in value but also no longer qualify for capital adequacy requirements of the banks who inventoried them.

Much will depend, of course, on the position supervisory authorities take. Will they look the other way as they did with the subprimes and irrational boom in derivative financial instruments? Will they act, and therefore end up with the choice to close banks with a weak capital base? Or will they follow the unfortunate policy of the British Treasury and the Bank of England, which poured £55 billion ($110 billion) into Northern Rock (Chapter 8) and ended by nationalizing the deeply wounded company?[27]

On Wall Street, the opinion of several analysts has been that those banks that were writing down their CDO holdings did so under the assumption that the monoline insurers won't face sharp ratings downgrades. That now looks an overly optimistic hypothesis. According at least to one expert opinion, in a worst-case scenario,

- Citigroup could face additional losses of as much as $10 billion,
- UBS would be staring at as much as $8.7 billion of red ink, and
- Overall writedowns could mushroom as high as $75 billion.[28]

These numbers come over and above the $22.1 billion already lost by Citigroup and $18.4 billion lost by UBS in 2007. A nearly 50 percent increase in that torrent of bad money suggests that the likelihood of a financial tsunami is far from being an academic question. Both US GAAP and Europe's IFRS require that holders of downgraded bonds have to mark them down under fair-value accounting principles.

Also severely hit will be entities like pension funds which are not permitted by law to hold non-investment-grade securities, raising the prospect that they may be confronted with forced sales. The loss of AAA credit rating would cost investors and borrowers up to $200 billion, suggested a news item at Bloomberg, the financial information entity.

The pros might say that, sovereign debt aside, it is not easy these days to find AAA-rated bonds; and in saying so they will be right. Taking euroland's bond rating of non-financial entities as a proxy, Figure 1.2 shows that from 1998 to 2006, AAA ratings become a rarity, closely followed in the downsizing by AAs. The As somewhat increased, but those which really boomed are the BBB, BB, and B ratings. (BB and B ratings are junk bonds, hence non-investment-grade.)

Since behind the bonds' credit rating hide those of their originators, this free fall in creditworthiness is an unmitigated disaster for credit

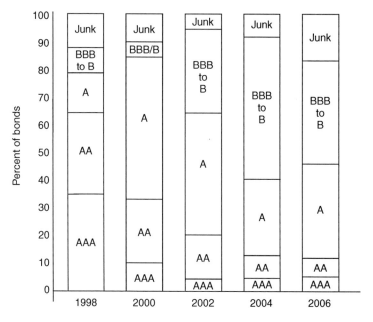

Figure 1.2   Rating of bonds issued in euroland by non-financial entities (statistics by European Central Bank)

default swaps, because it preannounces bankruptcies. The silver lining is that according to the Bank for International Settlements monolines have a very small percentage of the CDS business. The bad news is that the market is so vast that this still amounts to $95 billion of protection, most of it sold to big banks.

7. MBIA and Ambac: a case study

Investors, John Caouette, the former CEO of MBIA, told me during our meeting, can make more money by taking credit risk than market risk. The trouble is that, in the general case, investors understand market volatility – and, sometimes, risk and return associated with it – somewhat better than credit volatility and its exposure. Because of this simple fact, many people have been confronted suddenly with the question of what the subprime debacle means for the investment community at large, and the guarantor community in particular.

- MBIA and Ambac Financial, the subject of this case study, are the larger and better-known monoline insurers,
- Others, among a dozen guarantors, are ACA Financial, Assured Guaranty, CIFG Guaranty, Financial Guaranty, Financial Security, and more.

Till the end of October 2007, monolines were known as credit guarantors of municipals and mortgage bonds sold to a host of mainstream investors. When the news that they might be in trouble broke out, some analysts expressed fears that they, too, could be nursing unseen subprime-linked problems – thereby contributing to the already negative market psychology. The doubters were right.

The risk particularly came from the fact that MBIA and Ambac, as well as their smaller peers, had expanded their activities outside their original charter. Although they began life as insurers of municipal bonds, much of their growth in recent years had come from providing guarantees to structured securities such as asset-backed bonds and collateralized debt obligations. It is nobody's secret that these products:

- Have a higher rate of default than municipal bonds, and
- Are much more complex than those the municipals' guarantors knew how to manage.

Additionally, since many CDOs have been exposed to the stricken subprime mortgage market, where levels of late payment and default have far exceeded initial expectations, monoline guarantors have been faced with steep insurance claims. At the end of 2006, for example, Ambac had guaranteed $26 billion of CDOs with subprime mortgage bonds, while having a capital base of just $1.15 billion. At MBIA, the outstanding guarantees for its structured and municipal portfolio were said to amount to 150 times capital.

The market had a punishing response. As Figure 1.3 shows, the spread on MBIA's and Ambac's 5-year credit default swaps had a spike at the beginning of the subprimes crisis (July/August 2007), then calmed down in September, but in October 2007 started again to rise – and continued doing so in the following months.

Experts have been quick to comment that this is a piece of bad news for US states and cities, because of the high and rising probability that several of the largest bond guarantors will lose their AAA rating, and some might default. Massive losses on asset-backed securities that they had insured to the tune of more than $400 billion could wipe them out. Quoted by Bloomberg on 16 November 2007, the credit officer of one insurance company warned that this is the equivalent of *twenty Hurricane Katrinas* in insured losses.

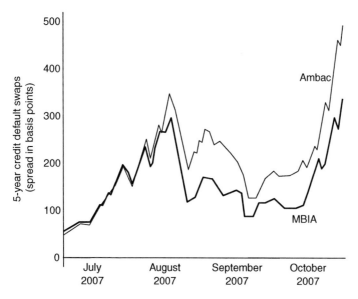

Figure 1.3 Basis points CDS spread of MBIA and Ambac Financial, July to October 2007

By late November 2007, the sense of the market was that the guarantors' credit rating was on the block. On 19 December 2007, Standard & Poor's slashed its rating of ACA Financial Guarantee, a relatively small insurer, to junk. The bigger companies in the industry have also been told to shore up their capital fast, or face downgrades which will:

- Drive down bond values, and
- Further cripple the lending ability of bondholding banks.

Another concern has been collateral damage. As a result of the huge exposure to subprimes which they unwisely assumed, both MBIA and Ambac – the leading bond guarantors with AAA credit rating – experienced significant share price declines, while the spread on their bonds widened. The risk confronting them could be expressed in two bullets:

- *If* a monoline guarantor were to see its rating slashed,
- *Then* mutual funds, which can only hold top-grade or very highly rated paper, would be forced to sell their municipal bonds.

Should this take place, it will lead to billions of dollars' worth of bonds being dumped into an already distressed market. Critics added that the monoline bond insurers had underpriced the risk they had assumed. As market psychology did not improve, in the first week of December 2007 the share price of MBIA slid by 16 percent after Moody's, the rating agency, changed its assessment of the bond insurer, saying it was "somewhat likely" to find itself short of capital.

A day after Moody's statement, MBIA said it could find capital to save its AAA rating. A week later it obtained some respite when it received a $1 billion boost in capital from Warburg Pincus, a private equity group. But at the same time the bond insurer faced losses which allegedly stood at $4.2 billion, leading its management into extra measures: flashing its annual dividend and selling $1 billion in debt to strengthen its position.

Analysts were not happy with debt gearing, because in a crisis the assumption of more debt is no way to strengthen the balance sheet. As the fear that both Ambac and MBIA might lose their AAA rating mounted, by 17 January 2008, compared with 2007 highs, their equity had sunk by 75 percent for Ambac, and by 52 percent for MBIA. In percentage points, the loss was practically at par with Merrill Lynch and Citigroup, the two financial groups which had lost the most from the subprimes.

The way some experts looked at what they considered to be a wider credit crisis was that the law of unexpected consequences was at work as guarantees for subprimes and collateralized debt obligations had reached into new corners of finance. This was considered to be of great concern to all investors, given that many transactions with debt instruments, not just those linked to CDOs, depend on the guarantee provided by Ambac, MBIA, and their peers.[29]

- *If* MBIA or Ambac were downgraded,
- *Then* all those transactions in portfolios of banks, institutional, and other investors would be in trouble.

By February 2008, this prospect caused several municipal bond auctions to fail, and also led to surging costs for borrowers. For instance, New York's Port Authority saw the interest rate on some auction-rate securities jump from 4.2 percent to 20 percent.

In the week of 11 February 2008, Warren Buffett made a rescue offer for monolines. Berkshire, Buffett's company, had recently formed a bond insurer with AAA rating, who proposed to assume the risk in the $800 billion of municipal bonds guaranteed by three troubled rivals: MBIA, Ambac, and FGIC. In return, it would receive several billion dollars of upfront fees, calculated as a percentage of future premiums.

Part of this plan was based on insulating the risk embedded in the monolines, who have acted as a credit risk transmission mechanism infecting America's $2.6 trillion municipal bond market with the disease they caught from CDO exposure. Working on a plan to raise $1.5 billion[30] as a likely prelude to a break-up, Ambac rejected the Berkshire plan; after some hesitation FGIC and MBIA came to the same decision.

Analysts said that had the plan succeeded, for $5 billion in capital, with which he endowed Berkshire's bonds reinsurance subsidiary, Buffett would have captured a third of the municipal insurance market. In the first week of March 2008, municipal bond markets rallied on news that Wilbur Ross and Bill Gross, two well-known investors, were betting big money into municipal bonds that were sold cheaply.

Appendix: credit default swaps defined

A *credit default swap* (CDS) is a bilateral financial contract in which the "protection buyer"[31] pays a periodic fee in return for a "contingent payment"[32] by the "protection seller"[33] following a "credit event"[34] of a reference entity – such as a bank or any other company. Should such credit event occur, the settlement can take place in either of two modes:

- *Physical*, with the protection buyer delivering particular obligation(s) issued by the reference entity, in exchange for a cash amount equivalent of the par value of those obligations.
- *Cash*, where the protection buyer receives from the protection seller an amount equal to the difference between the market value of defaulted obligation(s) and their par value.

Take as a very simple example the granting of a £10 million loan by bank ALFA to manufacturing company BETA, whose credit rating is AA. Bank ALFA buys protection for this loan from bank GAMMA, which will pay the protection buyer a compensation of 5 percent if BETA's credit is downgraded to A; 10 percent if downgraded to BBB; 25 percent if downgraded to BB (a junk bonds grade) and 100 percent if BETA goes bankrupt.

This settlement feature suggests that a simplistic way of looking at credit default protection is as an insurance contract protecting against losses from the borrower's loss of credit rating, all the way to bankruptcy. In a similar manner, credit default swaps (CDSs) allow credit risk to be unbundled from other exposures embedded in a financial instrument, and traded separately *as if* it were a stand-alone product.

That is what the pros claim about CDSs. Critics however answer that for trading reasons credit default swaps are mispriced, and with bankruptcies rising they may become an unmitigated disaster.

The use of CDSs

Default swaps were one of the first credit derivatives offered to the market, back in 1992, by Bankers Trust, being designed to address the bank's own concentration of risk with certain corporate *counterparties*.[35] An entity may use credit default swaps in order to hedge the specific credit risk of some of the issuers in its portfolio, by buying protection.[36] But it is also possible to enter into a CDS as a way of speculating on the likelihood of credit default by a given company. Essentially:

- The writer of a default swap becomes long on credit,
- While the buyer becomes short on credit.

> For instance, bank ALFA may buy a CDS from bank GAMMA, not for protection against default by its client BETA but for speculation about likely default, credit downgrading, or other event connected to some third party DELTA.
>
> BETA will be long on credit and ALFA short on credit in connection with DELTA. This is evidently speculation; which is unadvisable, but not illegal. The fact that banks can enter into such CDSs is plain failure of legislation and regulation in forbidding it outright.
>
> More than 90 percent of the $62 trillion of CDSs have nothing to do with commercial transactions. The regulators have allowed banks to shed their main function of intermediation, and turn themselves into speculators.

A default swap can be structured on a single credit name, or on a basket of names with the contingent default payment designed in different ways. For instance, it can be linked to the price movement of the reference asset at a predetermined level as "binary payoff";[37] or it may be in the form of an actual delivery of the asset at its initial price. The credit event may as well be different types of indebtedness manifested within a predetermined period of time.

In every case, the *credit event* must be material and objectively measurable, typically defined as: failure to pay, obligation default, obligation acceleration, repudiation, moratorium, restructuring. Alternatively, for speculative purposes an entity may buy protection under credit default swaps without holding the underlying assets. Or, it may sell protection to acquire a specific credit exposure.

Theoretically, credit default swap transactions are made only with highly rated financial institutions. Practically, this rule is often broken, particularly in times of crisis as the counterparty may not have the necessary assets to pay redemption proceeds connected to redemption requests; or meet its obligations resulting from credit default swaps and other instruments.

> Even *if* the CDS was connected to ALFA's loan to BETA, and therefore was protection bought for a commercial transaction, bank ALFA has not really got out of credit risk by paying a fee to bank GAMMA. It has simply transformed its credit risk with BETA, its loans client, into its credit risk with GAMMA – the protection seller.

The protection seller, too, may be assuming an absurd risk because quite often CDSs share the problem options have. They are greatly *mispriced* on the hypothesis that default rates are very low and that they will remain so in the future. To appreciate this event's impact on CDS pricing, it should be recalled that:

- In a CDS transaction, the buyer of credit protection pays to the seller of protection a periodic fee, which is the instrument's price, and
- This generally reflects the spread between the yield on a defaultable security, and the risk-free interest rate of a Group of Ten government bond.

Precisely for the reason presented by the second bullet, a CDS spread is taken as a proxy of *credit volatility*. In the event that the reference entity defaults, the buyer delivers to the seller debt owed by the defaulted party. Because credit default swaps are considered as similar to an insurance contract, insurance companies are quite active in this market, but without necessarily appreciating the full amount of assumed credit risk.

Are CDSs efficient?

Theoretically, but only theoretically, credit default swaps and default baskets seem to provide an efficient means of diversifying risk. To model credit correlations, analysts assume that transition occurs in discrete ratings, and the change in grades is the result of migration propelled by underlying factors. Other assumptions are:

- The underlying process is a good estimator of distance from default, and
- Distance to default can be transformed into a normalized risk score; that is, a score approximated by a normal distribution.

> In a substantial number of cases, the use of the normal (bell-shaped) distribution as an approximation to real-life distribution of risks is, to put it mildly, incorrect.
>
> CDSs are (at least allegedly) concentrated in the portfolios of some big banks like Bear Stearns and JP Morgan Chase in the US, Société Générale in France, and Unicredit in Italy. Their large and growing CDS exposure is not found under the normal curve but at the long leg of the risk distribution, which is populated by extreme events.[38]

Another hypothesis important in analysis is that of default correlations. Rocket scientists investigate the possibility of modeling joint rating changes through data regarding changes in historical ratings. Actual rating and default correlations can be derived from rating agency information, on the assumption that these tend to provide a rather objective measure reflecting actual experience. But the application usually suffers from:

- Sparse sample sets, and
- Lack of dependability of credit ratings, as demonstrated with AAA rating of CDOs' top tranche (Chapter 6).

Alternatively, analyst may employ bond spread correlations that give a relatively more objective measure of actual correlation in bond values and, by extension, in credit quality. The downside of this approach is that it suffers from data dependability problems connected particularly to low-quality issuers.

Another alternative is to use equity price correlations as proxy. Exchange-traded equity prices offer forward-looking market data as well as the advantage of good time-series. This approach capitalizes on the synergy which exists between equity market and debt market, *if* and where it exists. The disadvantage is that this method requires a great lot of computing time to yield reliable information about likely credit quality correlations; also, in a number of cases, the resulting correlations are low – leading to the mispricing of assumed exposure.

The aftermath of mispricing a CDS is that GAMMA the protection seller is not compensated for the credit risk it has assumed risk. Evidence of this can be found all over the $62 trillion CDS landscape.

But ALFA, too, may not be protected from its credit exposure to BETA, because the protection seller finds a way to shed its financial responsibility. For instance, according to the *New York Times* of 20 March 2008, another accounting charge awaited Merrill Lynch (already wounded by $24.5 billion in 2007 losses from subprimes), under its lawsuit against XL Capital Assurance, trying to enforce the guarantee (protection seller) of $3.1 billion in debt issued by CDOs. Shares in Merrill fell 11 percent, to $41.45, on the news.

2
The Fed Has Got It Wrong

1. Central banks lost control of monetary policy and of supervision

One of the important themes for the world economy discussed at the 2008 World Economic Forum in Davos, Switzerland, revolved around the fact that central banks have lost control of the economy by allowing commercial banks, investment banks and other financial institutions to do as they please. This attitude, which has been wrongly called *neo-liberalism*, has considerably diminished the central banks' clout and therefore their effectiveness as:

- Guardians of economic stability,
- Promoters of orderly economic growth through regulation of money supply, and
- Safeguards of value both of the money and of other assets.[1]

The basic issues behind all three bullets correlate. Economic stability requires watch over both systemic risk and inflation. Inflation concerns are also part of the second bullet, which focuses on the duty to manage interest rates in a way fair to all people. *If* interest rates don't cover the attrition of money through inflation, as it has happened in 2002 to 2004 and again in late January 2008, with the 125 basis points cut by the Fed in just 8 days, *then* a big part of the population is penalized to the benefit of the few:

- The savers don't see any more a reason to put their money in the bank, as the reward is less than the penalty.

It is not for nothing that since 2002/2003 when Greenspan's interest rate fell to 1 percent, savings by the American public were reduced to zero for the first time since the Great Depression of 1929–1933. This is counterproductive for the economy as a whole; and it also provides "ideal" conditions for Ponzi scams[2] which lead to the pyramiding of liabilities. Like Ponzi:

- Some banks devise a mare's nest of instruments to maximize their profits, paying lip service to the risk which accumulates into portfolios of investors and their own books.

An example of wrong policy not sanctioned by central banks and regulators is the commercial and investment banks' discovery that borrowing short and investing long can give them hefty profits – till judgment day. As for constantly inventing new instruments in plain disregard of their exposure, this has led to the absurdity of the subprimes and the deep financial crisis it brought along. Because, however, one example does not tell the whole story, let me name the cycle of crises which since the 1980s have become a 3 to 6 and 7 years' affair:

- Latin-American crisis of early 1980s.
- October 1987, stock market crisis.
- 1989/1990, savings and loans crisis, real estate crisis, and major financial crisis in Japan.
- 1994, crisis of bonds and of inverse floaters.
- 2000/2001, big stock market bubble.
- 2007, major bubble of the subprimes and of real estate.

While the reasons leading to the October 1987 stockmarket crash, a 14.5 standard deviation event, preceded the actions of Greenspan's Fed, the bond crisis of 1994 has been the result of a steady escalation in interest rates in a succession of more than a dozen steps, without paying attention to the fact that classically conservative bond investments were invaded by:

- Derivatives, and
- Leveraging.

Leveraging and an accommodating interest rate policy by Greenspan went into high gear in the late 1990s, inflating the stock market bubble of 2000. This was followed by rock-bottom interest rates, indeed the lowest for 50 years in the US, while the Fed did nothing to break up the party prior to the bursting of the 2007 subprimes bubble.

"Alan Greenspan became famous because nobody could understand what he was saying" – so in the Davos 2008 Forum stated Angel Gurria, the secretary-general of the Paris-based Organization for Economic Co-operation and Development (OECD; the former Marshall Plan). Gurria might have added that *quite likely* Greenspan also did not understand what he was doing, or otherwise he would not have brought the American economy to such a sorry state.

Another aftereffect of the long Greenspan tenure at the Fed has been the quasi destruction of the concept of bank regulation. As Joseph Stiglitz, former World Bank chief economist, Nobel laureate and professor at Columbia University, said during the same Davos meeting, bank regulators had established reasonably good operating conditions which remained in place till the late 1970s. All banks followed them. But the regulatory system:

- Got loose in the 1980s with free-market slogans, and
- It became even weaker in the 1990s, as well as in this century.

The big switch in downgrading bank regulation all the way to impotence came in September 2003, with bank regulators looking the other way when banks developed, packaged, and sold opaque financial instruments. Nothing was done to redress the balances, yet it was nobody's secret that with too fast innovation commercial and investment bankers were overtaking the regulators by a margin.

A further irony is that, according to some economists, the Fed even encouraged consumers to take part in the bankers' ball, for instance by advising the use of variable-rate mortgages, which Alan Greenspan himself had characterized as a very important instrument. With this and similar happenings taking place on a wide scale, including the free reign of hedge funds and the rapid growth of bank-to-bank over-the-counter derivatives (Chapter 1), central banks lost control of the economy. They also fell off the regulatory cliff when they allowed commercial banks to:

- Securitize,
- Collateralize, and
- Sell to people and companies instruments they did not understand.

At Davos in 2008, John Snow, former Treasury Secretary and chairman of the Cerberos hedge fund, answered Stiglitz's comments by practically saying that everybody is OK, thank you. Snow was seconded by a young fellow from Zurich Financial Services who suggested that the markets and their players should be left alone to do as they please (A formerly prosperous Zurich Insurance had done exactly that, namely transformed itself to "Financial Services," and went nearly bust – being downsized and saved only at the twelfth hour.)

What the former Treasury Secretary did not say, but many of his listeners expected to hear, was that because of financial globalization (Chapter 3) the freedom of US monetary policy is constrained by the monetary and exchange-rate policies of nations in upswing: China, India, Russia, Brazil, and more. As a result, decisions made in Washington, London, Berlin, or Paris are not filtering down the global financial system. Additionally,

- The world economy cannot even be decoupled from a US hard landing, let alone a major downturn, and
- Even if some nations are unscathed by the subprimes, they are not immune to a new depression.

Once the huge American demand for imported goods (and hence for exports by China and insourcing by India) wanes, neither of the latter countries will have enough internal demand to compensate for the loss. To the contrary, each will be under severe pressure to develop new employment opportunities which will be hard to find within its own borders.

Regarding the likelihood that the American financial and economic crisis spreads to emerging countries, Stephen Roach, chief executive of Morgan Stanley's Asian operations, pointed out that *if* market exchange rates were used, *then* US consumers spent six times more than China and India combined. Therefore, emerging markets would neither be immune nor would they come to the rescue of world growth even if consumption there rose rapidly. "Europe is not going to get a special dispensation from a US slowdown," Roach added.

Under present conditions of global production and consumption, Asia depends more on the US than what was the case 5 and 10 years ago. Having heard the different viewpoints, participants to the Davos 2008 special session voted with a majority of 59 percent that central banks have lost control of the financial markets. The sense of the meeting was the need to reinforce regulation, and do so at global scale. But there was a surprise (see Chapter 3, section 7).

2. The Fed rushes to protect the markets

Another conclusion from the aforementioned special session at Davos was that the Fed got it wrong on the economy. On other occasions, too, several economists suggested that since the mid 1990s monetary policy decisions have not been in the right direction, and this is documented by what has happened in 2007/2008 with big interest rate cuts; as well as at government level with the bending of fiscal policy (Chapter 5) and the uncertainty in the domain of bank supervision.

No bank's exposure has, or could ever have, zero risk weighting, because the financial industry builds its fortune on risk. Risk however must be steadily measured, subjected to limits, controlled, and audited. The problem today is that not only the management but also the supervision of banks, particularly of big banks, is wanting. In a televised interview on 1 April 2008 Dr Henry Kaufman, probably the best living economist, said that:

- If some banks are too big too fail,
- Then they should be very closely supervised.[3]

Kaufman proposed that for the 25 to 30 US banks and other financial institutions too big to fail, there must be a special regulatory authority which steadily watches over them (Chapter 10), and he is absolutely right. Once big banks, and with them the banking industry, get into a tailspin, postmortem official pronouncements, promises, reorganizations, and stimulus packages are hot air. Because of their effect on market psychology – for instance, "The Fed knows something that I don't know" – they amplify outstanding negative sentiment rather than contain it.

The fiscal stimulus enacted by the Bush Administration in February 2008 provides an example. Experts say that it has risks well beyond the US budget (which is anyway in the red), impacting upon the American current account deficit. A recession would have been an opportunity to bend imports and shrink that deficit. This move is seen by several economists as long overdue because the US has 5 percent excess consumption;[4] but the Bush stimulus package is precisely the opposite of what is needed to bring it under control.

- This 5 percent excess consumption reflects consumers' attitudes, and
- It feeds the trend in current account deficit, which does not reverse itself in spite of a cheap dollar.

The meaning of a consumption figure stuck at 67 percent of GDP, versus 62 percent in western Europe, is that the US economy never left the playbook, which brought it to the edge of the abyss with the subprimes. Low interest rates create a vicious cycle between US consumption and current account deficits. In a way similar to that of the Greenspan cuts of 2002, the message given by the Bernanke interest rate cuts is that the Fed is there only to protect the markets.

(It was as well said that the €4.9 billion ($7.25 billion) scam at France's Société Générale and the market volatility it brought along influenced the Fed's decision; while the announcement by WestLB, the troubled German public sector big bank, that it would get an emergency €2 billion ($2.9 billion) capital injection led to another steep fall in stock prices.)

"What we have now are the foreseeable consequences of bad economic management," observed Joseph Stiglitz. George Soros accused the Fed of cutting rates in a "rather panicky way...because people fear there are hidden problems." Most visible as well were the worries about monoline insurers (Chapter 1) and about the rumor that there might be a looming problem with money market funds. "Stop-gap measures to shore up world markets must be replaced by a coherent strategy for the real economy," said Guy Rider, general secretary of International Trade Union Confederation.[5]

Jean-Claude Trichet, president of the European Central Bank, emphasized the priority his institution attached to combating inflation, and a belief that euroland's problems were not those of America. Trichet's comments brought in perspective the contrast between the ECB and the US Federal Reserve. In Britain, Mervyn King, Governor of the Bank of England, suggested the latest volatility in markets would not change his institution's cautious approach to cutting rates. Highlighting the risks of inflation overshooting targets, he argued that:

- The adjustment under way in the British and world economy was necessary, and
- The continuing repricing of risk is not a process that "we should try to reverse."

Also eye-opening has been a comment by Charles Goodhart, a professor at the London School of Economics and former member of the Bank of England Monetary Policy Committee. He said that Britain's central bank faced acute difficulties in cutting rates when there was a significant risk of inflation rising well above target – a situation not unlike that prevailing in the United States and in euroland.

Echoing comments on the rate cut by Mervyn King, Edmund Phelps, the Nobel prize-winning economist from Columbia University, let it be known that he was skeptical of policies that tried to avoid a necessary workout of private sector problems. Phelps added that he worried over the call of politicians to prevent a recession *as if* interest rate cuts by the Fed and tax rebates could combat or undo the structural forces unleashed by weakness in the banking sector.

Outside the Davos Forum, in his 31 January 2008 televised interview on the US economy and the Fed's successive 75 basis points cut and another 50 basis points cut, Switzerland's Eric Faber phrased his thoughts in one short sentence: "Murky times ahead." His thesis has been that:

- *If* the Federal Reserve reliquifies the system without addressing the reasons for economic and financial problems,
- *Then* what the American economy will get is more of the same and even worse.

Faber traced the roots of the financial and credit risk crisis of 2007/2009 to too much easy money at very low cost, because of Greenspan's policies which undid what Paul Volcker had achieved by swamping US inflation in the 1980s. We are back in the economic environment of the 1970s, Faber said, and under these conditions neither equities nor bonds perform well:

- Bonds may offer safety for the next 10 days or a year,
- But long term, 30-year bonds are one of the worst investments, as their interest rate does not account for the coming inflation.

He also emphasized that, to his opinion, emerging markets are no place of safety, because the talk that they will be immune to a crisis in the west is nonsense (section 1 of this chapter). The financial sector, Faber added, had broken down, there were no more intermediaries, and therefore he felt sorry for Ben Bernanke because he was an academic and had been misguided in his monetary policies, with the aftereffect that:

- He did not recognize that the economy and financial markets had decoupled, and
- He kept on trying to shore up the falling financial markets, rather than focusing his attention on restructuring the American economy.

What Eric Faber brought into perspective is in tune with the thinking of many economists regarding the Fed's ongoing policies. They question particularly the policy of trying to avoid a recession at all costs, while recessions help in pruning the system from its own excesses.

Back in the realm of the 2008 World Economic Forum, Nouriel Roubini, of New York University, called for a more symmetric approach from the Fed: "There was a Greenspan put and now there is a Bernanke put," he said in reference to the market perception that two Fed chairmen got into the habit of always cutting interest rates when risk-prone investors lose money. In general, three criticisms emerged in the course of meetings at Davos 2008:

- That the timing of the large rate cut, just a week before a regular meeting of the Federal Open Market Committee, suggested panic.
- That the real motive for the move was an attempt to offer too much relief to equity markets, and
- Above all, that other considerations were kept in the back burner, particularly the likelihood that the policy of large rate cuts would not work.

The way Richard Cooper, of Harvard University, looked at this issue has been that there will be more economic pain in the US. Takatoshi Ito, of Tokyo University, voiced the fears of many in Davos, saying: "If financial turmoil spreads to local government bonds through monoline failures and other instruments, the situation would become serious."

Treasury Under Secretary for International Affairs David H. McCormick was cautious of the ability of the rest of the world to escape the forces impacting on the US economy. He emphasized that a housing downturn, a retrenchment of credit risk, and rising commodity prices were either global or widespread problems, so it would be difficult for other countries to remain immune. (See in Chapter 5 the wrong way out of recession chosen by the Bush Administration.)

3. Backwards into the Carter years

In late January 2008, David Rosenberg, of Merrill Lynch, was forecasting the Fed funds rate falling to 1 percent. Some analysts commented that, as they looked at the world at the moment, they would not make this a central scenario, in the hope that reasonable growth in the world would offset to some degree the recession in the US. Others, however, said that it is useless to believe the credit crisis is purely an

American problem. There appeared to be a growing global credit pandemic, and:

- *If* Rosenberg was right,
- *Then* we were facing a prolonged period of turmoil in financial markets.

The good news is that neither the stimulus by the Bush Administration (Chapter 5) nor rock-bottom interest rates are making unanimity. Several American economists and financial experts recognize their downside. The economics team at JPMorgan Chase has recently characterized the sharp interest rate cuts and stimulus as being "risk management on steroids." Those who challenge the "obvious" raise a key question for the American economic outlook:

- Does this high dose of anti-recession medicine fit the disease?
- Or, is it creating a new disease that may be far more lethal than the one it proposes to cure?

With headline inflation already at 4.3 percent in January 2008 (on a year-on-year basis) when big interest rate cuts were made, resulting in negative interest to capital, before 2008 has ended speculators could face a Fed suddenly intent on hiking rates. The trigger would probably be fear that an overly hot economy will push up stagflation to the level Jimmy Carter was famous for. As Edward Yardeni, one of the better-known American economists, put it in a note to clients: "I don't recall so much policy stimulus and so many bailout plans thrown at the economy so fast before there was compelling evidence of a recession."[6]

The risk taken by the US government and by the Fed is greater than what might have been otherwise, because there exists a global inflationary trend. In January 2008, Chinese inflation hit 7.1 percent, and rose to 8.5 percent a month later, with food price increases providing much of the upward surprise. Food prices also went through the roof in France and other countries in western Europe.

The Carter years' *stagflation* is a guide to what central banks should try by all means to avoid. It is always wise to remember errors and lessons from the past, and not only from the late 1990s. Also, in the early years of this century, short-term interest rates were lowered to extraordinary levels, with the Federal funds rate falling to 1 percent. The result has been a global credit bubble as capital became easily and abundantly available:

- On request, and

- Without credit questions asked.

At the time, a critical comment by an investment bank was that, with the funds rate down to 1 percent, the Federal Reserve would not necessarily reinflate the US economy but would instead give "free money to China." It did not only that, enriching the treasury of the Chinese government with a $1.4 trillion war chest; it also threw money at the market and we know the results (more on this later).

In the opinion of American economists whose judgment is not subordinated to election year politics, the Fed's 2007/2008 intense focus on interest rates is overdone. For practical reasons, central banks control only the price of credit and generally do not control the availability of credit. In other terms, they cannot force financial institutions to either start or stop lending. A study by Merrill Lynch advances two examples to demonstrate this point.

- The Fed could not force financial institutions to stop lending from 2004 to 2006 when it was increasing interest rates, and
- The Bank of Japan's decade-long attempts to persuade Japanese financial institutions to lend failed, even when the BOJ brought interest rates nearly to zero.[7]

In contrast to ineffectual headline measures, many investors and financial experts who want the system to survive have been pushing for greater transparency, including the accelerated disclosure of losses arising from the credit crisis. An overwhelming call has been for significant improvements in the information content of credit ratings, accompanied by action to address potential conflicts of interest for the rating agencies themselves (Chapter 6).

Another important request is addressed to the Basel Committee on Banking Supervision: to bring forward standards on improving the international management of liquidity risk, accompanied by more stringent capital requirements on banks. All financial institutions should be able to uphold their staying power in the face of losses similar to those of US subprime mortgages, leveraged deals, and other significant exposures.

This was supposed to happen with Basel II, the new capital adequacy regulation by the Basel Committee,[8] which has gone into effect. But it did not. Quite to the contrary, the safeguards Basel II was supposed to provide have melted away – while its models and its rules are now widely used by big banks for *regulatory arbitrage*, against all good sense.

4. LCBGs and systemic risk

The so-called *large and complex banking groups* (LCBGs) started the practice of regulatory arbitrage with Basel I, the first international capital
adequacy standard, which was based on compromises among central
bankers of the Group of Ten who constituted the Basel Committee
on Banking Supervision. With Basel II, cheating in terms of capital
adequacy became a science, as demonstrated by statistics in Table 2.1
(from the *Financial Times*), which contrast equity capital (core capital,
recently called "Basel Zero") to supergeared Basel II capital.

It has been a deliberate choice, in this text, to name LCBGs *big banks*,
because the label can be remembered better. More precisely, they are
mammoth *universal* banks, engaging in all sorts of financial activities
from commercial and investment banking to insurance, mortgages,
conduits, SIVs, hedge funds, and more. A 2007 study by the European
Central Bank has identified 36 of them; surprisingly 21 are located in
euroland.

The number of LCGBs increases over time. Two new big banking
groups have been added in 2007 in euroland alone, one resulting from
a merger and the other being the outcome of organic growth. There

Table 2.1   Regulatory arbitrage: Basel II and Basel Zero[1]

	Core capital ratio	
	Basel Zero	**Basel II[2]**
UBS	1.0	8.6
Royal Bank of Scotland	1.2	7.1
Barclays	1.2	7.6
Deutsche Bank	1.4	8.7
Société Générale	2.0	6.1
Credit Suisse	2.2	11.5
BNP/Paribas	2.8	7.3
Standard Chartered	3.5	7.5
HSBC	3.9	9.4
Unicredit	4.1	6.7

1. *Financial Times*, 8 February 2008.
2. In February 2008 there was no evident reason for disbelieving these
figures but, given the intervening events, by November 2008 they look
awfully inflated. By contrast, the core capital ratios in "Basel Zero"
seem to be about right. Several of the big banks in this list had mainly
toxic waste as Basel II capital, hence they urgently needed large capital
injections of taxpayers' money to survive (as explained in the footnotes
to Table 1.1).

were, as well, two new LCBGs outside euroland. However, if their number increases this is not true of their creditworthiness, as attested by the fact that their credit default swaps spreads widened significantly in July/August 2007 and again in early November 2007.

Using spreads of LCBGs' credit default swaps (Chapter 1), as well as equity returns, European Central Bank researchers made an empirical evaluation of simultaneous defaults. This provided a new financial stability indicator based on market perception of the likelihood of occurrence of an adverse systemic effect – a notion that should be looked at very carefully.

What has been found in this study is that in early November 2007 market turmoil was assessed by market players as having the potential for more far-reaching potential consequences for LCBGs than past events have had.[9] There should not be much doubt that one of the key reasons underpinning these results is the fact the LCBGs are thinly capitalized. Core capital, which is basically equity, is run down, while as Table 2.1 has shown Basel II capital figures have been inflated beyond recognition. Therefore:

- Economists, financial experts, and also bankers who want the system to survive ask that only core capital is accepted by regulators (*Basel Zero*).
- Every bank should report to regulators and the public both *core capital and liquidity,* leaving out the many tricks with leveraged instruments, "hybrids," "deferred tax assets," and the like.

Integral to honest financial reporting are both the need for new global *capital adequacy and liquidity* regulation, and, at national level, the need for new legislation. The rules for capital adequacy and liquidity must be few and very clear, aiming to control the wheeling and dealing by large and complex banking groups, like some of those shown in Table 2.1.[10] Moreover, their financial performances must be steadily monitored and analyzed by central banks for financial stability reasons:

- With globalization and rapid financial innovation, systemic risk cannot be controlled through old standards.
- Worse yet, with the current downgrading of supervisory watch it is the LCBGs that rate the regulators' compliance to their whims.

Not only should the supervisory tiger have biting teeth, but also a frequent review of control rules is needed to take into account the effects of operational and structural change. Crucial factors are: the extent of globalized operations; cross-border assets; universality of services; complexity and opaqueness of traded instruments; trading income, profits and losses; degree of leverage; increase in liabilities; deposits and other customer assets at risk; whether exposure is balanced; quality of risk management; as well as mergers, acquisitions and organic growth.

The gaps in regulations and legislation, which developed since the 1980s, are the basic reason that made it so attractive for banks to hide their gambles off balance sheet till heaven broke loose. In an article published in the *Financial Times* on 6 February 2007, Martin Wolf advanced the thesis that two major attributes qualify the financial system over the past three decades:

- Its ability to generate crises, and
- The mismatch between public risk and private reward.

These two issues converge to the fact that over three decades, from 1977 up to but not including 2007, none of the financial crises gravely damaged the global economy, though some devastated individual economies. Now, however, something has changed as a deep and prolonged US recession (or the beginning of a depression) not only hits savers, homeowners, and consumers but also has the potential to devastate several economies – with huge social and political consequences. This "something" is that practically the whole banking industry, not just investment banks:

- Has turned finance into a global Monte Carlo, and
- Losses of billions of dollars by the gamblers at the roulette table are hitting the bystanders.

The global financial markets, says a study by Merrill Lynch, are just beginning to head into a period when the *survival of the fittest* will be the order of the day. (Charles Darwin is often credited with coining that phrase, but prior to Darwin, Herbert Spencer used it in his 1864 book *The Principles of Biology*. Though Spencer did also use the phrase with respect to economies, one doubts if either Spencer or Darwin ever imagined their brainchild being employed to explain who of the LCBGs lives or dies in financial markets in free fall.)

In conclusion, taming the LCBGs is the *salient problem* of the global economy to which governments should bring their immediate attention, rather than trying to fix the broken wheel through rock-bottom interest rates. In the longer term, system risk will not be brought under control until the mammoth LCBGs are dismantled through the enactment of a new Glass-Steagall Act and other urgently required measures.

5. The need for a new Glass-Steagall Act

The study by ECB of the probability of simultaneous failures by LCBGs is most timely because one of the main contributors to the Great Depression of 1929–1933 and its aftereffects had been the massive bankruptcies of credit institutions and the volatilization of the American public's deposits entrusted to the banking industry. To face the challenge, the Roosevelt Administration instituted the Federal Deposit Insurance Corporation (FDIC), as the guarantor of bank deposits and the agent of preventing bank runs; and it also passed the Glass-Steagall Act of 1933.

Glass-Steagall separated the roles of commercial and investment banking, aiming to prevent commercial banks gambling in the securities markets with their depositors' money and other assets. The Act survived without much of a change until the go-go 1980s, when the advent of international financial markets led to a huge growth in cross-border capital flows and to its repeal in 1999, under the presidency of Bill Clinton.

A casino society replaced nearly seven decades of prudence. The Gramm-Leach-Bliley Act, which became effective in March 2000, permits qualifying bank holding companies (read: LCBGs) to become financial holding companies and thereby affiliate with a broad range of financial operations, instruments, and exposures. The Act identifies several activities as financial in nature, including:

- Retail banking,
- Commercial banking,
- Securities brokerage,
- Underwriting,
- Dealing in or making a market in securities,
- Investment management services,
- Insurance business, and more.

The Gramm-Leach-Bliley Act states that the Federal Reserve Board may impose limitations, restrictions, or prohibitions on the activities or acquisitions of a financial holding company *if* the Fed believes that the company is encountering difficulties with certain activities like mergers and acquisitions. The imposition of restrictions has not happened yet. What has surely taken place is free-for-all financial miserabilism, that has destroyed the American economy.

Critics of the Act say that the Fed was not even given full powers to intervene. Intervention might have happened had it believed that an LCBG did not have the appropriate financial and managerial resources to commence or conduct certain types of operations, for instance retain ownership of another company, but no mention was made of:

• An LCBG's inability to exercise risk management, and
• Its failure to be in charge of its exposure at each corner of its empire, each of its instruments, and each of its counterparties.

Yet, what these two bullets identify is by far more important than the big and complex financial entity's inability to make another acquisition. From 2000 to 2008 there had been plenty of reasons for corrective action, but only after the subprime mess of 2007 did some regulators start having second thoughts about the wisdom of mixing commercial and investment banking. The reason for establishing clear limits is not only the huge risks being assumed with other people's money, but also the moral hazard.

• The banks' executives, traders, investment managers, and other professionals get all the rewards if things go well.
• Depositors and taxpayers pay the bill when the bank goes to the wall, and the government bends over to save it.

It is not just star traders who through huge bonuses are given incentives to take inordinate risks (Chapter 6). Their bosses collect plenty of money, too, and they open their golden parachutes after their bank is in ruins. For moralization purposes, central banks, supervisory authorities, and governments should let a big bank go bust as an example to the others, providing a safety net only to smaller depositors. But the authorities don't take that step, because they do not wish to upset an economy already battered by the banks' excesses.

Rather than throwing money at the problem through salvage plans, rock-bottom invisible interest rates, and different "stimuli," it would be better to reign through an updated and biting legislation and regulation of the banking sector. This is an industry that has time and again demonstrated its capacity to generate serious crises – while having the political muscle to do away with supervision in the name of "free markets" (a misnomer).

Crucial to the success of a new Glass-Steagall Act would be that the change in legislation would prime assets over debt. Today, equity is taxed; debt is not. The fact that dividends servicing equity capital are taxed, while interest payments on debt capital are not, has given a great impetus towards leverage. (The legal convention of tax deductibility of interest emerged in the nineteenth century, without much of an economic rationale.) A number of critics, including the US Treasury, now argue that the priming of debt:

- Hurts productivity, and
- Distorts economic thinking.

Besides penalizing leverage to keep it subdued, the new Glass-Steagall Act should reward the financial institutions' ability to control future excesses. It should also explicitly state that risk management is key to the survival of the fittest, and provide the reference that in this specific mission nearly all of the 2002 to 2007 financial operators have failed miserably. They put up no money for:

- A proper risk control methodology,
- Extensive personal training, or
- Premium equipment for real-time response.

All their money has gone to the roulette table. The incentives themselves have been turned on their head, translated into inordinate bonuses and cashed every year – no matter the damage their miscalculated risk did to the bank, its other employees, shareholders, bondholders and the general public. Two sound principles are that:

- Incentives and bonuses should be paid only *after* the instrument expires and the entity has profited from its existence, and
- Bankers, traders, investors, and other financial operators should appreciate that incentives paid upfront no matter what may be the future damage are immoral, unethical, and counterproductive.

The late Steve Fosset, the adventurer, record-breaker, and former investment banker, has left us an excellent example of right incentives. His shrewdest move was to take out a $500,000 insurance policy that would pay him $3 million *if* his global balloon flight *succeeded* – which it did.

6. Fraud and punishment

Structured financial products are derivative instruments, by majority custom designed to appeal to a group of investors or market segment. The securitized subprimes are an example (Chapter 4). What the buyer of a structured product is not told by the vendor is that over the years it may present a number of problems that end in financial loss.

Part of the fraud with structured finance originated in severing the link between those who scrutinize the creditworthiness of borrowers and those who assume wholesale the risk when they default. There has been, so to speak, no origination certificate guaranteeing the quality of the underwriting – a sort of certified information issued by lender, broker, or servicer. Two bills pending in the US Congress aim to correct this deficiency.

One of these bills has an *assignee liability* provision that would hold the originators partly responsible for lax lending. Many banks and their lobbyists object to this bill, but not all bankers are against it. JPMorgan Chase has argued that some form of it is needed to counter the perception, if not the reality, that securitization is harmful.

The second bill would allow bankruptcy judges to alter the terms of struggling borrowers' mortgages. Banks are against it, saying that this would be "an intolerable violation of the sanctity [!!] of loan-pooling contracts," which is of course nonsense. Even without such bill, in the United States securitizers face probes by:

- The Department of Justice,
- Several state attorney-generals,
- The Internal Revenue Service,
- The Federal Bureau of Investigation (FBI), and
- The Securities and Exchange Commission (SEC).[11]

There are, as well, lawsuits from investors and a rising number of stricken municipalities. Between August and October 2007 the annualized pace of federal securities class-action lawsuits filed in America increased to about 270, more than double that of 2006. Some experts foresee that claims could easily exceed those of the dotcom bust and options-backdating scandal combined. Moreover, one thing that sets the subprime litigation apart from previous class actions is its breadth.

After the collapses of Enron (in 2001), and Adelphia and WorldCom (in 2002), lawsuits were targeted at a fairly narrow range of parties: internet firms which had gone bust, their certified public accountants, and some banks. By contrast, investors defrauded by the subprimes are aiming at mortgage lenders, brokers, and investment bankers as well as:

- Insurers such as American International Group (AIG);
- Bond funds – State Street, Morgan Keegan;
- Rating agencies – Standard & Poor's, Moody's;
- Homebuilders – Beazer Homes, Toll Brothers, and more.

Banks also turn against other banks. On 24 February 2008, Germany's HSH Nordbank sued UBS to recover millions of losses it incurred on a portfolio of credit derivatives sold to it by the Swiss bank. While it is rather doubtful whether a bank can prove it did not know what it was buying in terms of toxic waste, this is a good example on the flood of litigation about derivatives.

Bear Stearns, the investment bank, reckons liability insurers could lose up to $8 billion to $9 billion on claims related to such lawsuits. By all likelihood, the biggest losers will be those most exposed to complex and risky transactions. For instance, American insurers recently had to write down $4.9 billion of swaps, related to collateralized debt obligations; while Swiss Re had already written down $1 billion or so on two related credit default swaps, and also faces billions of dollars of write-downs on ill-judged investments in American mortgages.

Borrowers, are suing both their lenders and the Wall Street firms that securitized and sold them junk loans. Litigation has also become globalized. Local councils in Australia are threatening to sue a subsidiary of Lehman Brothers, over the sale of collateralized debt obligations.[12] Even lenders are turning on each other; and lawyers are practically assured to offer their spouse a new mink coat for Christmas.

With litigation becoming globalized, and given the reputational damage this can create, bankers should have been promoters rather than opponents of the bills pending in US Congress. By limiting the unreasonable amounts of exposure assumed by banks and other financial institutions in search of fat profits and ever greater end-of-year bonuses, such legislation will help first and foremost the institutions themselves in rebuilding their run-down risk control defenses.

It might not look so at first sight, but it is to everybody's interest not to repeat scams like the subprimes. Townships lose plenty of money on foreclosures. According to some estimates, on a foreclosure a house's value falls by from 20 cents to 60 cents on the dollar. Lenders say that they lose $50,000 or more on a foreclosure. Municipalities assert that they are faced with major costs, because foreclosed homes that become vacant provide sites for crime, and are raising:

- Police costs,
- Inspection costs,
- Court action costs,
- Fire department costs, and
- Costs of potential demolition.

There are also unpaid bills for water and sewage and for trash removal. Foreclosures also result in reduced property value and home equity for nearby homes in the neighborhood. Critics of the current lousy mortgage lending policies add that the attention of federal and state governments should focus on these issues, while current efforts theoretically intended at helping homeowners are actually aimed at slowing the collapse of the real estate market, to:

- Protect the values of the mountain of mortgage-backed securities, and
- Guarantee the solvency of the institutions that own them.

Therefore, rather than helping people, they perpetuate a system which has driven home prices and rents to unaffordable levels, ravaging the living standards of the economically weaker 50 percent of the US population. Precisely to help these people, on 25 February 2008 Alan Blinder, former Vice Chairman of the Federal Reserve and currently of Princeton University, came up with a proposal to create a new federal agency which will buy from its owner(s) real estate at the brink of foreclosure.

"We are back in 1933," said Blinder in a televised interview, with reference to FDIC and other Roosevelt-era federal agencies. He also added that neither Fannie Mae nor Freddie Mac can handle the mortgage crisis, and estimated that the new agency could take over between 1 million and 2 million house loans, and for this would need between $200 billion and $400 billion. (Most likely, it would end by needing double that money.) Some congressmen talk of an initial capitalization of around $20 billion, which will be a drop in the pocket.

An idea advanced by the Office of Thrift Supervision (OTS) is to give mortgage lenders a share of the upside if properties appreciate. Under this scheme, the Federal Housing Administration (FHA) would insure a new mortgage at a home's current value. The existing lender would get a *negative equity* claim for the difference between that and the original loan, which could be exercised if the house is later sold at a higher price. Opponents of this scheme say that:

- *If* the upside in value is taken away from home owners experiencing financial difficulties,
- *Then* they will abandon their negative-equity houses forthwith.

No matter which might be the solution, it would definitely ask for plenty of money. The taxpayer should not be asked to make that major down payment, intended to cover other people's faults and frauds. Instead, another Roosevelt-era solution must be used, with all banks writing mortgages paying the new agency's capital through a percentage of their profits past, current, and future (as with FDIC).

7. Sovereign wealth funds as lenders of last resort

At the World Economic Forum 2008, the Time Board of Economists remarked that the emergence of sovereign wealth funds (SWFs) may change the dynamics of the world economy. One of the questions debated during the Forum has been whether the SWFs are free-market players or state agents, since they depend directly on governments. Another was to what extent SWFs are power brokers and power centers.

A little joke explains the issue underpinning the latter query. It says that the $7.5 billion invested in Citigroup to save it from bankruptcy represented less than a month of Abu Dhabi's income from oil. Hence, there is no major problem if the big bank that got the money goes bust. On the other hand, however, it should not be lost from sight that the advent of SWFs is a shift of wealth to the developing world, which has:

- Serious geopolitical implications,
- A far-reaching economic aftermath, and
- A high likelihood that the transition period will be characterized by political, social, and financial instability.

In the past, banks needing money have turned to Western capital markets or borrowed from other banks. Today bankers don't lend freely to each other because they know their industry's accounts are opaque – while both on-balance-sheet and off-balance-sheet they have an enormous amount of risk. Precisely for the same reasons, national capital markets are most reluctant to act as wholesale funding sources, a role they have played since the mid to late nineteenth century.

Since their intervention in the fourth quarter of 2007 to save from bankruptcy mismanaged big American and European banks, sovereign wealth funds have earned for themselves two contradictory reputations: saviors of the financial system, and massive threats to national jewels of the west. Reality lies between these extremes: SWFs represent the rise of active sovereign wealth investors, and they cannot be ignored.

Therefore, one way of looking at a sovereign wealth fund is as an outcome of the globalization of markets, a sort of financial multi-national. The difference between SWFs and other multinationals lies in the fact that they are state-controlled and secretive – a reason why the US Treasury has been stepping up efforts to persuade them to be more transparent and accountable. This is supposed to counter unease about SWFs' investments in American banks as well as other businesses, adding to the fact that SWFs:

- Have largely been long-term stable, commercially driven investors, and
- Only in 2007 did they became a sort of *lender of last resort* to wounded western banks.

The message given by the first bullet is that the funds that come into SWFs coffers look for an investment home with reasonable security and good returns. The source of funds is not just the persistently high oil price. In addition to that are the global imbalances that continue to fuel foreign exchange reserves, which:

- Fill the treasuries of some nations to overflow, and
- Empty those of other nations because they don't care to be in charge of their current account deficits.

Compiling a league table of the largest funds is not easy, as most are highly secretive and do not even publish the size of their portfolios, let alone the type and spread of investments. What is not a secret, however, is that some of them are big and active. The list includes Abu Dhabi's ADIA, Singapore's GIC and Temask, the China Investment Corporation, Kuwait's Investment Authority, Qatar's Investment Authority, Dubai's International Capital, Russia's Stabilization Fund, and Norway's Government Pension Fund, among several others.

Saudia Arabia has a Monetary Agency, not a formal investment vehicle, though many bankers see Saudi Arabia as one of the largest potential sources of sovereign wealth. ADIA is widely believed to be the largest sovereign wealth fund, with assets worth over $800 billion. With half that money, Norway's Pension Fund has around 60 percent of its assets invested in bonds, with the rest in equities. It also has a large number of public company shareholdings, usually limited to less than 3 percent in each entity.

The investment policies of SWFs are most relevant because their war chests increase rapidly, and they have already taken substantial stakes in companies as diverse as Sony, EADS, and Union Bank of Switzerland. In September 2007, the Dubai Stock Exchange secured 28 percent of the London Stock Exchange (LSE), equivalent to most of Nasdaq's 31 percent stake. This has been a complex series of deals involving OMX, the Stockholm-based Nordic exchanges. The Qatar Investment Authority (QIA), which had failed to capture the Nasdaq stake, bought a nearly 20 percent holding from two hedge funds.

Other investments came in the aftermath of the banking industry's self-inflicted wounds. Citigroup, Merrill Lynch, Morgan Stanley, UBS, Barclays, HSBC and more – the "Who Is Who" of western big banks – have turned to government-backed investors in Asia and the Middle East for large slugs of capital. This new gold rush has served to underline:

- The shifting balance of global financial power,
- The growing confidence of sovereign wealth funds, and
- Political concerns in the west about the SWFs' influence, which tends to increase in proportion to western banks becoming gamblers.

For instance, in early December 2007 UBS "suddenly" found that the value of its investments linked to US subprime mortgages had dropped by another $10 billion. Reportedly, within 4 days, UBS had agreed the outlines of a $12 billion capital injection from the Government of Singapore Investment Corporation (GIC) and a Middle Eastern investor. (People familiar with the matter say the bank had potential commitments for three times that amount.)

Sovereign wealth funds are also joining forces with companies in mergers and acquisitions. Barclays turned to Singapore's Temasek and China Development Bank for help when sweetening its failed bid for ABN Amro, the global Dutch bank. SWFs are also bidding for whole companies, as in the case of Qatar's Investment Authority claiming control of JSainsbury, the British retailer, but failing to get it.

Slowly but unquestionably the owners of huge amounts of liquid money demand their dues, trusting no more empty promises but asking for "evidence now." Already some issues are rising in the horizon, and it is advisable to study them proactively rather than react late in the day using a fire brigade approach.

- One of them has to do with the so-called hands-off approach of SWFs as major investors.

Say that an SWF invested $10 billion in a big bank, trusting that its management would be in charge, but the bank went bust. What then? Should this be a matter of political negotiations? Admitting the SWF as a semi-sovereign party? Or, should it be a market decision, in which case the SWF could take legal action to recover its money?

- Another subject which should be settled proactively is that of trustees and of receivership.

This theme was debated at Davos 2008, and one of the expert opinions has been that the SWF may have good reasons not to accept the banking regulators of "this" or "that" western country as trustees. Will the International Court in the Hague become also a financial court, or should a new authority be instituted to dispense supranational financial judgments?

Notice however that at the end of the day sovereign wealth funds are not as dupable as western banks thought they are. The capital injections they have made to wounded western banks have strings attached to them, and breaking contractual clauses can be quite costly. Here is an example.

At the end of July 2008, Merrill Lynch said that it had taken steps to shore up its finances with an $8.5 billion share offering. Raising more capital brought the total since December 2007 to over $30 billion. This triggered a reset provision requiring it to pay $2.5 billion to Temasek, the SWF of Singapore, which had invested in an earlier Merrill equity offering (at a higher price) and poured another $3.4 billion into the late July 2008 equity sale.[13]

There is as well an important social issue concerning SWFs as lenders of last resort, which should be examined through a holistic approach. Millions of workers now depend for their livelihood on financial decisions made by SWFs and hedge funds. Should sovereign states apply rules of behavior? Or should this be left to the market?

There were no consensuses of opinion at the 2008 World Economic Forum on these issues. The reader should notice however that 81 percent of the participants to a special session voted that SWFs and hedge funds have become the world's new power brokers. Some participants also said that the relation of the west to the SWFs is a subject to be addressed *now*, not after it becomes too late to find solutions.

8. Central banks as repositories of last resort

In an effort to calm down the markets after the July/August 2007 blow-up of the credit bubble, and also buy time to figure out what to do, central banks injected lots of liquidity into the market. This started with the European Central Bank and (to a lesser extent) the Federal Reserve, but in December 2007 the British, Canadian, and Swiss central banks joined the ECB and Fed in a concerted liquidity plan; they repeated that same gesture on 11 March 2008 and several times thereafter.

Some experts saw in this policy an effort designed to preserve the fictitious values of subprimes, Alt-As, and other mortgage-backed securities, by reducing the need for holders of such instruments to sell them. As evidence, they provided the case of Merrill Lynch which had tried to sell the collateral of the two troubled Bear Stearns hedge funds, only to get offers as low as 20 cents to the dollar.

- A fire sale would have triggered a vicious cycle of writedowns and Merrill Lynch did not go ahead.
- Had it done so, brokers would have been obliged to issue margin calls prompting another round of asset sales, to raise the money.

Other experts brought this assumption a step further. In their opinion, in trying to alleviate the aforementioned problem by taking in much of this useless paper as collateral for loans they gave to commercial and investment banks, central banks have turned themselves into repositories if not outright *buyers of last resort* – a totally new role for monetary institutions.

The European Central Bank was best fit in assuming this role, because it is not as restricted as the Federal Reserve in the types of collateral it can accept for loans. The Fed, these experts said, probably contributed its share as buyer of last resort by means of its Term Auction Facility. The latter was set up to create inter-bank swap lines, which allow other central banks to draw dollars. Critics added that this new policy:

- Turned central banks into a mechanism for buying up worthless dollar-denominated securities, and that
- An extensive usage of this mechanism serves to obviate the need to sell worthless securities on the open market.

The way an article in the *Washington Post* had it, on 19 December 2007, the ECB's action was not just an injection of $500 billion, but $500 billion lent against almost any collateral, including a handwritten IOU from Uncle George in Baltimore or Uncle Ludwig in Dusseldorf. The problem of preventing a vicious spiral of asset writedowns was also addressed by:

- Bank of England markets director Paul Tucker, who called it a "vicious circle," and
- New York Fed chief Tim Geithner, who warned of an "adverse self-reinforcing dynamic."[14]

Down to its fundamentals, this action is akin to a *bad-debt-recycling* process, based upon the notion of taking out new loans to pay off old ones. It's a sort of Ponzi game, allowing banks to say that their debts are current; but at the same time it puts good money running after bad. This raises interesting questions in respect to:

- The extent the loan might be covered for the selected draining of some of the worthless paper out of the system, and
- Whether an alternative way has been found to overcome the banking system's *insolvency*, by exchanging worthless assets for cash.

On 31 January 2008 the *Financial Times* reported that €30 billion of securitized junk had been packaged by Holland's Rabobank (which still held an AAA credit rating), for the contingency of using it as collateral for borrowing from the ECB through its repo (lend and purchase) operations. Such a perpetual liquidity machine also served when in December 2007 Spanish banks issued securities for which there was no market, except at the ECB repo facility. In that month alone Spanish banks borrowed 63 billion euros through the use of anything other than prime collateral.

Had the Federal Reserve not intervened to save Bear Stearns, Fannie Mae, Freddie Mac, and AIG (but not Lehman Brothers), as well as to recapitalize Goldman Sachs and Morgan Stanley (among other big banks), another question would have been whether investment banks, mortgage outfits, and insurance companies qualify to receive taxpayers money. None of these firms were regulated by the Fed – and the extent to which they were really supervised by somebody is, at best, questionable.

A similar query can be posed in connection to hedge funds, and whether they qualify for taxpayers' money (which might happen in the coming months). This is by no means an academic question. The way an early February 2008 news item had it, hedge funds were on track for their worst month since the Russian default of 1998, which brought down Long Term Capital Management. In January 2008 alone the average hedge fund had been losing more than 3 percent of its assets, with event-driven funds which followed activist strategies being worst hit.

Severe losses were also taken by equity long/short funds, which are exposed to declines in stock markets. Hedge funds that had long positions on stock markets lost out as British blue-chips fell 6.6 percent and the S&P 500 index was downsized by 6 percent during the month of January. Pardus Capital, the activist New York hedge fund, lost almost a quarter of its value, some $800 million in November/December 2007 and January 2008, as its bets on US airlines and a number of European companies soured.

If it is that governments have decided to act as buyers of last resort, resurrecting banks and hedge funds with severe self-inflicted wounds, then why not to buy a couple of million cars to help General Motors, which made a net loss of $722 million in the fourth quarter 2007, and its loss for the whole year stood at $38.7 billion – more than anyone of the banks (at least so far). And in spite of all this 2007 red ink, the carmaker still managed to report a $15.5 billion loss in second quarter 2008 – *as if* it were a mismanaged bank loaded in subprime CDOs.[15]

Also in the queue for handouts will be Hollywood, which faced a walkout by writers in 2007/2008 and confronted another one by actors in June 2008. According to *Screen Digest*, the major studios' entire slate of 132 films from 2006 is set to lose $1.9 billion in cash over the 5-year cycle of cinema, DVD, TV, and new media income.[16] The idea of involving Hollywood is not so far-fetched:

- In the 1950s and 1960s the master of suspense was Alfred Hitchcock.
- Half a century later, the masters of suspense are the presidents of big banks who have ruined their institutions and hold the whole economy hostage.

Back to serious business, the original gesture by central banks to act as repositories of last resort, to ease the illiquidity strains of commercial and investment banks under their jurisdiction, has been turned into a new perpetual-motion machine of junk paper. Midway through 2008, the news that British banks were preparing up to £90 billion ($180 billion) of mortgage-backed bonds to send to the Bank of England created a doomsday mood in the markets,[17] and rumors spread about the quality of collateral the central bank will be holding.

According to JP Morgan Chase, as of mid June 2008, of €208 billion ($315 billion) of "eligible securities," created mainly to deposit in the vaults of the European Central Bank and take good money in exchange for bad money, only €6 billion had been placed with investors.[18] The fact is that having started this process of garbage collection, central banks have too few tools and procedures to cope with the problems it now poses.

In conclusion, a direct result of using central banks as *buyers of last resort* is that all citizens get penalized, since this money which serves to save the sinners from default evidently comes from taxpayers' pockets. Neither is it sure such a solution could be successful in the longer run, if it becomes a habit to use it "to calm the markets."

*   *   *

When this text was written, in August 2008, bailing out General Motors and its Detroit pals was considered to be a remote, unlikely and unpopular move. Attempting to spend taxpayers' money on the automakers would have been almost unbelievable.

However, by November 2008, in the aftermath of a financial storm which combined unprecedented poor management with an economic meltdown in the United States, GM was losing a rumoured $52,000 every minute. Over the previous four years the world's former No. 1 motor vehicle manufacturer had racked up losses of $75 billion, and by late November its share fell to below $3 from a peak of $75.50.

In early December 2008, Detroit's Big Three car makers asked the government – more precisely the US taxpayer – for a combined $34 billion. The US Senate rejected that request, but the Bush Administration agreed to shower GM and Chrysler (Ford opted out for the time being) with $13.4 billion drawn from the Troubled Asset Relief Program (TARP), intended for salvaging the US banks). What in late summer would have been unbelievable had now come to pass.

3
The Globalization of Credit Risk

1. Effects of financial globalization

Over the last twenty years, the globalized economic and financial system has changed to such an extent that central banks are on their way to becoming irrelevant. We are a long way from the supply-and-demand fundamentals of a merchandising economy, which characterized the multinationals in the 1960s and 1970s. As the credit crisis of July/August 2007 demonstrated, rather than central bankers and regulatory authorities, it is the global financial industry that holds the upper ground.

After the crisis of the subprimes started to spread to other mortgages, several experts expressed the opinion that the globalization of credit risk, and most particularly of credit derivatives, holds many surprises beyond what is already known (see Chapter 4 for evidence). This has proved to be one of globalization's negatives, as money center banks and other financial entities have been making loans at any level of creditworthiness because that's simply raw material for securitizing and selling structured products world-wide.

- The *originate to distribute* business policy (Chapter 5) calls for laxer credit than central banks would like, and
- In the aftermath of originate to distribute, central banks are struggling to police credit risk in the global economy, without a precedent to guide their hand.

Precisely because the global financial industry has escaped the supervisory authorities, the bust of subprimes, CDOs, CDSs, and other derivatives is as hard to control as the boom that preceded it in the wake of easy money and easy credit. Even in countries where central banks have tried to slow the glut of market liquidity by raising short-term interest rates, their efforts have had no major effect because:

- The market knows there are limits on how much interest rates can go up, and
- Market players are now at ease with cross-border transactions in all major currencies, and some minor ones.

As far as interest rates are concerned, even when they went up to 15 percent, as in Iceland, the central bank's initiative backfired. High rates made Iceland the beneficiary of the *carry trade* (Chapter 9). Investors borrow in low-yielding currency such as the yen and the Swiss franc, and invest the proceeds in a high-interest-rate jurisdiction – this being done in a massive way that could financially obliterate a small economy like Iceland's.

With financial globalization growing like wild cacti, the odds of new bubbles are growing too (Chapter 1). The banks themselves suffer from massive agency problems between their traders, investment experts, clients, shareholders, bondholders, supervisory authorities, and of course their own management. These problems are exacerbated further by the difficulty of monitoring risks embedded in novel internationally traded instruments that become known:

- Long after the event has taken place,
- After unreasonably large bonuses have been paid, and
- After plenty of toxic waste has accumulated in the portfolios of the banks themselves, and of their clients.

As Martin Wolf has it: "Given the number of agents and the wealth of information asymmetries, it is astounding how little went wrong."[1] A similar statement is valid regarding the fact that, as Figure 3.1 shows, the derivatives' growth is exponential while both the world's gross domestic product (GDP) and world trade have increased linearly.

The virtual economy and real economy are unstuck: We are increasing the debt while shrinking the productive base. Debt, particularly liabilities leveraged and traded through derivatives, has become the new Eldorado – not just in America and Europe, but worldwide. At government, business, and household level our economy operates on borrowed money. Therefore:

- Every major default carries the risk of triggering an avalanche of losses, and

- Failures of leveraged credit derivatives, traded as assets, can set off a global chain reaction.

How are the experts reacting to this likelihood of systemic risk? Nobel prizewinner Dr Merton Miller suggests that derivatives have made the world a safer place (though he does not explain how and why). But George Soros warns that, quite to the contrary, derivatives will destroy society. Other experts suggest that the number one risk with derivatives is that banks and other entities hide losses by rolling over unpayable debt and through other tricks. Therefore:

- Nobody really knows the actual dimension of toxic waste in the banks' trading books, and
- This worrisome reference to opacity includes the management of financial institutions, all the way up to the board.

The fact that nobody today seems to be in charge of financial globalization does not mean that an economy closed within its borders is a better alternative. It is not. Nearly two centuries ago David Ricardo, one of the influential economists of his time, railed against the doctrine of

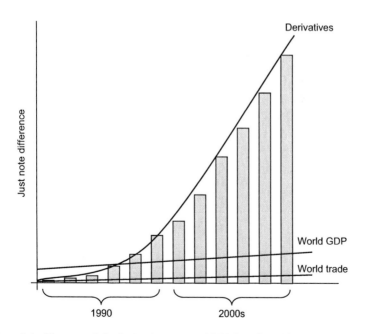

Figure 3.1 The growth in derivatives vs. world GDP and world trade

reinforced national borders by advocating free exchange of goods. Since then, his theory of comparative advantage has fed the free trade debate, gaining a large number of adherents.

Ricardo's central argument was that, even if one country could produce everything more efficiently than another – which is never the case – it would reap gains from specializing in what it was best at manufacturing and then trading its products with the other nations. What Ricardo did not say, but which the last 30 years has clearly demonstrated, is that for economies, societies, companies, and people, globalization has prerequisites:

- To survive they have to restructure themselves, improve their skills, become more flexible, and control their risks.
- For global trade to prosper, there should be a homogeneous system of checks and balances, including those for new financial instruments of creative but also destructive potential (subprimes are an example).

Technology has significantly improved the process of developing new products, and globalization has made it feasible to target new markets –, but while it increases mobility for individuals and firms, it also creates new unknowns which tend to have unexpected consequences. Five years ago, a study by economists of the IMF, which is in principle devoted to open financial markets, found no consensus that the ongoing financial integration yields any net benefits in growth.[2] Of 14 research papers reviewed in that study:

- Three said that financial integration has a positive effect,
- Four found that the effects are mixed, and
- Seven identified no effect, one way or the other.

Other studies, however, have contradicted these findings. Their conclusion has been that countries in the process of development, particularly in Asia, that have adopted a policy of globalization have grown faster than Western countries. In contrast, developing countries that retired into themselves, as has been the case in Africa, have stagnated or even became retrograde.

Clearly, there is cost and benefit with global financial integration, as with any other enterprise. Worldwide access to capital is likely to bring both advantages and drawbacks. Seeking the benefits of financial integration while suffering limited costs is an impossible task – because there exist plenty of tradeoffs (and many ironies) which make the choice of a strategy complex and uncertain.

One of the ironies is that while the global market has lots of freedom, central banks lack the freedom to take necessary measures in a timely manner. Were the West's central banks to tighten monetary policy aggressively, they would bring this process of money supply expansionism under control. But aggressive tightening is not feasible at the time of a major crisis (like the subprimes) because it could bring the financial edifice down single-handed.

Knowledgeable people also say that while Western central banks lose authority, other entities are not ready to take their place. For instance, in 2006 and 2007 credit rating agencies did not act swiftly to downgrade debt. Had they done so, they would have constrained households and companies from borrowing too much, as well as having discouraged banks from buying the upper tranche of junk mortgages as Tier-1 capital. (See also Chapter 6 on credit ratings.)

2. The instruments of financial globalization

A financial instrument is typically defined as cash; evidence of an ownership in an equity or debt; or a contract that meets certain criteria. Derivative financial instruments like options, futures, forwards, and swaps are examples (Chapter 1). The criteria to be met have to do with obligations and rights defined by contractual clauses. To a very substantial extent, the financial instruments of globalization have been:

- Cash, and
- Derivatives.

Plain cash in a base currency, cash in equities traded in exchanges, and other currencies are *spot* positions. While cash comprises only a small fraction of an entity's assets, it is the common denominator of all financial instruments, whether spot, forward, or options; and whether we deal in interest rates, currencies, debt equities, or other commodities. In the balance sheet a much larger segment of assets and liabilities consists of contractual obligations to deliver cash, and of rights to receive cash from a counterparty.

- *Cash flows* discharge these obligations, and
- They honor the contractual rights.

Future cash flows are dealt in *futures* or *forwards*, including future cash flows not just in a base currency but in any pair of currencies, as well as when an equity or other commodity is exchanged for a currency. Over-the-counter transactions are mainly forwards and options on interest rate, currency exchange rates, equity-linked contracts and commodities – with interest rates taking the lion's share. Figure 3.2 gives a snapshot on year-to-year increases in notional amounts outstanding of OTC derivatives.

Bonds are forwards, and the same is true of forward rate agreements (FRAs) and interest rate swaps (IRS). Bonds, bond options, and swaptions are subject to the uncertainties of the yield curve (more on this later). Their price is also influenced by spread risk, specific risk, duration, and market liquidity.

A favored instrument for global investing is equity trading. Many analysts look at shares as options on the commodity a company deals in, such as oil. Shares of gold mining companies, for example, are taken as options on gold bullion. This is incorrect because shares are also, and in a significantly way, influenced by stock market mood.

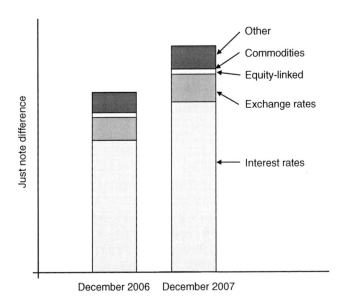

Figure 3.2 Notional amount of outstanding over-the-counter derivative contracts ($ trillions)

With the democratization of lending and the socialization of risk, which started respectively in the late 1920s and mid 1930s but became a force after World War II, more and more people were able to borrow, with an increasing amount of outstanding debt traded in the exchanges and off-exchange. In America, for example, in 2008 debt issuance increased by 70 percent year-on-year. Let's face it, some or even all of peoples' and companies' assets are other peoples' and companies' liabilities.

The democratization of credit and socialization of risk worked in synergy with financial innovation to conquer global markets, often in the form of structured instruments (section 3 of this chapter), but also through auctions (section 4 of this chapter) and private placements. This has created a sprawling market for "equity-looking" debt. Very few players and regulators have however appreciated that:

- Changes in market mood can create credit spread alarms (section 6 of this chapter),
- Global credit crises can spread widely like brush fires (section 7 of this chapter), and
- New, more effective methods are needed to manage debt investments, including (but not limited to) the existence of a global sheriff with significant authority (section 8 of this chapter).

Another key instrument of globalization is *transborder financial flows*, which constitute an alternative to borrowing from banks. In the short run, transborder financial flows sound easier and safer, but in the longer run they may well be more demanding and more expensive than plain banking loans.

In return for shouldering greater risk, including foreign exchange exposure, transborder investors require a much better income. Neither are transborder arrangements that straightforward. Banks that specialize in bridging the gap between investors and borrowers must not only do their homework in knowing them both but also pay attention to the fact that many investments require a close long-term relationship between:

- The investor, and
- His counterparty.

A case in point is foreign direct investments (FDI), which bring the recipient of capital inflow not only useful money but also useful technical and managerial knowledge. There is as well moral hazard if the receiver of FDI expects to lose some of the value of his investment because of following risky policies, or as a result of operating under the changing fortunes of political leverage in a corrupt business environment.

Moral hazard and corruption correlate. Corruption discourages effective wealth management. A big question in this case is how corruption is measured. When a fair system of risk and rewards cannot be assured, the likelihood is high that investors as well as bankers will be defrauded of their money.

3. Global structured products

Structured financial products are an increasingly popular instrument of globalization. They are often custom-designed bonds, whose origin could be traced to *repackaged asset vehicles* (RAVs), a term used by Morgan Stanley in the early 1990s to identify the produce of its efforts to restructure classical securities into derivatives. Also known as black box transactions, RAVs put securities into a trust company (the black box) which proceeded to issue new assets of a higher and leveraged profile. These are:

- Marketed as premier instruments (which they were not), and
- Theoretically aimed at "sophisticated" investors, who often lack risk management skill.

Collateralized debt obligations (CDOs; see Chapter 6), asset-backed securities (ABS) and mortgage-backed-securities (MBS) are examples of structural products. Up to the July/August 2007 subprimes crisis, their market was growing almost exponentially, as shown in Figure 3.3. To my experience,

- The more complex is a financial instrument's structure, the lower the investor's benefit that can be achieved and the greater is the risk of misunderstanding risk and return.
- As Figure 3.4 indicates, no two structured products have the same secondary market performance, even if they share similar characteristics.

Additionally, few people truly appreciate that structured products may involve an inordinate amount of credit risk. Some of these products are enhanced in terms of credit exposure by a guarantor; that's good, but

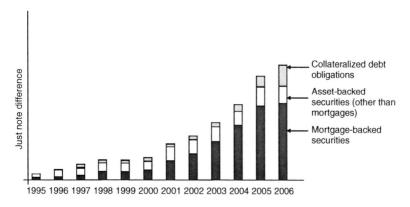

Figure 3.3 Global structured product issuance in $ trillions (statistics by IMF)

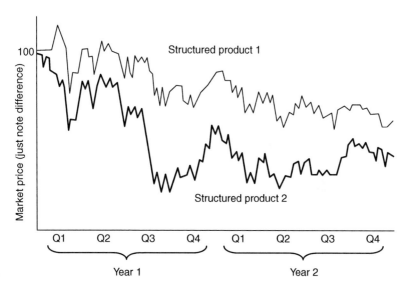

Figure 3.4 Secondary market performance of two structured derivative instruments, bought at 100 percent at issuance

guarantors, too, have credit risk (see Chapter 1). Another party's protection is needed to warranty the creditworthiness of the issuer.

In terms of financials, instead of receiving a fixed coupon or principal, the structured note sees to it that its owner gets amounts adjusted according to a fairly complex formula. The underlying may be an index of a yield curve. Many investors in a structured note lack the notion that the bet they are making, by buying it, is one against a set of *forward yield curves* which tend to slope:

- Upward, or
- Downward.

An interesting example of structured products is principal-exchange-rate-linked securities (PERLS). These are disguised like bonds, but they are derivative instruments targeting changes in currency rates. They are structured like debt instruments to make it feasible for investors, who are not permitted to play in currencies, to place bets on the direction of exchange rate changes.

Instead of just repaying principal, a PERLS may multiply such principal by the change in the value of the dollar against the euro; or twice the change in the value of the dollar against the Swiss franc or the British pound. This repayment, linked to the foreign exchange rate of different currencies, sees to it that the investor might be receiving more than an interest rate on the principal alone – or a lot less.

Examined from an overall perspective, the concept of structured financial instruments has been given several interpretations, depending on the timeframe the vehicle was brought to the market. Traders tend to distinguish between three different generations of structured notes. The elder, or *first-generation*, usually consists of products based on just one index, and includes:

- Bull market vehicles such as inverse floaters and cap floaters.
- Superfloaters, which are usually bear market instruments.

Bear market products became popular in 1993/1994. The superfloater has a small coupon at the beginning, which improves only if the London interbank offered rate (LIBOR) rises. A coupon that is below current market levels until LIBOR goes higher is however harder to sell than a big coupon that gets bigger every time rates drop. Another superfloater might pay twice LIBOR minus 7 percent for two years. The risks embedded in these instruments have never been fully appreciated by their investors.

Second-generation structured notes are different types of exotic options – more complex still than superfloaters. Examples of second-generation structured notes are *range* notes (with embedded binary or digital options). Their investors are at risk for an entire coupon period if LIBOR goes outside a set band. With *quanto* notes, investors can take a bet on, say, sterling LIBOR rates but get paid in dollars.

You-choose range notes have been designed for a bear market. Every quarter the investor gets to choose the range, this being a responsibility which requires considerable skill. For instance, *if* the range width is set to 100 basis points, *then* the investor has to determine at the start of the period the high and low within that range. This is far from being a straight job, though he may be given an option to change his mind in the next quarter.

Surprisingly enough, there are investors who like this sort of ambiguity because they figure their risk period is really only one quarter. But they are badly mistaken. In reality, even for banks *you choose* notes are much more difficult to hedge than regular range notes, because the hedges are both dynamic and imperfect – a fact very few people appreciate.

There are as well *third-generation* notes offering investors exposure to commodity or equity prices in a cross-category sense. Such notes usually appeal to a class other than fixed-income investors. For instance, third-generation notes are sometimes purchased by fund managers who are in the fixed-income market but want to diversify their exposure. The heavy hammer that hit the Orange County Fund, and brought it to bankruptcy in December 1994, talks volumes of the exposure taken by buyers of such complex instruments.

Yet, in spite of the knowledge that these globally circulating, so-called sophisticated financial products can too often be misunderstood, and that they are highly risky, a horde of equity-linked and commodity-linked notes are being structured and sold to investors. An example is the *London Interbank Offered Rate floaters*, designed so that the coupon is "LIBOR plus," counting in basis points every day that the spread between, say, the 2-year Treasury bill and 6-month LIBOR is less than 100 basis points, and zero when it is out of that range.

The pros say that even if they are complex, structured instruments can still be useful to investors seeking to manage a particular portfolio, and/or have an interest in trading risks. However, as a result of exposures being assumed, and also the likelihood that there is no secondary market, structured transactions are not suitable for investors with statutory limitations on risks they can assume; or who are not able financially to bear the exposure which comes with them when worse comes to worse. Investors beware.

4. Auction-rate securities and the attorney general's reaction

A brief reference to auction-rate securities, and to the early August 2008 settlement between big banks and the New York attorney general, has been made in Chapter 1. *Auction-rate securities* (ARSs) are debt instruments – typically municipals, state-sponsored, or corporate obligations[3] – with a long-term maturity. However, their interest rate is reset short-term through an auction held daily or every 7, 14, 28, 35, 49, and 91 days, semi-annually or annually.[4] Interest is paid at end of the auction period.

- Broker-dealers submit bids on behalf of potential buyers and sellers of the obligations.
- Based on submitted bids the auction agent will set the next interest rate, as the lowest rate to match supply and demand.

Fair enough? For some years it looked *as if* it were so. (The first auction-rate security for the tax-exempt market was introduced by Goldman Sachs in 1988.) As in the twenty-first century the supply of ARS zoomed to over $330 billion in mid 2007,[5] banks marketed them to institutional and retail investors as money market paper *without any risk*. Yet, roughly half the issues have been corporate debt, with all this means in credit exposure.

The credit crisis saw to it that the market for ARS disappeared while risk reached for the stars. This led to the early August 2008 settlement by Andrew Cuomo, New York's attorney general, which obliged big banks to reimburse to the nominal price the ARS they had sold to investors. The fine banks pay, over and above refunding, helps them avoid accusations of malpractice. Other parties to the settlement have been the Securities and Exchange Commission (SEC), Massachusetts Securities Division, and state regulatory agencies represented by North American Securities Administrators Association (NSAA).

Beyond the early August 2008 first cases, the Securities and Exchange Commission is examining about twenty firms over their sales of auction-rate securities, and the New York State attorney general's office plus twelve other US state regulators are conducting at least a dozen similar investigations. Part of the regulators' bet is that without an ARS settlement with their clients, banks will be reputationally at great disadvantage. At least one big bank faces additional allegations that its executives sold personal holdings of their securities, even as their salespeople told clients the investments were safe. Therefore,

- Regulators have been examining how brokers sold the notes and whether they fully disclosed the potential risks to buyers.
- But at the same time they appreciate that buying back all of the ARS at once would be a big burden for the banks, many of which have

been weakened by multibillion-dollar losses and writedowns stemming from mortgage-linked bad deals.

The first three banks to sign the agreement to restore liquidity to their clients connected to ARS transactions have been: Citigroup to the tune of $7.3 billion and a $100 million penalty; Merrill Lynch $12 billion; and UBS $19.4 billion and a $150 million penalty. Cuomo also asked for settlements by Morgan Stanley and JP Morgan Chase. Each of them committed itself to buy back $7 billion of ARS. Other big ARS market players were Goldman Sachs, Lehman Brothers, Wachovia, Bank of America, and Royal Bank of Canada.

The presence in this select list of UBS and Royal Bank of Canada documents that the affair of auction-rate securities is one with international dimensions. There are as well similarities between ARSs and CDOs, at least at the commercial paper end. It is indeed intriguing that the ARS market collapsed (February 2008) 6 months after the commercial paper market had gone to the dogs – which suggests that after August 2007 short-term financing previously done through conduits was switched to the auction-rate securities.

For the time being, under pressure from attorney generals and regulators, different banks have offered different plans. UBS committed itself to purchase a total of $8.3 billion of ARS, at par, from most private clients during a two-year time period beginning 1 January 2009. Private clients and charities holding less than $1 million in household assets at UBS will be able to avail themselves of this relief beginning 31 October 2008.

In addition, UBS has also committed to provide liquidity solutions to institutional investors and will agree, from June 2010, to purchase all or any of the remaining billions of the settlement from its institutional clients. This comes over and above the firm's intention to repurchase $3.5 billion of tax-exempt auction preferred stock, announced on 16 July 2008. One can only hope that nearly worthless ARS will not find themselves in the vaults of the Swiss National Bank, since central banks have been acting as repositories of last resort (Chapter 2).

For its part, Merrill Lynch plans to create liquidity for some 30,000 clients who hold municipal, closed-end funds and student loan auction-rate securities to the tune of about $12 billion. The investment bank expects this amount to be reduced to under $10 billion by January 2009, as a result of announced and anticipated issuer redemptions to retail clients – including individuals, charitable institutions and many family-owned and small businesses. Clients would have a year, beginning on 15 January 2009 and ending on 15 January 2010, in which to sell their ARS.

From September to December 2008, Citigroup would buy back auction-rate securities from individual investors, charities and small and midsize businesses – about 40,000 entities in total – who have been unable to sell their securities since mid-February 2008. As in the case of the other institutions, a company spokesman said at a news conference that the settlement reflects "a truly favorable solution" for investors and clients. The big question however is how this large amount of repurchases will be financed by banks badly wounded by the subprimes and other CDOs.

Given the condition of the banks' balance sheets it is reasonable that regulators have considered their ability to absorb losses that might result from the settlements. Even so, however, banks need to find ways to dispose of the repurchased auction-rate securities and recoup their money. US big banks have overgamed the Federal Reserve's Term Auction Facility.

- In mid 2007, prior to the credit and banking crisis, 91 percent of the Fed's assets were invested in government bonds.
- In mid 2008 their share has dropped to 52 percent.[6]

Which might be the alternatives? According to some opinions the strategy used by a couple of market players may provide a partial solution, but this is far from being a fail-safe course. Boston-based Eaton Vance, Chicago's Nuveen Investments, and New York's BlackRock developed new preferred shares that carry a put option. The latter is supposed to guarantee that an investor can sell back its securities "when needed."

- The hypothesis is that money raised from the sale of these "new securities" will help to retire the auction-rate preferred shares.
- This hope however is based on the wrong assumption that the banks' clients will once again be taken for stupid.

The time when suckers come forward is, at least temporarily, over. The dual effect of credit crisis and of false assurances given by the bankers to their clients has caused the market to shrink. Since February 2008, for example, almost all of the student-loan and preferred securities have been frozen while half of the municipal auction-rate paper reportedly remains locked up.

Even heavy discounting may not induce investors into buying the massive amount of ARSs banks have to repurchase from their clients at par. Bonds sold by local governments, hospitals, and colleges currently trade at 90 to 96 cents on the dollar, some auction-rate preferred shares issued by mutual funds sell at about 80 to 85 cents, and debt backed by student loans is valued at 70 to 80 cents. Experts suggest that moreover Citigroup, Merrill, and UBS will be repurchasing securities that have already lost as much as 30 percent of their value, or more.

Therefore, according to some accounts, the three banks may have to write down the ARS debt they buy from customers by $4 billion; others comment that the final bill will be more than three to four times that amount. "These are developments of gigantic, historic proportions," James Cox, a securities law professor at Duke University in Durham, North Carolina, said of the auction-rate agreements. "Never have we witnessed defendants who created a product that isn't inherently illegal, being required to buy back such a large market."[7] The debt product itself might not have been illegal; what were illegal were the fake promises about *zero risk* to get it sold at massive scale.

5. The search for yield weakens credit ratings

Bonds always carry issuer's risk and, for this reason, investors have been demanding a risk premium. But, in the early 2000s, in the search for yield by bond investors at a time of exceptionally low interest rates, the latter have accepted exceptionally low risk premiums. In reality the risk has been created primarily by the Fed's policy of low interest rate over the longer term – rather than by risk-prone investors.

A brief historical review helps in understanding this statement. As companies restructured their balance sheets after the year 2000 stock market bubble, the global issuance of new corporate bonds in the international capital market declined. It even declined by roughly 20 percent in the first three quarters of 2004, compared with the same period of 2003 (this statistic does not account for bond issuance by banks).

Examples of large issuers who reduced their indebtedness are companies in the telecommunications sector, which accounted for a large share of outstanding bonds after they were privatized (prior to the 1990s in Europe, telephone services were under the thumb of the government as part of the PTT). Also, the smaller number of mergers and acquisitions which followed the equity market's bust led to less debt paper being issued.

From 2002 to 2006, there has been a silver lining for those entities which continued issuing bonds: they had found themselves in a sellers' market. Additionally, with interest rates already falling because of monetary policy decisions, they were able to reduce the cost of new debt, while strengthening their hand in regard to clauses associated to:

- Negotiating new loans with banks, and
- Offering debt instruments to the capital market.

It was almost too good to be true, but wise bankers and investors should have known that these conditions cannot last forever. Particularly in America, the shrinking of credit risk premia did away with basic tenants of finance. Bond investors forgot that they should examine with attention an issuer's credit quality, and they paid dearly for it a few years down the line.

A nearly global rush of unreasonably high ratings of debt instruments contributed to this unrealistic situation. Independent credit agencies such as Moody's and Standard & Poor's, which operate the world over, are exempt from the SEC's fair disclosure rules and therefore enjoy privileged access to company financials. Their ratings, however, did not always reflect the true credit quality.

- Companies were willing to cooperate with rating agencies in their research because an entity's borrowing costs fall as it moves up the rating scale.
- But they also profited from the fact that in their dash to lock into interest rates a little higher investors did not question the validity of credit ratings, and paid scant attention to quality.

Too much lenience in rating is counterproductive. On 26 February 2007, Moody's Investors Service was accused of undermining its own ratings system because of the massive upgrading of sixteen European banks to top triple-A status. Moody's surprised both analysts and investors with the scale of its credit changes, which led to questions over the seriousness attached to a credit watch. The general market opinion has been that the rating agency gave much bigger upgrades than thought likely, forgetting that:

- Issuers of debt instruments never object to free upgrades,
- But other market players are unlikely to be pleased by the removal of the ability to meaningfully discriminate between higher-quality and lower-quality debt.

In a note on the aforementioned credit rating changes, Royal Bank of Scotland said Moody's was rapidly making itself redundant; adding that while defaults in European banking have not exactly been legion in recent years, creating AAA-rated banks across the board meant that essentially there is no risk in investing in financials.[8] Some months down the line, the subprimes debacle proved that these upgrades were premature – as practically across the board banking stocks were under water in the last quarter of 2007.

It is nevertheless interesting to note that the new system, in which ratings on banks have been massively upgraded, aimed to take account of the willingness and ability of a state to support a troubled bank. Critics looked at this as being a concept unfit for the market economy because it bypasses a basic criterion of credit – that the entity can stand alone.

Furthermore, while traditional credit ratings tend to focus on probability of default, accounting for state support is an assessment of the likelihood that taxpayer money will bail out a particular bank – largely a socialist practice adopted by the US. For instance, in the case of the three Icelandic banks that received the biggest upgrades, Moody's saw state support as highly likely, but it did so without considering political risk.

6. A credit spread alarm

In Wall Street in mid March 2007 Dr Henry Kaufman, whose vast background and experience makes him the *doyen* of economists, gave a speech distinguished by a clear diagnosis. The current economic and market challenges, Kaufman pointed out, have their origin in the changing definition of liquidity. Classically, liquidity has been an *asset-based* concept (see Chapter 9). Companies were liquid *if* they had on hand cash and easy marketable other assets.

- Today, however, firms and households often blur the distinction between liquidity and credit availability, and
- At the same time, securitization and new banking technology have stimulated risk appetites among broader strata of investors.

Prior to July/August 2007, a rising risk appetite has fostered the (wrong) attitude that credit is usually available for the asking, and at a reasonable price. This hypothesis is only on-and-off true because eventually the market discovers that *credit matters*; and with overleveraging credit can quickly disappear long with market confidence, as happened in 2007, first in the US and then in Europe and globally.

A sudden rise in risk aversion unnerved equity markets in many jurisdictions, reversing a state of mind where complacency in regard to assumed credit exposure had taken hold, promoted by a rally of the subprimes which had been underpinned by the false belief that global liquidity had made it safer to invest in risky assets. With subprime debt spreads on the rise shattering this conception, investors were also worried by contradictory events in the so-called "high-yield" (read: junk) debt market.

Over the years in which Alan Greenspan's second bubble, that of ultra-low interest rates and very easy credit, got momentum the junk bond market was especially strong. Spreads were falling to record lows, which is the very notion of easy credit. (A *credit spread* is a spread in which the value of an option sold exceeds the value of an option bought. The inverse case is known as a *debit spread*.)

With bonds, a *real spread* is derived from market prices of credit risk-free bonds, after deducting inflation rate from the market interest rate. Corporates usually offer a premium over the real bond spread. (Corporate bond spreads are computed as the difference between 7-to-10-year corporate bond yields, and 7-to-10-year government bond yields.)

The spread between Group of Ten government bonds and corporate bonds shrinks when there is easy money, as happened in the early 2000s in the United States. This induces investors into taking credit risk and, contrary to all investment logic, to stuffing up relatively low-yielding debt from companies with:

- Poor credit ratings, and
- Shrinking profit margins.

Risk aversion grew gradually. After the late February/early March 2007 shocks, the fear of "What comes next?" started making investors a little more careful and lenders less keen to extend cheap, no-strings-attached credit to risky borrowers. The market started factoring in anticipation that the era of cheap credit might be ending, while economists debated *if* and *when* the piling up of low credit quality debt would be followed by a bubble.

Nearly every month after July/August 2007 saw renewed concerns over subprime and other knock-on impacts. Interbank markets were also affected as credit institutions and brokers looked to manage their balance sheets over the year-end. In addition came the effect of the severe widening in late October 2007 in CDS spreads of the leading US monoline insurers (Chapter 1), which would lead eventually to additional losses for all banks that had bought protection insurance from these firms.

The rush to quality had an evident impact on credit spreads, reversing lax policies of the preceding years. Figure 3.5 dramatizes the easy money market sentiment with the collapse of euro junk bond spreads starting in late 2002/early 2003 and continuing in 2003, 2004, and 2005. From a peak of 1,550 basis points in 2001 right after the stock market bubble, the spread of junk bonds shrank to slightly over 300 bp, then hovered around 400 bp.

Notice that the spread of AA-rated bonds also shrank from 50 basis points to about 20 bp, another signal that investors were hungry for credit risk. Because the spread of companies other than financial is calculated against AAA G-10 government bond yields, this meant that

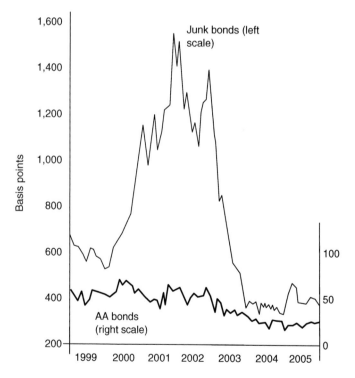

Figure 3.5   Bond spreads of corporates other than financial: euro-denominated junk bonds and AAA bonds (statistics by European Central Bank)

20 bp did not even represent the difference between AAA and AA credit ratings. The global financial market had a ball. But 2007 was the year of rude awakening.

7. The impact of globalized crises

There was a time when political, military, or financial crises were confined within the borders of the country or countries where certain events took place. This was, for instance, the case of the first panic of the twentieth century. After Wall Street spent a cliff-hanging year, turning negative on 25 March 1907, with massive selling roiling the New York Stock Exchange, the real equities nightmare at NYSE came a few months later, in October of that same year.

The 1907 stock market crash in New York, as well as those that had preceded it in the late nineteenth century, were American events more or less confined within the borders of the US. After World War I, however, panics have been internationalized, as the 1929 Great Depression documents – a reference that is valid for market behavior way beyond stock market crashes.

The two major oil events of the 1970s created a tsunami of inflation in America and Western Europe, and required concerted action by several government and central banks to bring undercontrol. More dramatic has been the global spread of political anxiety in the aftermath of 9/11, which rapidly morphed into a financial crisis-to-be, obliging the Fed and central banks in Europe to inject plenty of liquidity in order to calm the market.

The disruption created by the terrorist attack at World Trade Center and Pentagon also had a great impact on global emerging markets, particularly those running big current account deficits that render them more dependent on foreign capital. Because of a compound effect in a market already characterized by low confidence, reality for investors changed as the aftershock hit consumers, corporations, and the economy at large. The reaction of policymakers to such a devastating psychological event was to assume that:

- No previous experience was comparable, and
- The then existing analytical tools were useless because they did not factor in the market's psychological response.

On Wall Street, analysts said a global panic-prone line of thinking could lead quickly to an emotional and highly risk-averse response on the part of equity investors. Subsequently, because the initial reaction was usually short-lived, traders and investors tried to define the principal challenges of spikes to the economy and equity markets, as well as potential offsets that might emerge over the next few quarters.

"Within a year, we will find ourselves in a totally different macro environment than the present," said Isaac Souede in the 21 September 2001 teleconferencing at Merrill Lynch. Ten days after 9/11, there was no doubt globalization and global supply chains were significantly affected by the terrorist attacks. One of the big issues in financial discussions thereafter has been the extent to which 9/11 was not only a murderous enterprise but also a way to hurt or defeat globalization. Nobody could say the precise extent to which the attacks would impact:

- Trade flows,
- Free cross-border movements of capital,
- Global supply chains, and
- Foreign direct investments.

Neither were foreign markets buoyant; after having observed the stress at Wall Street. Frankfurt dropped 9 percent on 9/11, beyond the losses it had sustained in the previous months. Economists and investment experts suggested the way to bet was that as a result of terrorist attacks at the heart of America:

- Investors would want to go into more liquid and more defensive portfolio positions, and
- Even the best-managed portfolios, which were already defensively positioned, would have to slim down in whatever credit risk and market risk they had.

The pain investors were willing to accept was conditioned further by the tendency of some parties to benefit from the majority's stress by short selling. To better appreciate the psychological impact of this event, it is necessary to bring into perspective a key notion underpinning the virtual economy in which we live.

Economic value, and therefore wealth creation, is no more built exclusively around the production of material goods. Increasingly, it depends on the utilization of services both within and outside the better-known design, manufacturing, distribution, and maintenance processes. As a result, risk and return is less and less that defined by the Industrial

Revolution, and its notion of price equilibrium. Instead, it depends on the ability to:

- Cope with uncertainties and vulnerabilities implicit in the financial system, and
- Experiment on how and how much selected events find themselves at the core of economic action.

Understanding today's global economy for what it really is, is fundamental to longer-term success in business life, because it permits holding the high ground as competition intensifies, the bastions of the industrial economy lose their grip, and crises (financial, political, and social) are getting increasingly globalized. Statistics help in trying to quantify the state of the global financial system.

A well-timed warning about a latent but coming global financial crisis has been given by the Bank for International Settlements (BIS), the institution that is owned by central banks and practically functions as a central institution for the global central banking system. In its Annual Report issued 24 June 2007, the BIS suggested that the current rapid expansion of money supply coupled with a fast credit swing would have to be ended to keep inflation under control.

Big developing economies like China, India, Russia, and Brazil are flooding the global money supply rather than showing restraint – a reason why, in all likelihood, a global financial crisis would be brutal and bloody. Yet, eventually, this might prove to be the only option. Those who believe that the global financial system has been virtualized to the point that one can control its disintegration are painfully mistaken.

Stated in a different way, while high gearing brings along with it a great deal of worry, just as challenging in terms of financial stability is how the global economy, and most particularly the overleveraged global banking system, is going to cope with deleveraging after the time for high financial stakes has passed. Experts suggest that even managed deleveraging would require painful dislocations over and above:

- The unavoidable risk repricing, and
- The reassessment of global exposure which has been created by the growing risk appetite of bankers and investors.

Assets and liabilities adjustments are anyway overdue, because the need for pruning the balance sheets has been delayed by a financial system kept afloat with unprecedented levels of debt. As long as the going was strong, this delay generated little alarm even if hedge funds and private equity outfits have been embracing debt with great enthusiasm – unconcerned by the fact that the seven first years of the new century:

- Have been marked by a sharp decline in the level of returns expected by investors, and
- This has happened in spite of the risks they are being asked to assume in order to see an improvement in their return on investment.

Moreover, as the subprimes debacle has demonstrated, the faith in mathematical formulas and market manipulation is misplaced. The system cannot be fixed from within. The solution to the crisis lies outside the realm of finance and in the catching up of the productive sector of the global economy – which is not yet a goal of governments, companies and a substantial part of the Western population. Beyond this, there is an urgent need for a global regulator endowed with enough authority to catch the thieves.

8. The global sheriff of George Soros

George Soros does not need an introduction, and though not everybody likes him few people would dispute his experience. A thesis he presented at the World Economic Forum 2008 has been that we currently find ourselves at the end of a 60-year period based on the dollar. The weakness of the American currency and persistence of the country's current account deficit see to it that:

- The rest of the world is no longer willing to accumulate dollars, and
- Therefore many economists outside the US are now thinking in terms of a basket of currencies.

One of the reasons is the persistent dollar weakness, unfit for the global economy. As a Merrill Lynch study shows, from December 2006 to February 2008, compared with an index comprised of the euro, yen, British pound, Canadian dollar, Swedish krona, and Swiss franc, the US dollar fell from a rating of 87 to 75.[9] It is not the euro's (unreasonable) strength but the dollar's inherent weakness that turns investors away from it.

As the dollar's former might is eroding, economists cope with the fact it would not be easy to bring to an end the 65 steady years of its reign. This worry includes the pricing of crucial products and services based on dollars, as well as checks and balances that the global economic and financial system has built for itself. Yet a basket of currencies may be a better solution than returning to barter agreements and bilateral deals, which:

- Will significantly increase currency exchange risk, and
- Be most difficult to control without a central, global authority endowed with mighty powers, which simply is not in place.

Soros stressed the point that the need for a central authority able to be in charge of, and exercise control over, the globalized economy is pressing since one can now reasonably argue that financial speculation pulls the strings. Precisely because globalization has so much changed the real world, as well as its economics and financials, at Davos 2008 Soros's thesis was that the world needs a sheriff to:

- Police the global markets, and
- Save them from themselves.

The meaning of this proposal has been that, to continue operating in an orderly manner, the financial markets urgently require a global regulation and one authority – not a mosaic of regulatory agencies with conflicting aims. If they are left to their own devices as they have been for several decades, the markets will continue going from euphoria to despair, back to euphoria and then to the precipice – as the July/August 2007 events have shown.

A number of participants in the Forum's conference, which centered on this subject, were not alien to the global sheriff concept because they appreciated that financial markets have to be regulated, contrary to the policies followed since the 1980s which have been characterized by total disregard of market fundamentals. Lack of global regulation, Soros insisted, has gone too far. Because of it, central banks became a moral hazard as they adopted the practice of bailing out banks that failed because of:

- Their legendary imprudence in credit risk and market risk, and
- Plain bad management which has run a number of big banks down.

On the other hand, however, the question of a global regulator is a subject which raises resistance and controversy. A basic question was posed by one of the participants to the conference, a senior executive of India's Infosys: "Will the different nations give up part of their sovereignty in financial matters?" In his opinion, they will not; hence there is no place, he said, for a global sheriff.

Of course, the need for global regulation of financial activities is not a question to which there is a simple answer, and indeed if one exists it is far from being self-evident. Rather than having a new global sheriff, some participants to Davos 2008 proposed to use an existing structure, for instance revamping the International Monetary Fund (IMF) and giving it new powers.

To this Soros objected, and for good reason. He said the IMF had not been designed for that purpose, and moreover the US had used its veto power at IMF; it would do it again, and follow whatever steps were needed to continue having the dollar as world currency. The US had abused this power, Soros added.

The suggestion made by Fred Bergsten, director of the Washington-based Petersen Institute for International Economics, was for a new regulatory structure based on today's three big economic powers:

- The US;
- Euroland;
- China.

The Indian executive who had challenged Soros's arguments about a global sheriff objected, asking "Why not also India?" Bergsten responded that India had not yet integrated itself into the global economy, as China had – which is true, as is documented by European Central Bank statistics.[10]

This classification should be kept in perspective, because *if* there is a basket of currencies *then* it must definitely include the currencies of countries best integrated into the globalized market place. The problem of the global sheriff, however, goes well beyond the basket's frame of reference.

Answering to an example advanced by Soros on the need for a global financial regulatory authority endowed with the power to take action, the Infosys executive said that the subprime crisis should not be seen as a global issue, because it has been a US problem. Soros objected to such a narrow view, and brought forward the fact that globalization has allowed the US to suck up the savings of the world, consuming 6 percent more than it produces and paying for it by securitized subprimes.

Other participants to the conference commented that, in their judgment, the world had become too complex to deal with it at international level, which is an argument against globalization. Still others said that there might be a solution, but this was an issue which had not been studied and therefore no proposal was forthcoming.

According to Lawrence Summers, the former US Treasury secretary and former president of Harvard University, Soros was right when he said that in the immediate post-WWII decades there had been a consistent economic and financial policy, which was presently missing. The proof, Summers added, was the prevailing current seesaw in global economics and finance.

As the discussion proceeded, the sense of the meeting was that the ongoing absence of global policing of the financial system was a rolling disaster. But then conflicts of interest set in and, at the end of the day, Soros's proposal for a *global sheriff* of the financial industry fell way short of the participants' majority. Only 25 percent of the people present to this conference voted for it, while 59 percent had voted that the central banks had lost control of the economy and they could no more make monetary decisions right. In other terms:

- The majority recognized that the current situation is disastrous and unsustainable,
- But when confronted with the prospect of a global regulatory authority, one out of three participants changed his vote, because as always "control may be good for others, but not for one's own self."

The best epilog has been written by one of the participants, who pressed the point that lack of global regulation creates a swarm of risks, and failure to police prudential rules increases lust and greed. As he put it: "All sort of bonuses are at the origin for the current mess. Not even chairmen and presidents of ruined financial institutions feel responsible for the risks which they have been assuming and for their reckless management."

Part II

The Subprimes Crisis

4
Earthquake in the Subprime Mortgage Market

1. The banking industry's self-inflicted wounds

Capital is an instrument – not a profound pleasure. As executives from the Securities and Exchange Commission (SEC), Federal Reserve, Federal Deposits Insurance Corporation (FDIC), Office of the Controller of the Currency (OCC), and Office of Thrift Supervision (OTS) underlined in meetings we had in Washington and Boston, a top responsibility of senior management is the preservation of assets.[1] This is true even if speculation has joined industry as one of the economy's pillars.

Judged under the present perspective of the economy and of the banking industry, the mid 2007 developments in the United States, and generally in international financial markets, give plenty of cause to essentially revise the way we have been looking at global banking and innovative financial instruments. The rapidly growing amount of exposures associated with problems in:

- The US subprime[2] mortgage market, and
- The credit crisis which followed on its heels

derive from the wider mispricing of credit risks, excessive use of leverage, and lip service paid to the control of counterparty exposure – which has traditionally been the main pillar of banking. The US mortgage securities bubble exploded to an estimated $20 trillion in just five years, with a terrible impact on homeowners, as well as on the financial industry because mortgage-based assets are 49 percent of the US banking system.[3]

A common feature of bubbles, like the Great Mississippi Bubble and the South Sea Bubble of the early eighteenth century, as well as the dotcom mania in late 1990s and the early twenty-first-century housing boom, is that most people refuse to believe they will burst until they do so. After the blow-up, many market segments experience extreme nervousness and overreaction. Jan Hatzius, chief economist of Goldman Sachs, has forecast that American bank losses in 2008 will be $400 billion, and the total drop in the ability of banks to lend will be $2 trillion.[4] (Since then these figures have increased significantly.)[5] Contrary to previous crises:

- This explosion has been generated by the banking industry itself, rather than being due to an external event like emerging markets meltdown, and
- Among other credit institutions, Barclays, Citigroup, HSBC, and UBS have been paying 2 percent above Treasury to borrow money because investors are scared of losses that are still hidden.

The banking industry created the subprimes hecatomb not just because of lust and greed but also as aftereffect of generalized bad management in the credit creation arm of the economy, with the result that a negative economic outlook has caused concerns about many other business sectors. Belatedly, the market has recognized that the different forms of structured debt are far from being secure investment assets.

No wonder therefore that plenty of bankers and investors are now licking their wounds; and some of them have fallen twice in the same vice. Such is the case of California's Orange County, which in 1994 was responsible for America's largest municipal bankruptcy, after losing $1.6 billion through repos and other ill-advised derivatives trades.[6] In 2007 Orange County:

- Had $860 million in subprimes, out of a $2.3 billion fund; a 37.4 percent high risk exposure, and
- It lost $460 million from this $860 million in toxic waste – which amounts to a wholesome 53.5 percent of invested capital.

A principle which seems to have been totally forgotten in the first decade of the twenty-first century is that policies and practices of investors, as well as of the banking industry's leadership, are about judgment and understanding of counterparties and stakeholders, with a little arithmetic tossed in. Misunderstanding and mismanagement saw to it that, also unlike in previous financial crises,

- The one which started July/August 2007 has been centered on *debt* not on equity, and

- In a meltdown, because debt is much more leveraged it is far more dangerous than an equity bust.

Plenty of experts now say that to put the US economic landscape back in order the debt-to-equity ratio has to be significantly reduced. What they fail to explain, however, is by whom and how the huge difference between current and projected debt ratios is going to be paid – because at the end of the day, short of bankruptcy debt always has to be paid.

A question on everybody's mind – from the US government to Wall Street, main street, and private home owners – should be: who will pay for the mess? The losses of big banks, primarily US and European, will compete with those of American households for the dubious prize of number one position. In late November 2007 JP Morgan Chase said that losses from collateralized debt obligations (CDOs; see Chapter 6) in the banking industry alone may reach $77 billion. Analysts immediately commented that this is a conservative estimate and an intermediate figure, since we are not yet at the end of the red ink torrent.

It should be kept in mind that the first sign of a coming upheaval due to overleveraging in mortgages, and most particularly in subprimes, showed up in late February 2007. Market optimism relegated that event to only a blip, and the same has been true of the April 2007 worrisome sign. The nervousness of bankers and investors, as well as their growing unwillingness to trust one another, reappeared in June 2007 and became a major worry in July/August when market upheaval turned into a fivefold disaster:

- Subprime crisis,
- Banking crisis,
- Crisis of liquidity,
- Crisis of collateral, and
- Crisis of credit rating.

All of these crises, and the credit crunch they brought along, have happened at the same time. Both the European Central Bank (ECB) and the Federal Reserve rushed to inject liquidity in an effort to calm the market players' worries and avert a deepening of the crisis, which might have led to severe recession. (Moreover, on 12 December 2007, the Fed, the ECB, the Bank of England, and other central banks of the Group of Ten started a concerted action to provide liquidity to commercial and investment banks.)

This fire brigade approach became necessary because of the commercial bankers' and mortgage bankers' lack of care about borrowers' *credit rating*[7] and the exposure their clients were assuming. Also blamed were some aspects of financial engineering which allowed a small number of people working for investment banks to create a great amount of illusion among investors (see Chapter 2).

Released on 22 October 2007, a report on the US mortgage blowout, by the Congressional Joint Economic Committee (JEC), documented that half the people who got mortgages with initially very low interest rates (*teaser* rates; see section 3 of this chapter) did not know that the rates they would pay in the future would increase. To ensure that the banks would not be able to hide their losses by marking to model (which Warren Buffett once characterized as being sometimes marking to myth), on 29 November 2007 the Financial Accounting Standards Board (FASB) announced a new Statement of Financial Accounting Standard 157 for the estimation and reporting of fair value of inventoried positions:

- The fair value of assets in the portfolio must be documented with market data, and
- For financial reporting purposes, dependence on different fair-value hypotheses fed into models will be significantly reduced.

With SFAS 157, and the always-in-force Sarbanes-Oxley Act of 2002, banks producing fair-value estimates for subprimes and Alt-As[8] in their portfolio are in for unpleasant surprises. In early December 2007, Moody's Investor Services cut or placed in review for downgrade the ratings on $64.9 billion of debt sold by Citigroup's structured investment vehicles (SIVs; Chapter 5). Champagne corks are popping at trial lawyers' offices.

2. Institutionalization of subprime mortgages

Banks, thrifts (savings banks), and subprime mortgage companies always face legal risk. A new mortgage law of late October 2007 allows borrowers to hold liable Wall Street banks which have securitized their home loans. As the subprimes crisis has unfolded it has become evident that in their drive to *originate to distribute* (Chapter 3) debt instruments for profits, commercial banks and other entities violated the two cardinal principles for extending credit for family houses and apartments:

- Credit history, and
- Equity in the asset by the owner.

Both were massively (and unwisely) disregarded with subprimes and Alt-As, where mortgages were approved on just the borrower's declaration without any examination of his or her credit – while the classic requirement that the borrower must have equity on a new home was put in the backburner.

In parallel to this has been the advent of specialized *subprime mortgage houses* which lend to people whose credit records are poor, credit history is spotty, or income is too low to qualify for a loan to finance the purchase of a house – whether old or new. The subprime lending industry:

- Zoomed in the 2002 to mid 2005 years, while interest rates were the lowest in five decades, then
- Slowed down as interest rates rose in 2005 and 2006, and house prices started tapering off, and
- Went through first shocks from February to April 2007, with the Mortgage Bankers Association reporting that 13 percent of subprime borrowers were behind in their payments.

Because interest rates rose and house prices stagnated, life suddenly became much harder for subprime borrowers and their lenders. In the first months of 2007, New Century Financial, the second-biggest subprime institution in the US, shuttered its offices as clients defaulted on their loans. Others, like Accredited Home Lenders, saw their capitalization dive from January to March 2007. Within a short span of time, Accredited's equity lost more than 90 percent of its value.

Within the same timeframe Fremont General, one of the smaller American subprime lenders, said it would agree with the Federal Deposit Insurance Corporation to stop making risky mortgage loans and end other violations, adding that it planned to exit the subprime business. The way news items had it, several other subprime lenders were near the end of their power to survive financially.

In early 2007 HSBC, a big international bank and owner of US-based subprime lender Household, issued its first profit warning. On the back of US bad debts, writedowns had been £1.8 billion ($3.6 billion, €2.6 billion) higher than expected. The vows of HSBC with securitized subprimes and other structured financial instruments did not end with these losses. In November 2007 it announced that it had absorbed three of its SIVs with billions of red ink in their books. Just as depressing in financial terms was the case of Countrywide Financial, a big prime and subprime mortgage lender.

Investors who in the past bought mortgage-backed bonds of sub-primes, even accepting a much lower interest rate margin that would have been rational for the assumed credit risk, also lost plenty of fea-thers. For different pools of credit investors, the securitization of sub-prime mortgages diced up the credit risk into tranches. But with houses boarded up and auctioned, investors were in disarray.

As the subprime crisis proved, the top-of-the-line "AAA" credit rating given by independent credit rating agencies to the senior tranche of a securitized pool of subprimes meant nothing; that was just upper-tranche junk. Wrong credit rating has been done:

- Against all good sense, and
- In spite of the fact that these pseudo-AAAs, which supposedly boost returns, can easily turn belly-up.

Worse yet, to show investors a good financial performance, hedge funds borrowed heavily from the banking industry and made leveraged bets. Essentially, they tried to magnify by 10 or 20 times what appeared to be a "win–win" scenario. The irony in the 2002 to 2007 timeframe has been that as hedge funds, pension funds and other investors piled up subprime CDOs, the cost of leveraged financing fell, making it possible for risky borrowers to gear more cheaply and further conduct deals:

- All the way up to a crisis point, and
- From there to the inevitable crash.

Over this 2003 to 2007 timeframe, Alan Greenspan's second bubble assumed king-size dimensions. This has been a curious time for the financial industry, not just in America but worldwide. The global phe-nomenon that brought the mid 2007 crunch has been characterized by two trends, which worked in synergy:

- A rapidly *decreasing* credit quality, and
- A just as fast *increasing* money supply, blinding investors in terms of the creditworthiness of the paper they buy.

Both trend lines are shown in Figure 4.1, from 1992 to 2007. Notice that after the bonds crisis of 1994 the quality of credit conditions improved; and the same happened with the equity bubble of 2000. At the same time, after the 1994 debacle the growth in money supply fell below the 4.5 percent per year target of G-10 central banks. But after the equity

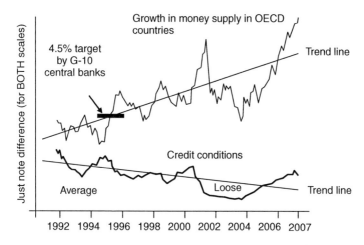

Figure 4.1 A bad omen: the diverging trend lines of money supply and credit conditions in OECD countries over 15 years

bubble of 2000, and most particularly at the time of the tragic events of 9/11 in 2001, money supply grew exponentially.

In 2006 and 2007, as dollar interest rates rose and the cost of CDOs followed on the way up, the money supply increased because banks became more willing to lend greater sums to hedge funds and other entities, against collateral often consisting of securitized subprimes. Up to the July/August 2007 blow-up, that practice allowed them to buy even more leveraged debt instruments – with dramatic consequences.

Highly rewarded individuals, heading all sorts of financial institutions, paid practically no attention to the fact that the perpetual machine set up by subprime lenders, commercial banks, and investment banks in the early years of this century would one day fall apart. The concept underpinning this perpetual-motion machine's dynamics worked on the principle that, at each stage of debt, issuance risks can be converted into securities which may be subsequently:

- Sliced up,
- Repackaged,
- Sold on, and
- Sliced up again.

This has led to endless opportunities to write contracts on underlying debt instruments whose stripes have changed many times. In its way, the policy of multiply, divide, then multiply again explains why the outstanding value of credit derivatives contracts rocketed to $26 trillion in early 2007, and shot well beyond that level in a few months.

The inflation in the value of credit derivative instruments (Chapter 5) amounted to an estimated 700 to 800 percent increase of their worth in just four years (2003–2007). Over this time, regulators had taken no corrective measures to bend the curve (Chapter 7), while brokers earned a high fee for selling subprimes with floating-rate loans (adjustable-rate mortgages, ARM; section 4 of this chapter).

After the July/August 2007 crash of the subprimes, banks suddenly became wary of lending not only to their clients but also to each other, owing to a concern about a correspondent bank's leveraged off-balance-sheet positions. For their part, investors lost faith in the so-called "innovative techniques" that enabled the very fast rise in gearing. The aftereffect has been a vicious downward spiral that produced a liquidity freeze, while:

- Signs of recovery remained fragile, and
- It became less than clear whether the deleveraging process, which inevitably follows excesses, would spill over.

As Martin Wolf wrote in an article, at best big adjustments lie ahead. At worst, the world economy may face a period of upheaval. Should industrial and emerging countries fail to adjust to the challenges ahead, a sharp and unpleasant global economic slowdown may follow.[9] No one knows when the subprimes mess is going to hit bottom.

3. Borrowers at the edge of bankruptcy

While subprimes loans are smaller than mortgages taken by the better off, the subprime borrowers are poorer and their credit is often questionable. Therefore, contrary to fixed rates of higher credit, subprime mortgages usually feature flexible (variable, adjustable) interest rates – intentionally starting at very low teaser rates, often 1 percent. Additionally, subprime borrowers have tended to join the housing market late, when house prices were already high or near their pick. They did so because:

- Willingly or by mistake, they underestimated the risk of default, and
- They were encouraged to take out loans by brokers more concerned about their fees than their clients' ability to repay their debts.

Pushing down the throat of a borrower a mortgage he or she can ill afford had two evident consequences. One is the aforementioned lowering of credit standards, which with time became a practice of the banking industry at large. The other is the marketing need for inventing newer but less secure debt-based financial products with esoteric characteristics that even their designers understand only poorly.

Additionally, getting the client to self-certify his or her income sees to it that lenders are left with no credit evidence at all. These curious types of mortgages, known as "liar loans," became quite common as borrowers stretched their budgets – a practice which happened not only in the American real estate market but elsewhere as well. In Spain, mortgage lenders have been courting the country's army of young immigrants:

- Who have short or non-existent credit histories, and
- Often work on these building sites themselves.

Among European countries the case of Spain is the nearest to the American subprime boom and bust (though Italy, too, has some problems with subprimes). Low interest rates and a buoyant real estate market have produced the illusion that home ownership is affordable to lower-income citizens. Fierce competition has driven some Spanish banks into the riskier segments of the market, consisting primarily of Spain's 4-million-strong immigrant population.

- At the beginning of 2003 lending for house purchases in Spain stood at €235 billion.
- At the beginning of 2007, in less than 4 years, it hit €550 billion – a 234 percent increase.

Spanish lenders are staffed with Moroccans, sub-Saharans, Chinese, and Latin Americans who sell subprimes in immigrant neighborhoods, supposedly tailoring mortgages to their clients' special needs. Outdoing American subprime lenders, Santander, the largest Spanish bank, has offered 40-year mortgages with a 5-year "grace" period on capital repayments. To the economically weak,

- This sounds too good to be true,
- Even if in reality it is nothing else than unwarranted leverage.

It should not come as a surprise that subprime borrowers are under stress. In Madrid, Roger Saavedra, a 34-year-old Peruvian, said he has had to let out one of the tiny rooms in his 50-square-meter (540-square-feet) two-bedroom apartment to keep up with his €160,000 mortgage. "My wife stopped working after the birth of our second child, and even working extra time I cannot make the repayments on our mortgage," he was quoted having said.[10]

Subprime real estate boom and baby boom seem to correlate among themselves, but not with rational thinking. Saavedra works as a brick-layer, and his biggest fear is becoming unemployed as most jobs in the construction sector are short-term and Spanish homebuilders suffer setbacks. Being unemployed is precisely the kind of fear gripping American subprime borrowers, making one wonder:

- *How* they got themselves into such an impossible situation in the first place, and
- *Why* lenders were not more careful in examining whether their clients would be able to pay interest and repay the loaned capital, as every banker should do.

Nicknaming these mortgages "Alt-As" is making fun of people who (unwisely) loaded themselves with a mortgage through self-certification of wealth and income. Experts have been suggesting that in the US the volume of Alt-A mortgages has been even greater than that of subprimes. Many economists believe that the worst in US mortgages is still to come in 2008 and 2009, with teaser rates eventually jumping from 1 percent to 12 percent for non-creditworthy borrowers – while government measures announced (Chapter 5) essentially benefit only those better off.

During August and September 2007, the Federal Home Loan Bank (FHLB), a New-Deal-era government-sponsored enterprise (GSE) like Fannie Mae and Freddie Mac, was compelled to lend to deeply troubled institutions like Countrywide Financial and Washington Mutual. FHLB reported that they issued so much short-term debt in those 2 months that it pushed their outstanding bond debt up 21 percent, to a record $1.5 trillion, half of which comes due before 2009.

Asset correlations present another potential problem. After the July/August 2007 sharp downturn, analysts were quick to point out that, because of uniform sell-off, assets with little in common became almost perfectly correlated. One opinion has been that the impact of money managed by quantitative risk models is itself at the origin of tight correlation, which challenges reliance on:

- Judgment,

- Reason, and
- The ability of models to manage risk.

On 16 October 2007, in a comprehensive speech on the downturn of the American housing market, Hank Paulson, the Treasury secretary and former CEO of Goldman Sachs, warned that the US economy will suffer further damage. He also said the conduct of some mortgage market participants had been "shameful" and called for nation-wide regulation to replace the current fragmented oversight of US home loans. Paulson also outlined:

- Short-term steps to mitigate the damage (Chapter 5), and
- Long-term measures to improve damage control in a financial downturn.

In the background of the Treasury secretary's statements has been the belief that the housing downturn would continue to impact adversely the US economy, capital markets, and many homeowners for some time yet. The ongoing housing correction is not ending as quickly as it might have appeared late the previous year (2006), Paulson added, even though the US economy remained "healthy and diversified" and would continue to grow.

This was a speech detailing a learned opinion about a severe crisis, with Paulson sounding a note of caution over banks' exposure to off-balance-sheet units, saying that: "Our bank regulators must evaluate regulatory capital requirements applicable to bank exposures to off-balance-sheet vehicles"[11] – and suggesting the Treasury would review the accounting rules for these entities. The speech also emphasized that America needed to ensure that yesterday's excesses are not repeated tomorrow.

4. A mare's nest of low quality housing loans

According to some opinions the events that led to the subprime mess can be traced to a tandem of changes in mortgage lending. In 2002 in the United States, the share of adjustable rate mortgages (ARM) to all new mortgages was just over 10 percent by number of new mortgages granted and about 20 percent in dollar volume. These numbers peaked at around 35 percent and 50 percent in 2005, and though since then they have declined somewhat, the difference from 2002 remained significant.

The aftereffect of this change combined with the fact that starting in 2005 a substantial number of subprimes were given to individuals with poor credit histories, or none at all. Another ominous sign for the future is that delinquency rates on subprime mortgages increased markedly, especially on loans that were originated in 2005 and 2006. According to experts this has happened because of five reasons:

- Usually subprime borrowers are not very creditworthy;
- They are often leveraged, with high debt-to-income ratios;
- Mortgages extended to them have typically relatively large loan-to-value ratios;
- Priced to sell, an increasing number of subprime mortgages were characterized by a teaser interest rate; and
- After an initial period of grace of 2 to 3 years, this low interest rate is reset to a much higher rate, not affordable by low-income borrowers.

Analysts at Credit Suisse have estimated that 80 percent of subprime loans made in 2006 included low teaser rates designed to increase their appeal. As such, they have led many financially weak individuals to overleveraging. The result has been one of piling bad debts upon bad debts – a practice that opened the door to the subprimes crisis. Unwisely, the US banking industry discarded danger signals.

Based on statistics published by Merrill Lynch (ING,[12] 16 November 2007), Figure 4.2 exhibits the failure curves of 90-day-plus *serious delinquency* ratios for Alt-As. Notice that for mortgages originating in the 2002–2005 timeframe, 2002 was not a good originating year, since serious delinquencies exceeded 4 percent over a 24-month period.

- The best Alt-A loans year was 2003, with serious delinquencies slightly above 1 percent 24 months later.
- This ratio increased to 2 percent for 2004 and 2005 loan originations, with the doubling of serious delinquencies being a danger signal.

Since credit institutions did not pay attention to the alert, Alt-A loan originations continued as usual. Not surprisingly, delinquencies connected to 2006 US mortgages hit a 3 percent ratio in just 12 months; thereafter statistics on serious delinquencies moved up most significantly.

By 2006, all over the United States house prices had become less affordable, particularly in states characterized by high rates of house price inflation. Nationwide housing starts were down from their peak, and residential building shrank from a record of 6.3 percent of GDP in

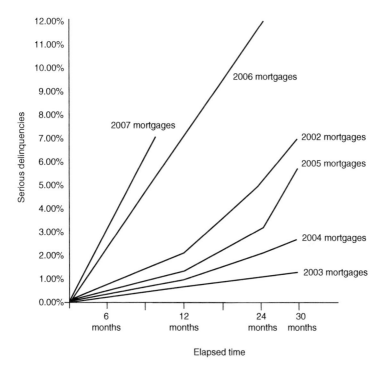

Figure 4.2   Alt-90 day + serious delinquencies as percentages of Alt-A loans in a given year, as of end 2007

2005. Yet, trading in subprime liabilities still boomed, aided by excessively loose credit standards all over industry – not just on the part of mortgage originators.

To better appreciate the extent of price inflation it should be recalled that from 1997 to 2007 house prices had much more than doubled in real terms. When, after April 2005, the rate of US house price inflation began to decline, many mortgages exceeded the worth of the house. At the same time, the drop in house price inflation limited opportunities:

- Of borrowers wishing to pay off debt through selling their house, and
- Of people in the habit of using their house as collateral for a big increase in borrowing for different personal needs.

What the second bullet practically means is that as long as the subprimes party lasted, the system's weaknesses were hidden. Investors only demanded higher-yielding assets, and the illusion of getting higher yield through residential mortgage-backed securities (RMBS) and collateralized debt obligations boosted the low-creditworthiness paper. At the end, investors paid dearly for their lack of attention to the exposure that comes with structured instruments.

For their part, banks and brokers earned fat fees by pooling and slicing the credit risks in loans to borrowers of low or no credit history. It was like bottom-fishing at the credit ladder, said an expert – who also expressed his surprise that subprime lenders, and the investment banks pooling and slicing their mortgages, found so many buyers who accepted yields just about 0.2 of a percentage point higher than Treasuries. There has been a total failure in pricing assumed exposure, because:

- House prices had skyrocketed, and
- Investors were silly enough to believe the upside would never end.

This investment philosophy, which stands on its head, collapsed when the market woke up and treated mortgage-backed securities based on Alt-As as as risky as those based on subprimes. Indeed, by July 2007 the foreclosure rate for homes priced above $800,000 has reached over 2.5 percent, higher than the national foreclosures average. With almost 80 percent of Alt-A loans being liar loans:

- Loan-to-value ratios often reached over 90 percent, and
- To trap the client, even a second piggy-back loan[13] was routinely thrown into the mortgage deal.

In Britain, too, subprime lending, called non-conforming or adverse-credit lending, proved to be highly risky, though the market, which grew at astonishing pace, from 6 percent of all new mortgage lending in 2005 to about 10 percent in 2006, was profitable overall. Yet, in Britain, as in the US, mortgage borrowers had failed to notice that a non-confirming loan is not a free lunch. The interest rates on it is usually 50 percent (or more) higher than that charged to a prime customer and this further weakens the borrower's finances.

Over a certain period of time, the boom in British house prices has been instrumental in driving repossessions to unusually low levels, as homeowners made paper gains on their equity and therefore were more inclined to pay off their mortgages than to walk away from them. Economists, however, had been asking how long this could last, and by December 2007 the market's answer came that the party was over.

While the conditions in Britain have been less bust-prone than those in the US, they have still been risky. In the end, the combined result of financially stretched borrowers, higher interest rates for lower-credit borrowers, and reduced opportunities to do cash-out refinancing for delinquent loans (because of declining house prices anywhere else than London), saw to it that delinquency rates increased.

5. Economic aftermath of subprimes

The trend towards higher interest rates, which started in 2005, put in question the viability of highly leveraged mortgages. Higher rates were a "must" because of the risk of inflation, which penalizes everybody and most particularly the economically weak segment of the population. Central bankers have been also worried about the slackness of lending standards which prevailed in the market when the going was good. Of particular concern to monetary policymakers were the facts that:

- Inflation and low creditworthiness correlate, and
- Confronting them calls for tighter money, not for an easier monetary policy.

Critics of the loose monetary policy that followed the 2000 internet and telecoms bubble say that subprime lending has been promoted by what Alan Greenspan once called the *democratization of credit*. (This has not however been a late-twentieth-century phenomenon. Lending to private individuals started in the mid 1920s in America.[14] The Great Depression (1929–1933) put a break to the acceleration of private lending, but it took off again after World War II and rose exponentially during the last two decades.)

Particularly worrisome to those economists who have been critical of Greenspan's easy-money years is the fact that the former chairman of the Federal Reserve had failed in foreseeing the unwanted consequences of loose monetary standards – this being his second major failure in a row. (The first was Greenspan's monetary policy in the mid to late 1990s, which led to the great equities bubble of 2000.)

The pros answer that monetary policy failures happen all over – they are not only Greenspan's. In trying to pull the moribund Japanese economy up by its shoestrings, the Bank of Japan has fallen into the same trap of easy money for nearly two decades, a blunder which saw to it that the global carry trade has grown by leaps and bounds (Chapter 9), while the Japanese economy is still in its coma.

As if it were the *alter* ego of the subprimes, in terms of economic exposure, the carry trade has reached the retail banking level most particularly in the housing market. Because Switzerland and Japan have among the lowest interest rates worldwide, their currencies have been used to give homebuilders a boost and (supposedly) new house owners a break.

At least theoretically, the carry trade has enabled vendors of real estate to discount their mortgages by as much as 300 to 400 basis points a year. Home buyers in Hungary, Latvia, and other EU countries are certainly not aware that in taking out such an "attractive loan" they are becoming global carry traders, rubbing shoulders with hedge funds who have made tremendous profits:

- Borrowing in currencies where interest rates are low, and
- Investing in those countries where they are high, all the way down to the level of mortgage loans.

Opinions are divided on how hard may be the fall of the real estate market. Back in June and July 2007, optimists answered this query by saying that bad as the subprime mortgage mess might be, its aftereffects would not spread because the number of mortgages at risk was too small for defaults to threaten the American economy, let alone that of Europe. According to this opinion, even if the *then* 13 percent of crisis loans grew to 20 percent, this:

- Would mean just a fifth of America's $650 billion of flexible rate subprime loans going to the dogs, and
- It would prove to be a blip in the $40 trillion US market for debt instruments.

Pessimists, and many realists, contested these assumptions because in their opinion what was known at the time about the red numbers of subprimes was not even the tip of the iceberg. In December 2007, financial news proved them right, as they indicated that, in all likelihood, less than a third of the huge subprimes losses were known then – and even this amount had left many big banks bleeding (Chapter 6).

Another argument by optimists made in June and July 2007 was that even if repossessions extended the housing downturn, this would not derail an economy that remained healthy with unemployment between 4.5 and 4.7 percent. Pessimists however answered that it does not take much to unnerve the market, and they gave as an example the smaller meltdowns of late 1990s: East Asia, Russia, and LTCM, which led to the big stock market crash of 2000.

What particularly worried some economists was that defaults by subprime mortgage borrowers, including those with poor or limited credit histories, had changed the prospects of a quick housing recovery. (One estimate says that house prices will not return to their past peaks before 2014.) Nobody can be sure how far and how fast market blues can spread to other sectors of the economy. An argument often heard in the last quarter of 2007 was that subprime mortgage bankruptcies have not hurt commodities, because US housing is a small part of their global market, China included. Still,

- Home construction accounts for 5 percent of the American economy, and
- When furniture, home-improvements spending, and utilities are included, this rises to about 15 percent.

Beyond these figures, the cataclysm brought with the massive securitization and wide distribution of doubtful credit amounted to nothing less than a revolution in banking with unknown consequences. Michel David-Weill, the French investment banker, is quoted as having said: "We don't like to make revolutions. When you have to do that, it means that you have somehow failed."[15] Greenspan should have taken notice.

When he was active, David-Weill designed his moves to be incremental rather than to lead to radical change, but nowadays many bank CEOs follow precisely the opposite policy – judging from obtained results. Take as an example the financing of the US housing market. Between 2004 and 2006, 86.2 percent of home owners who took flexible-interest-rate mortgages had less than 30 percent equity in their house. Of these:

- 69.5 percent had less than 20 percent equity;
- 51.3 percent had less than 10 percent equity;
- 25.4 percent had *zero* equity;
- 12.7 percent had up to 5 percent negative equity; and
- 6.5 percent had *up to 10 percent* negative equity (!).

This *negative equity* is pure poison to the balance sheets of the banks that gave such silly loans. Additionally, when securitized and sold it is corrupting the balance sheets of investors and of other banks. It is indeed surprising that more than a quarter of "house owners" don't really own their house; it owns them. Such statistics, and some other facts, add up to the projection that if the worse comes to worse, millions of American families will lose their homes because they have fallen prey to predatory lending.

At the end of March 2007, more than a quarter prior to the financial earthquake, Mike Calhoun, president of the Center for Responsible Lending – a Durham, North Carolina-based nonprofit entity – testified to the US Congress that a sea of foreclosures *was* a possibility.[16] By marking the start of a broader credit crunch that could bring the US economy into deep recession, the July/August 2007 crisis proved Calhoun right.

On Wall Street, critics of the policy of low credit standards pointed out that in 2000 the implosion of a few hundred internet ventures sparked a much broader stock market correction, and a recession came on its heels. Today, not only the subprime borrowers are overleveraged and bankrupt but also the US economy is too much indebted. Something similar is true of the British, French, German, Italian, Spanish, and other Western economies.

Repairing the balance sheet of a bank or a household is usually done by deleveraging. But though this is the better way to repair the financial position of individuals, companies, and governments, the cost is not going to be negligible. The price of deleveraging is recession, and that's what Dr Greenspan meant when at the end of February 2007 he said there was a one-third risk that the US economy would go into recession late in that same year. Had he said depression, for once he would have been right.

6. Impact of the subprime crisis on the economy

One of the major differences between the first and second half of 2007 was the severe drop in market confidence, as the financial news became increasingly dismal. The S&P homebuilding index dropped from nearly 1300 in January 2007 to 700 a month later. Already by June 2007 US homebuilders' confidence had fallen to about 25 percent, from 75 percent in 2004 and 2005, amid worries about:

• The future of subprime mortgages, and
• A sharp drop in home construction.

Lennar Corp., the biggest US homebuilder, reported a 73 drop in first quarter 2007 profit, with no improvement in the second quarter, while other homebuilders faced similar challenges. Bankers, however, paid no attention to the construction and other industries' woes; or for that matter to the fact that a drop in house prices was bound to make a discernible dent in US families' wealth and therefore consumption growth. Their attention focused on rate cuts by the Fed, not on the risk that falling house prices can be an ongoing drag for years.

In the first months of 2007, particularly March and April, rate cut speculation hinged on the assumption that the subprime lending debacle would force the Fed into cutting rates aggressively, as a way of damage control. These were one-sided expectations; still the calls for major rate cuts persisted even in May 2007 while subprime fears subsided as positive and negative economic data cancelled each other out.

Businessmen who found themselves on the wrong side of the balance sheet qualified their urging of rate cuts as "their worry about costs to be paid by home owners." In March 2007, based on his firm's database of most American mortgages, Christopher Cagan, an economist at First American CoreLogic, suggested that 60 percent of all flexible-interest-rate loans made since 2004 would be reset under the following conditions:

- In the general case, payments would be 25 percent or more higher.
- But a third of this 60 percent would see monthly payments soar by 50 percent or more.[17]

Such percentages meant that the exposure faced by consumers in the housing sector was quite likely going to drag US economic activity for some time. That has been the opinion as well of Wendell Perkins, who oversees $1.6 billion at Johnson Asset Management in Racine, Wisconsin;[18] Perkins was reasoning on the basis of surging defaults.

Other wealth managers, as well as several economists, felt that the meltdown in mortgages given to borrowers with poor credit histories would spill over to the broader economy – and most particularly to consumer debt in securitized credit cards and auto loans.[19] As early as April 2007, US statistics indicated that more than thirty mortgage lenders had halted operations, gone bankrupt, or sought buyers, as defaults on subprime loans surged. A month earlier (March 2007), concern about foreclosures had pushed the Conference Board's index of consumer confidence down from a 5-year high.

Still, in the earlier stages of the subprime crisis other economists were not too pessimistic. Their thesis was that the US residential mortgage market is huge, and around three-quarters of residential loans were already repackaged into mortgage-backed securities (MBS), mainly by the government-sponsored Fannie Mae and Freddie Mac. Instead, they worried about the buyers of securitized mortgages like insurance companies and pension funds,

- Which found themselves in the frontline as mortgage losses pile up,
- But might not have enough financial depth to withstand the shock of the subprimes.

(It is bad policy to take lightly the stress of Fannie Mae and Freddie Mac. At the end of 2007 both reported heavy quarterly losses because of higher defaults on loans and rising foreclosures. Yet, in late February 2008 the Bush Administration said it would consider lifting a cap on their ability to invest capital imposed on the pair because of accounting irregularities. The "lifting" delighted the markets.)

Apart all other considerations, there has been an exchange rate fall-out as well. After the July/August 2007 subprimes crisis optimistic projections on the US economy faded out, and the Fed cut interest rates three times in 2007: first by 50 basis points then twice by 25 bp. Some economists however considered the 11 December rate cut unnecessary, because:

- It weakened an already very weak dollar, and
- It came at an inopportune moment, as the Fed would have done better to keep its powder dry for events that might unfold in 2008.

A different way of making this statement is that while an uncertain scenario characterized interest rate expectation in the US, there has been no calm in the currency markets. Already in April 2007 the dollar dropped through several landmarks, falling 4 percent against the British pound in 6 weeks, and even more against the euro. With a whole range of moves fresh in their memory,

- Analysts looked at short-term risks,
- While economists took a longer-range view.

Whether examined under the short-term or longer-range consequences, one thing has become clear. The price of gambling with poorly conceived and badly controlled derivative instruments:

- Is astronomically high, and
- It threatens to bring the Western banking system to the ground.

Wrong top management decisions, risk control failures, and a dismal credit quality in lending have been key issues raised by the subprimes debacle. People critical of the way lending policies developed during the last two decades, and most particularly in this century, stressed the point that subprime borrowers of all sorts – not just in housing – are the fastest-growing segment of America's market. By 2007, in mortgages they accounted for:

- 20 percent of new loans, and
- 10 percent of all mortgage debt.

By lowering the standards of their lending policy, banks, and other financial institutions brought upon themselves the cataclysm, they are the parties responsible for orchestrating the disaster. When the US housing market began to slow, lenders stepped up the pace of home sales by further loosening credit standards.

Banks cut the need for credit documentation, lent more against each property, waived the equity requirement for lenders, and assumed an even greater amount of risk. At that time Wall Street cheered them; but all these exposures had been piling up and the dam holding them broke down, flooding the vaults of European banks and then unleashing a global financial crisis.

7. A business opportunity for distressed-debt artists

According to the opinion of a growing number of individuals know-ledgeable about where the market is going, starting with America and following up with Britain then Spain (among continental European countries), a huge business is about to come into being, namely that of buying and restructuring *distressed debt*, with all sorts of mortgages at the core. Experts also predict that this restructuring into novel financial instruments will bring outsized returns for those who know:

- How to thrive on credit risk, and
- How to trade in financial casualties.

Capitalizing on distressed debt was once the reserve of a few specu-lators, but it now seems to attract mainstream bankers and a lot of other debt artists. According to some estimates, in the US alone there are presently some 170 institutions that invest primarily in distressed debt turnaround, having among themselves an estimated $300 billion as their war chest. By all accounts, this massive approach to financial alchemy is a first in the history of banking.

Among the distressed debt specialists are entities known as vulture funds, and those who manage them reportedly believe that they currently find themselves at the start of a bright future. Defaults in mortgages present them with business opportunities greater than those of junk bond defaults (an estimated 17 percent of senior, unsecured junk bond issues are at the edge of the precipice, and this is an 850 percent increase over the 2 percent prevailing in 1990).

It is not necessary to explain that distressed-debt artists don't find the tools of their art in textbooks. Faced with rich pickings, they bet on the fact that when after a long bull run market sentiment turns negative, even seasoned market players usually tend to overreact. By so doing, they are losing the sense of distinction between:

- Basket cases, and
- Risky but viable debt.

Distressed-debt artists, however, will need a great lot of ingenuity to pull their deals through, because of the novel situations they face. According to some accounts, one of the reasons why the next wave of distress will be unlike those we have already known is that commercial banks no longer dominate the lending process. Instead, non-banks like hedge funds:

- Now make roughly half of all high-yielding leveraged loans, and
- They also hold the bigger share of the secondary market for such debt.

An interesting hindsight, as well, is that the money to save troubled companies, including traditional financial institutions, comes from banks and it only transits through hedge funds seeking high returns. When, after banks withdrew support, Farallon gave to Accredited $200 million, it did not do so because of being a good Samaritan.

Reportedly, Farallon charged a credit-card-like rate of interest – which in practice means around 18 percent – beside which it secured the right for 10 years to buy over 3 million Accredited shares for $10 each. Such a deal will bring huge returns if the lender pulls through and the borrowers survive. Specialists say that this is a "loan-to-own" strategy, which has become popular among hedge funds and now finds its way into policies by sovereign wealth funds (Chapter 2):

- Credit is extended on the basis that it can be converted to equity under favorable terms, and
- This allows the lender-turned-owner to thoroughly restructure the firm, make it profitable, and sell it.

Both bullets lead to the second major change characterizing twenty-first-century financial markets. Unlike under the conditions prevailing in the past, the capital structures of borrowers, which classically consist of various layers of debt and equity, feature a complex plurality of rights. Untangling them in the event of default becomes much more complicated than it has ever been, therefore:

- Making it difficult to know who is entitled to what, and
- Opening up some significant opportunities for profits.

One of the reasons why over the years complexity has increased is that conditions attached to loans vary from one case to the next as many are bilaterally negotiated. Another reason is the explosion of second-lien lending. Textbooks say that such loans are secured against a company's assets, but with fewer rights than in the case of more senior loans. Financial wizards are ready to prove that textbooks are wrong.

Because it usually happens that these rights are not always clearly spelled out, second-lien lenders have begun to exploit the prevailing legal fuzziness, to challenge those investors who theoretically stand above them, particularly those in the first-lien pecking order. While theoretically second-lien loans give a lesser claim to an owner's assets than prior loans, as assumed debt is increasingly covenant-lite, the practical result is that a team composed of shrewd lawyers and ingenious analysts may be able to recast, to their client's favor, who owes what to whom.

5
The Industrialization of Credit Risk

1. Credit derivatives

Credit derivatives are financial instruments enabling the trading of credit risk separate from other types of risk. This is achieved by appropriately designing, securitizing (section 2 of this chapter) and distributing credit exposure to willing investors. A simple form of a bilateral credit derivatives deal is that two parties agree to exchange predetermined cash flows associated with a given credit event, over a defined maturity.

While in the way they are currently traded credit derivatives are relatively new instruments, dating back to the 1990s, the concept underpinning them is much older. Predecessors of credit derivatives, as financial products featuring default risk, have been all types of bonds and syndicated bank loans. There are lovers and haters of the credit derivatives concept.

- Many analysts consider them to be financial products instruments whose time has come.
- Others believe that they are a push product, sold aggressively by banks, because vanilla-ice-cream lending no longer has the profitability of the 1960s.

Whichever opinion one adopts, the reason why trading credit risk is not so different from trading market risk (though both the characteristics and mechanics vary) is that lending has become nearly as risky as trading.

Examples
Examples documenting this statement are the Latin American debt crisis of the early 1980s; the Texas and New England real estate bubbles

of the late 1980s/early 1990s; the East Asia debacle of 1997; the Russian meltdown of 1998; and the subprimes crisis of 2007.

Underpinning the trading in credit derivatives is the market's appetite for credit risk, which has increased over the last fifteen years. Classically, banks assumed credit risk with their loans. Now they both buy credit risk and sell it short. In a market that has grown by leaps and bounds, as shown in Figure 5.1, success depends on finding counterparties willing and able to assume the unbundled credit risk in exchange for a cash flow.

Critics say that because credit derivatives let banks pass off to other parties the risk of default on their loans, they have created a banking anticulture which pays scant attention to borrowers' creditworthiness. Therefore, investors must be very sensitive to the likelihood of bankruptcy, and able to come up with a dependable method for calculating the risk of default – a tough job given that the counterparties' creditworthiness is often a well-kept secret.

In spite of an opaque creditworthiness, insurance companies and other entities, including other credit institutions, provide the originators of credit exposure with protection by assuming their credit risk

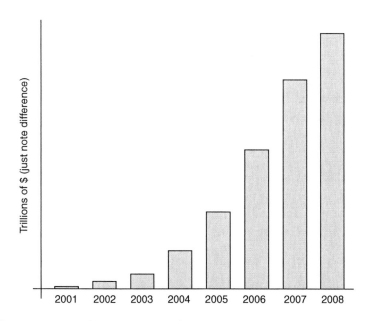

Figure 5.1   Notional amounts outstanding in global credit derivatives

against a fee. Typically, the originator is the *risk seller*, who offers compensation to the *risk buyer* for his agreeing to the transfer of credit risk in his books, with or without inclusion of guarantors. It's a risky game, and to be ahead of the curve buyers must:

- Understand and analyze the risk and return profile of each underlying instrument;
- Model this risk and return using market response to past negative events and their aftermath; and
- Stress test market information and model results through outliers and extreme conditions.[1]

Stress analysis is a "must." Advanced experimental techniques are necessary for credit risk transfer practices which have little to do with the traditional, time-honored policy of commercial bankers: "I lend to the people I know, in places I know." But as the events of July/August 2007 and subsequent months have shown, not even banks (let alone the wider spectrum of investors and speculators) are ready for this new methodology.

A short item which appeared in a public affairs weekly captures the depth of the problem with credit derivatives. It reads like this:

> Rumor has it that when you open a new account at one of the big banks these days, you are offered a choice between a $1 million mortgage-backed security and a toaster, and that most people are taking the toaster.[2]

Enlightened spirits have seen the pitfalls well before the 2007 meltdown of the subprimes. As early as 2000, Dr Brandon Davies, a former treasurer of Barclays Bank, advised that credit derivatives contribute not to the distribution but to the *concentration of risk*, because the main clients are (and will continue being) institutional investors, insurance companies, and the banks themselves.[3] This is precisely what has been documented with the 2007 credit crunch. Since our economy operates on borrowed money, concentrations increase the risk of default and a high rate of defaults can trigger an avalanche of losses. Even were the creditworthiness of the pool of loans being securitized not in doubt, the perils associated with concentration of risk would rise because *credit volatility* is much more opaque than market volatility.

- Market volatility is more or less an established notion in the consciousness of bankers, traders, investors, and regulators.

There are by now well-studied metrics and ways to measure it, while some educated guesses could be done on the correlation between liquidity and market volatility. Additionally, indices and established exchanges help in the discovery of market volatility.

- Credit volatility, which amounts to the impairment of the credit-worthiness of an obligor or group of obligors is, so to speak, a concept in search of analytical definition.

One of the unknowns is the exact way in which it correlates with *liquidity* (Chapter 9), an issue that has not yet been adequately researched in terms of its nature, extent, and impact. Also, dependable metrics are missing. The nearest proxy is credit rating but, as the subprime events have shown, credit rating is subject to bias; it is therefore much less reliable than it was expected to be (Chapter 6).

Yet, a sound estimate of credit volatility is an important factor in pricing credit derivatives, because, like options, forwards, and swaps, these are both financial contracts and means of actuating a pricing mechanism that is credit-sensitive. Such is the case of credit default swaps (CDS, Chapter 1), which are seen as a credit insurance scheme.

2. Risk associated with securitization

The broader definition of *securitization* includes any transaction that involves the packaging and productization of credit risk (or other commodity), as well as the act of transferring it to third parties: a pool of loans with credit exposure is put together, the whole being separated into two or more *tranches*. Each tranche is characterized by a credit risk quotient, with the higher tranche having *seniority* and being, at least theoretically, less risky than that (or those) which are lower. As a rule:

- The securitized asset's performance depends on the performance of underlying exposures, and
- At the bottom line, all or most of underlying exposures involve financial-type risk which will reside in the buyer's portfolio.

While securitization started around 1912 with real estate assets, the ways and means for doing a neat pooling job developed some 60 years later with *mortgage-backed securities* (MBS). Subsequently it extended to other types of assets, examples being credit card receivables and auto loans. A general label for this type of securitizations is asset-backed

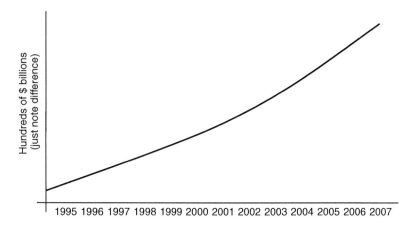

Figure 5.2   Issuance of American asset-backed securities

securities (ABS) – a debt instrument which has grown almost exponentially during the last dozen years, as shown in Figure 5.2.

In principle, but only in principle, institutional and other investors who buy securitized instruments have been demanding. Speaking from experience in the 1980s and early 1990s, investors in securitized mortgages will not put up their cash until the underwriter gives them the option-adjusted spread (OAS; the computation of which requires Monte Carlo simulation). But slowly attention to detail waned, with principle and practice taking divorce in the first years of this century.

The opportunity for divorce has been presented by the subprimes. No better words can characterize securitized junk loans and their buyers (including the top management of the bank or other entity which reached the fateful decision to acquire them) than those made by two different, indeed opposing, political forces regarding Sun Yat-Sen, generally considered as the theoretical father of the Chinese Republican revolution.

Lenin once described Sun Yat-Sen as a man of "inimitable – one might say virginal – naiveté." That's precisely the profile of CEOs who brought their banks to the edge of bankruptcy by going for securitized subprimes in a big way. For its part, the British Foreign Office had concluded that Dr Sun was a mere windbag,[4] which is exactly what subprimes, Alt-As, and the "AAA-rated senior tranches" of securitized subprimes have been.[5]

The reader should moreover notice that, creditworthiness aside, all securitized instruments carry *basis risk*. The term expresses the relationship in exposure between the *underlying asset* and the *reference asset*, which is usually a publicly traded security. Basis risk comes from the fact that the reference asset will not necessarily track the real risk against which it is hedged. As such, its presence is of major concern to everybody:

- From originators,
- To investors, and
- To regulators.

A third major risk comes from the vast amount of investments made in securitized credit instruments. As has been brought to the reader's attention, one of the problems encountered with securitized debt is that the evaluation of creditworthiness at origination of loans is often superficial. With "originate to distribute" operations (section 3 of this chapter), bankers rarely if ever apply the "Stern principle" in granting a loan – which means questioning not only the rationale of it but also the absolute level of exposure.

Michel David-Weill used to make reference to an elderly and wise banker (the grandfather of Edward Stern, his son-in-law) who was on the board of Banque des Pays Bas (today Paribas). In a session, the board was reviewing credits to major clients and one of its members said: "We are lending 100 million francs to the Ottoman Empire." The old banker jumped on his seat: "What?...A hundred million francs? I would not lend that to myself!"[6]

When he spoke to bankers, David-Weill cited that incident, because he knew that they frequently forget that there are sums you should not be lending even to the credit you may adore the most: your good self. You should just say "No! This loan is ridiculous." Had the Stern principle been applied in the case of the subprimes, the horde of banks and investors who suffered the deep wounds would not have lost a fortune by granting, productizing, and superficially buying other peoples' garbage.

Sound evaluation principles should apply not only to each loan in the pool, but also to each tranche of securitization, including: terms, covenants, pricing, and yield. And always one should keep in mind that the credit risk quotient is not the same from one pool or one tranche to the next.

- Additionally, banks are wrong when they think that securitized credit risk is off their books.

- Regulators can put some or all securitized exposures back on their balance sheet.

There exists, of course, regulatory arbitrage. One of the loopholes in Basel II, the new capital adequacy norms, has been that banks servicing securitized residential mortgages do not need to hold capital against the undrawn portion of eligible servicer cash advances. Another gap in supervision is that with the internal-ratings-based (IRB) approach of Basel II, for each tranche credit risk exposure must be rated by an independent credit rating agency (or have an inferred rating). Originators need two ratings, investors only one, with risk weights depending on:

- Rating,
- Seniority, and
- Granularity.

But as the subprimes debacle documented, credit ratings can be biased, to the point that they don't mean much. Another interesting issue is multiple exposures to single securitization. Risk capital requirements for all securitization exposures held by a single bank associated with a single securitization cannot be greater than the sum of IRB capital for underlying exposures and the bank's expected credit loss for underlying exposures. This seems to leave out of the equation of exposure the frequently disastrous effects of:

- High leveraging, and
- Significant correlations between risk factors.[7]

The supervisory rules say that a credit institution with multiple duplicative securitization exposures must apply the risk capital treatment to the position that results in the highest capital requirements. For securitization exposure in the form of an MBS, or participation interest resulting from a mortgage loan swap with recourse, the bank must bifurcate the position into:

- The retained recourse obligation, and
- The percentage of MBS, or participation interest, not covered by the recourse.

But while the risk-based capital requirement for each component should be separately calculated, trivial attention is paid to the fact that two or more of these components may correlate, augmenting by so much the exposure quotient. Instead, the total risk capital requirement is capped at the risk capital requirement for the underlying exposures *as if* they were held directly on-balance-sheet, in a theoretical way abstracting from the leveraging and correlation effects, and simply forgetting about off-balance-sheet commitments.

3. Originate to distribute

One of the financial processes characteristic of the twenty-first century has been the so-called "originate to distribute" model which, in a short span of time, has been embraced by many banks worldwide. The concept underpinning it is that of originating loans on a scale resembling Henry Ford's production line, which are then securitized and sold on. Therefore, at least theoretically, they require limited capital adequacy on the originator's side.

- The originate-to-distribute strategy deals with temporary exposures accepted with the intention of productizing and selling the asset within a short period.
- This is the exact opposite of "take and hold" positions in the loans book, which have been the foundation of the banks' strategy as financial intermediaries.

Banks securitizing their loans book know that, in the general case, not every credit transaction entering into a pool will be ultimately creditworthy. The exact proportion of defaults will vary significantly with company and debt rating. For their part, people purchasing these originate-to-distribute debt securities assume more than one sort of exposure. The four most important are:

- *Counterparty risk* – whose presence is evident, but not its extent.
- *Collateral value risk* – what the securitized product will be worth in the future when used as collateral.
- *Collateral illiquidity risk* – which may not be compensated by covenants in the contract (if any).
- *Legal risk* – particularly present with global asset pools, and under a growing number of circumstances associated with all sorts of securitized loans.

For instance, a major worry relates to the legal structure of credit derivatives, because such instruments often fail to lay down clearly what would constitute a default for the purpose of triggering payment by the credit risk buyers to the credit risk seller (see also the discussion on legal risk in Chapter 2). Investors who buy securitized credit risk can be divided into five main classes:

- *Corporate treasurers*, who look for diversified tools to manage or hedge exposures on their balance sheets.
- *Insurance companies* and investment funds, which target new products and annuities to sell to their retail clients.
- *Pension funds*, wanting to capitalize on somewhat higher yields, or to have a credit risk exposure as distinct from market risk experience.
- *Other banks* and their special investment vehicles, which inventory and trade debt instruments.
- *High-net-worth individuals*, and increasingly medium-net-worth private banking clients, lured into debt- (and equity-) type structured products by their bankers or by hedge funds.

Beyond these five classes are the hedge funds and traders who get into derivatives transactions not for investment reasons but for the profits to be made from dealing; and for commissions. In the same category also fall investment managers and other professionals who make most of their money from commissions in the credit derivatives market and from fat bonuses on imaginary profits. (More on this in Chapter 6.)

Rather absent from the originate-to-distribute process has been the need to keep a close watch over the risk outlined in the preceding paragraphs. The July/August 2007 subprimes debacle has demolished the concept that by the magic of pooling them, poorly researched and *covenant-lite* loans turn into a creditworthy asset. Banks have been simply careless in evaluating creditworthiness and in providing the foundations for risk control.

In fact, credit institutions have been imprudent not only towards their clients, but also towards themselves – because they have not always transferred as much credit risk as they thought they did. Quite unexpectedly, some of the assets held in off-balance-sheet vehicles like *conduits* (section 5 of this chapter) have been forcing them to hold more capital against assets they have distributed. An example is loans that have been sold, but on which the bank retains a reputational risk.

The 2007 to 2009 events have also shattered the notion that for temporary exposures the critical factor is the potential for distribution assessed as part of a transaction's approval. The subprimes abyss demonstrated that being factual and documented about the distribution function is even more important than doing so in the originating side of the business, because it conditions the type and amount of commitments a bank should make. Generally, though not always: the easier is the distribution of securitized loans, the lower are the average credit ratings of positions remaining in the bank's portfolio; and therefore, the banking book's credit risk concentrations increase, with exposures rising within a relatively short time. Because of these concentrations (whether assumed credit risks are seen as temporary or as take-and-hold), good governance should see to it that both the origination and distribution sides of the business:

- Are well documented, and
- That for each of them there are comprehensive limits to exposure.

A variety of stress loss limits, which encourage greater attention on the quality of assumed credit risk, should be integral to a sound policy. This is not what happens in the majority of big credit institutions, which count on their distribution leverage to free up capacity for further loans. Yet, both credit and market conditions suggest that greater care is required than in the past, away from the so-called covenant-lite lending policies.

Typically, *covenant-lite* transactions are lacking maintenance covenants, which means that banks have much less control on borrowers when business turns bad – a very poor management practice. The disturbing news of mid 2007, when the subprime market turned sour, has been that the total amount of covenant-lite loans issued in the first two quarters of that year in the US alone was $105 billion, which tops by a wide factor the $32 billion of all covenant-lite loans written from 1997 to 2006.

An ironic aspect of this situation has been that the largest users of covenant-lite policies were not consumers for their mortgages, but private equity firms able to dictate terms to lenders. In May 2007, just one buyout company, Kohlberg Kravis Roberts (KKR), filed to raise a record $16 billion of such loans to finance its buyout of First Data.[8]

Banks tend to answer criticism of carelessness by saying that they employ risk mitigation techniques for most of their credit portfolios. Theoretically, they do so by taking security in the form of cash, marketable assets and so on; or through risk transfers, including the purchase of credit protection. Banks add that, depending on the product and the type of mitigation, this is reflected in their policy:

- By recognizing its existence in determining the exposure they are prepared to carry, or

- By directly accounting for risk-reducing effect of credit protection, in reported credit exposure.

This is an argument open to different interpretations. True enough, as a matter of policy, banks take financial collateral in the form of marketable securities and generally apply *haircuts* (discounts) to current market value, reflecting the asset's quality, liquidity, volatility, and other criteria. As Figure 5.3 shows, the types of collateral instruments are wide-ranging.

All loans, however, are not secured by collateral. Unsecured lending consists predominantly of exposures to public authorities, as well as to other banks and corporate clients with enough clout to apply their own conditions. Besides this, covenants are just as important to credit risk control, and their dilution may be hiding major future exposure.

Critics say that the dilution of prudential criteria and covenants for loans has not been properly factored into the new capital adequacy framework of the banking industry; and that is one of Basel II's several downsides. Though stress tests may help in partly answering this requirement, they have been relegated to Pillar 2 (national supervision). They are no more globally uniform and therefore their results are not necessarily comparable from one jurisdiction to the next.

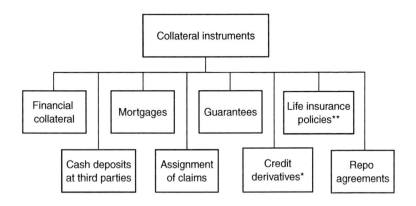

* Here is exactly where the subprimes mess, and overrated AAAs, hit the most.
** For personal collateral.

Figure 5.3   Eligible collateral for credit risk mitigation

4. Variable-interest entities

As if the quadrillion dollars in derivatives, crisis of the subprimes, coming debacle of credit default swaps, and monolines credit rating woes were not enough, on 26 February 2008 there appeared on Bloomberg. com a worrisome article by Mark Pittman. In it, the author suggested that even Goldman Sachs and Lehman Brothers – who so far had sailed through the subprimes crisis without major losses – might find they had not escaped the descent into Dante's hell. The new source of potential losses was said to be *variable-interest entities* (VIEs)[9] that make it possible for financial firms to keep assets such as subprime mortgage securities off their balance sheets. According to this estimate:

- VIEs may contribute another $88 billion in losses to the subprime mess which followed the collapse of the housing market,[10] and
- Goldman, which had no part in the banking industry's huge write-downs, may incur as much as $11.1 billion of losses from these instruments.

The article explained that VIEs, known as *special-purpose vehicles* (SPVs) before Enron's collapse in 2001, finance themselves by selling short-term debt backed by securities, some of which are insured against default; and one type of VIE has already been forced to unwind or seek bank financing, namely the *structured investment vehicle* (SIV).

This soup of names is too confusing, and it does not need to be so; we will see why in section 5 of this chapter. Important for the reader to appreciate is that, no matter how they are called, these vehicles are (and have been) opaque off-balance-sheet instruments characterized by an inordinate amount of exposure. They are also a widely practiced way to game the bank's capital requirements:

- Supervisory authorities control the bank's balance sheets, which are audited and on which are based their financial statements.
- Off-balance-sheet is a visible blight of failed supervision. The practice started in the 1980s with derivatives. It is a cheat, and contrary to official pronouncements it continues being condoned by regulators.

Many VIEs (and therefore SPVs) have been designed to provide off-balance-sheet financing to clients and/or to invest in real estate. Theoretically, assets held by VIEs where one bank provided financing and is the primary beneficiary, must be recorded in loans, notes, and mortgages in the consolidated balance sheets. But assets held by VIEs where a bank has invested in real estate partnerships or other financial products, and is the primary beneficiary, are a loophole. Also, theoretically, the beneficial interest holders in these VIEs:

- Have no recourse to the general credit of the parent bank, and
- Their investments are paid exclusively from the assets in the VIE.

Practically, however, a VIE is thinly capitalized; therefore, it is not self-supportive. Other entities must provide it with financial backing, and one of these other entities should be the primary beneficiary. This means that at least one of the entities which have variable interests in the VIE must assume more than half of the expected losses and the expected gains:

- *If* neither entity assumes more than half of expected the losses or gains,
- *Then* there is no primary beneficiary, and therefore no consolidation exists. Even a camel can pass through this needle's eye, contrary to the Biblical saying.

The full extent of the accounting loophole can be better appreciated by knowing that in their financial statements banks need to consolidate such VIEs if, *and only if*, less than 10 percent of the investment is provided by "outside investors," who can be manufactured at will. Beyond this significant help in escaping prudential supervision, banks do their own interpretation of off-balance-sheet assets.

This is one of the reasons why Tanya Azarchs, managing director for financial institutions at S&P, was quoted in the same Bloomberg article as having said:

> The disclosure on VIEs is hopeless ... You have no idea of the structure or how that structure works. Until you know that you don't know anything. It's like every day you come into the office and another alphabet soup has run off the rails.

Azarchs was making reference to the fact that predictions for losses vary widely because banks are not required to specify the type of assets being held in the VIEs or how much they are worth. Goldman Sachs, for instance, had earned a record $11.6 billion in the year ended in

November 2007. At the time, it avoided writedowns by setting up trades that would profit from a weaker housing market. Two months later, the threat stood at $18.9 billion of CDOs in VIEs, as the firm stated in its regulatory filing on 29 January 2008.

Lehman Brothers, which had already written down the net value of its subprime securities by $1.5 billion, had guaranteed $7.5 billion of VIE assets as of 30 November 2007, according to a filing also made on 29 January 2008. "We believe our actual risk to be limited because our obligations are collateralized by the VIE's assets and contain significant constraints," Lehman said in its filing; but it would not elaborate.

By the end of the first quarter of 2008, the greater fear in Wall Street was that a combination of subprime collateralized mortgage obligations (CDOs), SIVs and conduits would result in a flood of assets in fire sales into an already stressed market. The widely expected result would be price collapse, with some banks being damaged much more than others.

Financial analysts suggest that the battered Citigroup, which till late February 2008 incurred $22.4 billion in losses from the subprime crisis, had an additional *$320 billion* (!!) in unconsolidated VIEs. This information comes straight out of its 22 February 2008 filing. By contrast, Merrill Lynch, which recorded $24.5 billion in subprime write-downs, had $22.6 billion in VIEs, according to CreditSights.

The aforementioned statistics are significant because, according to a learned opinion, the securities in the VIEs may be worth as little as 27 cents on the dollar once they are put back on balance sheets. David Hendler of CreditSights based this estimate on the recent sale of $800 million of bonds by E*Trade Financial. In this case:

- Merrill Lynch may be bleeding another $16.5 billion, and
- The hemorrhage at Citigroup will stand at $233.6 billion, meaning that, if these estimates are right, for all practical purposes the credit institution is bankrupt many times over.

Ironically, this wholesale disaster is no event that could not have been foreseen. It is the way the global debt machine works, when fed with plenty of unsustainable loans by a management which has lost all sense of reality. The "good work" of VIEs, SPVs, SIVs, conduits, CDOs, and CDSs is layers of leverage based on debt whose repayment is theoretically backed by an income stream whose whereabouts are lost in the meanders of leverage.

5. Structured investment vehicles[11] and conduits

The careful reader will recall that a basic method of structured finance is that of separating the holder of a loan from its originator, by means of pooling and distributing credit risk. Section 4 of this chapter presented to the reader the poetic story of the VIEs, also known as *special-purpose* vehicles (SPVs) with *structured investment vehicles* (SIPs) as subsets of the great financial swindle where one opaque instrument is interlinked with a myriad of others.

The first two SIVs, Alpha Finance and Beta Finance, were created for Citibank by Nicholas Sossidis and Stephen Partridge-Hicks. The latter also wrote a book, *Synthetic Securities*, portraying SIVs as extremely advanced financial vehicles – which they are not. What is true is that their number has been rapidly growing because of the banking industry's desire to manipulate balance sheets, hide sour transactions, free up capital, do maturity transformations, and proceed with risk transformations. Special-purpose vehicles can be divided into three main classes:

- Structured investment vehicles (SIVs),
- SIV-lites, mainly fed with MBS subprimes, and
- Asset-backed commercial paper (ABCP) conduits.

These three are related. SIVs and SIV-lites refinance themselves in the money market, through asset-backed commercial paper. However, *if* credit risk rises or there is market panic, *then* SIVs face liquidity problems – and eventually a torrent of red ink. Up to a point, but only up to a point, accumulating losses are hidden from public eye because:

- *Conduits* are carried off-balance-sheet by the bank that creates them, and
- *Structured investment vehicles* are supposedly independent of the parent company.

Conduits and structured investment vehicles are freely set up by a credit institution for its own use and that of its clients. Because there is no regulation in their regard, they make possible high leverage, satisfying risk appetites, and allowing investment in equity and debt with greater than statutory exposure. In this sense, conduits are *high-risk* instruments employed to make a fast buck, since:

- The underlyings are cheap, often rolled over every few months, and

- The money is employed in buying what is actually junk but has been incorrectly rated as high-quality assets, like the upper tranches of collateralized debt obligations.

The result is a double exposure, one to the *credit risk* of loans such as subprimes and the other in regard to *liquidity* (Chapter 9), because banks buy medium-term instruments, financing them through short-term credit. According to Moody's Investors Service, conduits had $784 billion in commercial paper outstanding at end of February 2008.

That's financial policy turned on its head, and it is interesting to notice that the first high-risk conduits saw the day just a decade ago. They were established in 1998 by WestLB and BayernLB, two German state banks (*Länderbanken*) supposed to act as safe keepers of local savings banks treasuries as well as being state banks – but generally known to take inordinate risks while covered by taxpayers' money. They do so without asking for any permission since the German states have lost control over them.

Up to March 2007 (latest available statistics), there was an estimated $507 billion of fake AAA assets in European conduits, in a global market estimated at $1.3 trillion (double its size in 2004). WestLB had an exposure of €35 billion ($51 billion). Sachsen LB had an exposure of €17 billion ($25 billion),[12] and it went bankrupt.

The people who designed these conduits were long in financial alchemy but very short in risk management skills, particularly with regard to liquidity exposure. As so frequently happens with short-term funding, with the subprime debacle of July/August 2007 the conduits have been confronted by a severe liquidity dry-up, including the aforementioned fake AAAs:

- Liquidity was not expected to be a problem with AAA-rated assets held by these conduits.
- But their "AAAs" were just the upper tranche of securitized debt obligations with high credit risk, hence junk.

The way a Merrill Lynch study had it:

The financial community is more exposed to subprime mortgage assets than what is implied by the static amount of subprime debt currently outstanding. The problem of lower asset-backed securities (ABS) prices has been exacerbated by the fact that these securities were bundled into structured debt instruments like collateralized debt obligations (CDOs). Attracted by the high credit rating and wide relative spread, financial institutions both here and abroad bought these bonds using off-balance-sheet entities, which meant that little or no capital provisioning was needed.[13]

As the malaise spread to the sponsoring banks, providing what is incorrectly called "temporary backup credit," the liquidity switch of commercial paper was turned off. Ironically, the crisis of conduits surprised many experts because they have been hugely popular in both America and Europe, but the irony does not end with the disappearance of the commercial paper market.

Most irrationally, many banks were hoping that with Basel II the conduits' "high ratings" might enable them to reduce their regulatory capital: they were rated "AAAs," of all things, and they paid better than similarly rated American Treasuries till half or more of the capital invested in them was lost. The subprimes hecatomb proved that both these AAA ratings and the logic behind them were, to say the least, a cheat.

Neither have the conduits been the only way in which to hide investment positions of high exposure from the eyes of the market and of regulators. In off-balance-sheet terms the structured investment vehicles have been similar to conduits, but they also have:

- A more general purpose, and
- Higher leverage, which makes them even more failure-prone.

SIVs became a pole of attraction because theoretically they feature little credit-line support by banks, relying on a sort of insurance known as *credit enhancement*. This theory, however, has been shattered by the subprime crisis.

As long as the story of SIVs being entities operating at arm's length of their parent was believable, to reassure their lenders special investment vehicles said that their assets were marked-to-market *daily*. This statement was at least halfway a fake, because no one in the market knows the SIVs' assets value, as they are scarcely traded – their main operation consisting of borrowing short-term to buy long-term high-yielding junk securities.

So as to keep up their reputation as a financial innovation, but with the freedom to behave as mini-hedge funds, SIVs have been by large majority deliberately incorporated in the British Cayman Islands: offshore and off-balance-sheet. As such they are outside the control and regulation of government authorities. But with the subprimes crisis, the SIVs were hit by a triple whammy:

- Falling market values of financial debt products,
- Difficulties in valuing complex structured bonds they invest in, and
- The virtual impossibility of raising funding in the short-term debt markets on which they rely, as investors have deserted high-risk instruments and entities.

Equally damaging for the SIVs has been the fact that after the subprimes debacle many analysts started looking at them as rather primitive structures. They fell off the cliff with other instruments supposedly designed for and sold to sophisticated investors. This was a failure waiting to happen because, since the start, to maximize profits for their holding (not for the investors), SIVs superleveraged themselves, borrowed money short-term, invested in long-term products, and bought the most speculative assets.

6. State funds pay the bill: the case of Florida

The heavy bill of the subprimes has to be paid by somebody, and little by little the "Who Is Who" in silly high-risk investments is becoming known. After devastating the homeowners and the banks themselves, the subprime contagion hit the investment pools of American states: from Connecticut to Florida, Maine, Montana, and Washington; as well as many US municipalities. Their treasurers had bought billions of dollars of debt of SIVs, in commercial paper and medium-term notes.

The failure of SIVs' supposed "assets" impaired the revenue funds of public authorities that held them. On 4 December 2007 it was announced that in the state of Florida, the Local Government Investment Fund (LGIF) has suffered a torrent of red ink. An audit made by BlackRock, an investment firm, revealed that:

- 14 percent of positions in its municipal fund had defaulted, and
- This represented the loss of $2 billion out of $14 billion in audited municipal fund holdings.

This is not the first bad experience of the state of Florida with real estate. In the twentieth century, in just one year (1924/1925) its real estate prices quadrupled with nearly everybody having become a real estate investor or agent. The bubble blew and Florida's real estate market collapsed in

1926, producing mass foreclosures on mortgages and giving a warning on future painful events.

Eight decades later, in 2007, both the state of Florida and local governments have been hit by huge losses in untrustworthy investments, depriving countries and municipalities of a major source of income in funding schools, fire departments, and other public services. The loss of an estimated 20 percent of the value of the state's money market fund comes over and above the loss of revenue which is usually collected, because of:

- Sinking home prices and real estate taxes,
- Falling home sales and consequently disappearing fees,
- Submerged construction activity, and
- The economic impact of mass home foreclosures.

The sin committed by the LGIF managers is that, hungry for extra yield, they gobbled up several billion dollars of debt issued by SIVs. As with the Orange County fiasco and so many others, these structured investment vehicles had heavily invested in subprime mortgages, with the extent of this exposure slowly revealed in November 2007. As (belatedly) rating agencies hastened their downgrading of SIV borrowings, nerves frayed. Investors pulled out $13 billion, nearly half of the fund's assets, before state officials froze withdrawals (on 29 November 2007).

These unfortunate "investments" violated state policies, since Florida, like other states, required that its short-term investment positions had to be top-rated liquid securities, able to assure that taxpayer money is not placed at risk. Contrary to this directive, Florida's wealth managers had been investing in hedge funds and in structured vehicles committed in mortgage-backed securities. Among the state's investments which have been downgraded are:

- $400 million of Axon Financial Funding debt, cut to junk status by S&P;
- $850 million of KKR Atlantic Funding Trust, cut to default by Fitch Ratings;
- $577 million of KKR Pacific Funding Trust debt, cut to default by Fitch; and
- $319 million of debt issued by Ottimo Funding cut to default by S&P.

According to expert opinions, nearly a thousand Florida school districts, cities, and countries invested in this ill-fated LGIF. Florida is not alone in this huge mismanagement; still, its story is an example of what should never be done.

As the news broke on 4 December 2007, Charlie Crist, the state's governor, approved a rescue plan forged with help from BlackRock: the wounded investments were put into a distressed fund, while those less damaged were poised to reopen at least partially. US municipalities, of course, have no exclusive license in bad management of their wealth. Municipalities overseas, from Norway to Australia, have also been caught out.

What these references document is that the subprime crisis has put in question the ability of the financial industry to serve social needs; while the regulatory treatment of banks' balance sheets proved to be substandard. A basic reason why banks have been gaming credit risk rules is that regulators now allow them to hold less capital against loans, if they have sold these to "outside" entities – even if these entities happen to be their own subsidiaries (section 5 of this chapter). At the root of this huge loophole lie the following facts:

- Conduits and SIVs have off-balance-sheet status;
- Hedge funds are not regulated; and
- Each of the big banks owns a number of conduits, SIVs, and hedge funds, effectively avoiding supervision.

Therefore, not only has the imperfect treatment of hedge funds, SIVs, and conduits to be rethought, but other issues, too, must be urgently addressed. These definitely include the quality of management of state and municipal wealth funds – and the liquidity shocks to which they are exposed because of poor investment decisions as well as the non-existence of risk control.

7. The US government looks at the subprime mess

Chapter 4 made the point that unlike previous global crises, the one that hit the global financial system like a hammer, in July/August 2007, has been of the banks' own making. Additionally, the banks were so successful in *mismanaging* their own assets, and those of their clients, that 2007 was the first time American real estate prices:

- Fell nationally, and
- Can fall altogether by 20 percent to 40 percent, according to investment experts.

Worse yet, if contagion from the subprimes and Alt-As spreads to other forms of consumer credit, the signs of strain will greatly multiply. Analysts at Goldman Sachs reckon that credit card losses could reach billions, and practically all banks are exposed to credit card receivables. The credit crisis is also threatening to hit auto loans, and from there finance companies by way of car write-offs, as well as insurance firms.

There are indeed many questions which remain to be answered about the subprimes crisis and its aftereffect, as by all likelihood what has been revealed in the third and fourth quarters of 2007 has been only the tip of the iceberg. Statistics are chilling. In the US alone, there are an estimated two million adjustable-rate subprime mortgages, due to be reset till mid 2009.

- They are worth a dazzling $350 billion, and
- They hang like Damocles' sword over the global financial system.[14]

These facts and figures are known to the authorities. In the week of 15 October 2007, Hank Paulson, the Treasury secretary, gave a strong warning that the slowdown in the US housing market and the concurrent crisis in the credit and mortgage markets posed a significant risk to the American economy. He also pointed out that the problems did not stem *only* from the subprimes, or only from the millions of homeowners finding it difficult to make other types of mortgage payments.

A combination of sliding house prices and loose lending standards for non-qualifying borrowers gave birth to a hydra whose killing needs a new Heracles. Not only did the aftereffect of the subprime crisis leave homeowners and investors nursing mounting losses, but also the mood of millions of borrowers changed greatly as they belatedly found that they were unable to make credit payments which became due. For the American public at large, a Fox News poll revealed that:

- 70 percent of respondents were against using taxpayer dollars to help out troubled homeowners, and
- 80 percent were against a bailout for banks, mortgage companies, and generally institutions that had created the subprimes mess.

In California, Governor Arnold Schwarzenegger struck an innovative deal with four big mortgage loan servicers. The companies will extend by several years the period at which thousands (but not millions) of borrowers can stay at initial teaser rates. (Who is to pay the cost is still unclear.)

A bolder but less sustainable suggestion came from Sheila Bair, the CEO of the Federal Deposit Insurance Corporation (FDIC). Her concept has been that most borrowers who face resets but are paying their dues should be given a chance by servicers to switch to fixed-rate loans for 30 years – also at starter rates. Neither Bair nor Schwarzenegger specified who would save the mortgage servicers from bankruptcy as:

- They borrow short-term at high rates, and
- Will be supposed to support 30-year subprimes at low rates

Other government officials, too, have come up with suggestions, but stop short of putting up the money. One of the solutions being suggested is to sort subprime borrowers out into "needy" and "not-so-needy." Good luck to anyone who tries to do so. Henry Paulson has been more realistic, having concluded that servicers lack the resources to deal with case-by-case mortgage modifications. "We are going through uncharted territory," the Treasury secretary said.[15]

The chances that a selective salvage plan can succeed were reduced by the fact that there is currently no industry standard for modifying mortgage terms, and discussion on restructuring may lead nowhere, particularly at a time when house prices are falling. Securitization, too, adds a great deal to the challenge, by requiring the figuring out of the value of mortgage pools within a CDO owning a diversified aggregate of securities.

Some voices also add that in many cases preventing foreclosure is a bad idea, because not all defaulting borrowers are suffering families. In the hottest property markets, many mortgages are held by investors who were speculating on higher home prices. For instance, in Florida an estimated 25 percent of all defaulting loans were held by non-residents, many of them being investors who made a bad bet.

Other people expressed the opinion that the US government is responsible, because it wanted to increase the number of homeowners since owning the house in which one lives is a sign of higher social standing. Therefore, the Bush Administration looked the other way as the housing bubble was fed by easy credit and rock-bottom interest rates; and it took no corrective action in spite of the fact that the housing bubble grew by leaps and bounds.

In conclusion, there are no easy answers to a recession caused by a huge real estate bubble combined with a credit bubble that has affected, in one way or another, a huge number of American households and devastated the big banks' balance sheets. Additionally, as if this double tsunami of bad news was not enough, a classical cyclical bear market has been unfolding in equities with the potential to create the deepest and broadest deflation in the post-World-War-II years.

8. The way out of recession is not paved with more debt

The medicine provided by the Bush Administration to the housing crisis is reminiscent of 1929, and Herbert Hoover's great stimulus package. After the stock market crash, but before the Depression went into full swing, then President Hoover and Treasury Secretary Andrew Mellon summoned some of America's top industrialists and merchants to Washington to agree on measures to stimulate the economy. That plan included:

- $160 million in Federal tax relief,
- Promises from the Fed of cheaper credit,
- Increased government construction spending,
- Promises from labor unions not to seek higher wages, and
- Promises from different industrialists for greater capital expenditures.

Promises, promises, and promises. Sounds familiar? It is so, starting with the $160 million Hoover package which with inflation became $168 billion under Bush. But we know how all that turned out, with the economy plunging into the deepest depression the modern world had ever known. (The first ever banking meltdown happened in the Roman Empire under Tiberius.)

Some economists look at the $160 million of handouts as the brainchild of Treasury Secretary Henry Paulson and Fed chairman Ben Bernanke. On 17 January 2008, appearing before the House Budget Committee, Bernanke called for fiscal and monetary stimulus, saying that it was most important that such measures be implemented quickly. Critics however commented that:

- What Paulson and Bernanke proposed is another round of debt increases, which will only make matters worse, and that
- A stimulus promoted by deficits is leveraging and carries with it the possibility of a cascading sequence of negative events.

According to the European Central Bank, a Fiscal stimulus carries the

risk that tax cuts or spending increases that are intended to be temporary will, in practice, become permanent ... This raises the risk of

government debt accumulation and long-term fiscal sustainabil-
ity ... The build-up of debt that has plagued many countries is a reflec-
tion of the difficulties associated with fiscal activism ... Moreover, the
rising budgetary costs from an aging population underline the need
to take the risks of an unintended permanent rise in deficits and debt
seriously.[16]

As an article in Executive Intelligence Review put it:

> Our descent into bankruptcy is reflected in the balance on current
> accounts, which shows our increasing dependence upon foreign
> goods and investments ... A comparison of the growth of debt and
> GDP shows that since the beginning of this decade we have incurred
> nearly $5 in debt for every dollar increase in GDP, giving the lie to
> the claims of the "fundamental soundness" of the US economy.[17]

While several American economists are cynical about the Bush stimulus
plan, Paul Fabra, a French economist, denounced it for weakening the
dollar. Writing in *Les Echos*, the financial paper, on 1 February 2008,
Fabra stated:

> The successive, massive lowering of interest rates by the Fed will bene-
> fit banks, and banks alone. The new tax breaks [stimulus policy] and
> increasing budget spending proposed by the Bush Administration
> contain the awful threat for the outside world of a supplementary
> weakening of the dollar. One would like to scream: "Please stop
> resuscitating a rotten system ..."

Japan provides a scary precedent regarding stimulus packages. The
ghost of its "lost decade and a half" haunts American policymakers as
the consequences of the burst housing bubble are felt through financial
markets. Nobody wants to repeat Japan's awful experience of boom-
and-bust, but is pumping money into the economy the right medicine?
(Japan's property-and-stockmarket bubble burst in 1990, creating bad
loans equivalent to about one-fifth of GDP. The cost of the economy's
resurrection has been 100 percent of Japanese GDP – with no results.)

During the early February 2008 meeting of finance ministers and
central bank governors from the Group of Seven leading economies,
speaking with reference to attempts to spend Japan out of recession and
deflation in the 1990s, Fukushiro Nukaga, Japan's finance minister, told
reporters: "We have learned what such fiscal spending could mean from

our experience after the burst of the bubble," adding that the important thing "is to stabilize markets and create a relationship of trust by promoting information disclosure such as losses at financial institutions."

Like in Japan in the mid to late 1980s, over the 2002 to 2007 timeframe in America the government, central bank, and supervisory authorities can be blamed for inadequate oversight of the booming financial market. Nobody seems to have cared about the massive slicing and dicing of mortgages. The difference from Japan has been that rather than being simply apathetic its government was deeply complicit in hiding the ensuing mess for years.

Nukaga was not alone in his objections to using fiscal policy as a lifesaver. In Berlin, Thomas Mirow, deputy finance minister, insisted Germany's economy was robust, saying: "There is no reason for additional measures." In London, a Treasury spokesman made clear that it saw no grounds for a sizable fiscal stimulus[18] – a proof that other G-7 governments were not going to follow Washington with a big loosening of their fiscal policies, even if Keynesian economics stage a comeback at least in America. Indeed, the adoption of budget deficit policies by a Republican Administration was odd:

- As a result of prudent fiscal policies by a Democratic Party administration, in 2000 America ran a structural surplus.
- But eight years later, under Bush Junior, it had an underlying deficit of 3 percent of gross domestic product.

Theoretically at least, this $168 billion stimulus, over and above previous large deficits, is aimed at cushioning the economy's downturn by getting cash into consumers' pockets and encouraging firms to spend. Critics however say that more than anything else it will increase by so much the US current account deficit with China.[19] Other economists have argued that, even if well timed, a temporary stimulus will not work because people will hardly adjust their spending in response to a one-off tax cut.

Curiously enough, George W. Bush got a helping hand from the IMF. Traditionally a guardian of balanced budgets, in February 2008 the IMF was pushing for a broad and global fiscal loosening. Monetary policy may be less effective in this downturn, argued Dominique Strauss-Kahn, its new managing director (and French Socialist Party leader). But Ken Rogoff, the IMF's former chief economist, said Strauss-Kahn's easy-money plan seemed dubious.

It has also been quite interesting that in emerging economies the call for budget loosening seemed to be falling on deaf ears, even if high commodity prices and better economic management could have permitted China, Russia, Brazil, and Mexico to loosen their budgets. Only in Spain, where in 2007 inflation hit 4.1 percent, more than twice the target rate of the European Central Bank, was the government thinking along the line of budget deficits, putting together a fiscal-stimulus package as the country's economy slowed in the aftermath of a construction bust.

Outside America and Spain the reason for prudence with red ink has undoubtedly been that past experiences of the effects of stimulus through red ink were not positive. Analyses of America's stimulus efforts in the 1970s have come to the conclusion that they were poorly timed and ineffectual – while, in Europe, activist fiscal policy brought permanently higher public spending and a zooming of the national debt. As for Japan's experience, when in the 1990s it tried to break deflationary stagnation with a tandem of fiscal packages,

- Debt soared to a level that surpassed the national debt of Italy but the country did not really recover, and
- Milton Friedman famously used Japan to argue that fiscal pump-priming does not work.

There have been plenty of reasons why Jean-Claude Trichet said bluntly that discretionary fiscal policy should be avoided. Joaquin Almunia, the European Commissioner on economic matters, gave warning against succumbing to the easy-money siren song. But *what if* the American government continues pumping money, the Fed chooses rock-bottom interest rates, the dollar descends to the abyss, and economic miserabilism is the end result?

6
Leveraged Instruments, Their Credit Ratings, and Other Unorthodox Practices

1. How to lose your money with collateralized debt obligations

To appreciate the wider impact of the debacle in subprime mortgages it is important to understand the explosion in supply of leveraged financial instruments; also, the negative aftermath of a steady policy of low interest rates and low credit ratings which followed the year 2000 stock market bubble. A combination of these factors saw to it that between 2001 and 2005, the annually issued amount of securitized mortgages of all sorts tripled in terms of dollar value.

The booming credit derivatives market (Chapter 5) set the tone for many trading transactions at the fringes of sound banking practices. In 2006, in America, $600 billion worth of derivatives were created in the form of *collateralized debt obligations* (CDOs), which are a fairly recent financial instrument and arguably the most complex ever to become mainstream. By one estimate, some 40 percent of CDOs are mortgage-backed. Innovation has been on fast track; on the global financial market:

- In 1999 synthetic balance sheet CDOs were introduced;
- In 2001 synthetic arbitrage CDOs appeared;
- In 2003 cash and synthetic CDOs were traded;
- Also in 2003 came synthetic single-tranche CDOs;
- In 2004 the new financial product was synthetic index-linked CDOs, and so on.

All CDOs are structured instruments, which, with issuance of rated debt securities (by *tranche*), fund the purchase of other assets. Their particular characteristic is that they enable market players to readily transfer very significant amounts of credit risk to third parties, often through highly leveraged transactions. Unlike traditional securitization, the number of assets backing a collateralized debt obligation is rather low. Additionally, CDOs are heterogeneous and lead to significant concentration of exposure. Figure 6.1 gives a snapshot of CDOs underlying collateral used in 2006 and part of 2007.

Another set of eye-opening statistics regarding the amount of toxic waste that enters into residential mortgage-backed securities (RMBS) and collateralized debt obligations are shown in Table 6.1. In the wrongly named "high-grade" asset-backed CDOs, 50 percent of underlying assets are subprimes and another 19 percent are other risky CDOs. The share of subprimes rises to 77% with mezzanine CDOs (more on

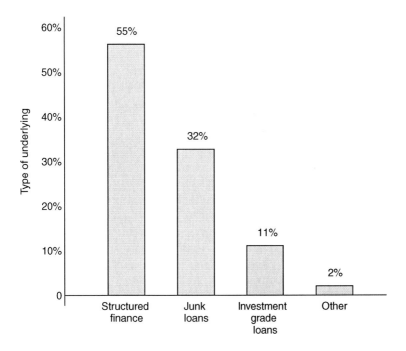

Figure 6.1 Underlying collateral of CDOs used in 2006 and up to September 2007 (Deutsche Bundesbank, *Financial Stability Review*, November 2007)

Table 6.1   Typical collateral composition of asset-backed securities CDOs

	High-grade ABS CDOs[1]	Mezzanine ABS CDOs[2]
Subprime RMBSs	50	77
Other RBMSs	25	12
CDOs	19	6
Others	6	6

Source: Bank for International Settlements: Basel Committee on Banking Supervision, The Joint Forum. "Credit Risk Transfer," Consultative Document (April 2008).

1. Typically rated as AAA by independent rating agencies, though their creditworthiness is no more than BB–. See also section 5 of this chapter.
2. Usually rated BBB by independent rating agencies. A more accurate credit rating would have been B–.

these in section 2 of this chapter).

- Simply stated, it is garbage-in/garbage-out, and
- There is no wonder that not only investors but also the banks themselves that played such dirty games have lost a horde of money.

On 17 July 2008, Merrill Lynch announced a $5.7 billion second quarter 2008 loss from writedowns. A short time earlier, to cover expected shortfall in its capital base it had sold its equity in the Bloomberg financial network for $4.8 billion (much less than the $5.5 to $5 billion it had hoped to get), and raised capital through equity.

Additionally, to stop further bleeding because of writedowns from junk securities in its portfolio, the investment bank also took the unprecedented step of a fire sale of the huge amount of CDOs it owned. Reportedly, this brought Merrill to the 14th rank of exposure to CDOs from the top-three level which it shared with Citigroup and UBS. The announcement said that $30.7 billion of CDOs were sold for $6.7 billion – a huge discount that means for less than 22 cents to the dollar. Acting on these news items:

- The Bank of America commented that this transaction may establish a pattern for other companies who want to get rid of their CDOs, and
- Goldman Sachs allegedly saw in it an opportunity to sell a new supply of American junk securities of "very high yield" to lightheaded European banks.

But was it really 22 cents to the dollar? Subsequent information indicated that the discounting of Merrill Lynch CDOs was much worse than that. Lone Star Funds, a Dallas-based vulture fund, agreed to buy the aforementioned collateralized debt obligations at that very low price *if* Merrill financed three-quarters of the purchase.[1] This left just 5.5 cents to the dollar in real money, the balance being an exchange in credit risk, from inventoried CDOs to the Lone Star loan.

While Merrill Lynch the company, its shareholders, clients and the American economy at large lost a fortune with the CDOs, its CEO of the go-go years, his pals and plenty of traders had made one through bonuses and options by way of accumulating and warehousing all this toxic waste in the company's vaults. None of those ladies and gentlemen has yet been:

- Brought to justice,
- Publicly reprimanded for unwarranted and fraudulent bonuses, or
- Paid a penalty for his or her acts, which ranged from silly to odious.

Yet, the US 2002 Sarbanes-Oxley Act (SOX) has an interesting section, number 304, which has been applied in other cases, albeit only partially. It states that companies can recover money taken by managers and other option and bonus receivers whether these unwarranted rewards were due to fraudulent reasons or accounting errors.

A study done by The Corporate Library (TCL) suggests that by mid 2007, some five years after SOX, only 14 cases were found in American industry where section 304 was put into effect. But with the subprimes and credit crisis in 2007, just a year later this number had grown to 297 companies. This is still only 14 percent of the sample considered by TCL; still it is more than twenty times bigger than fraud uncovered and penalized during the previous years.

Experts suggest that even companies applying section 304 of the Sarbanes-Oxley Act do so only partially. Still, it is interesting to note that, according to the TCL study, in US industry:

- 44 percent of unwarranted bonuses and benefits from options are due to outright fraud;
- 39 percent are linked to performance which has been badly presented due to accounting error rather than plain fraud; and
- The remaining of cases have a variety of causes in the background, but still resulted in significant loss to shareholders as companies paid out money to the wrong parties.

Nor is the torrent of CDO red ink at Merrill Lynch, which we followed in this section, one in a million. Overfat salaries and unwarranted lavish bonuses have been awarded all over the financial industry, while "profits" are pie in the sky, dividends are paid even when the company has suffered heavy losses, and banks have wounded themselves badly by taking silly risks (see also section 7 in this chapter, on the racket of options and bonuses).

Not only have "profits" from CDOs been non-existent for anyone other than the insiders who raped the system, but also the aftermath has also been a very bitter pill to swallow. This *5.5 percent to the dollar plus credit risk* (assumed with the loan to the vulture fund) is proof that Merrill's CDOs were worth practically nothing. It is also a cold shower for all those banks and other entities that hoped to get rid of their most unwisely assumed exposure to toxic waste.

Another irony is management's inability to realistically price assets. UBS allegedly believed that its CDO holdings were worth between 30 and 40 cents to the dollar, and rumor had it that Citigroup valued its CDOs at 45 cents to the dollar. The price offered by Lone Star Funds provides plenty of food for thought on how far from reality such estimates tend to be. If they can do better than 5.5 cents to the dollar why don't they try to sell them?

Neither are the woes of Merrill Lynch and of the other overexposed banks ending here, because the bond insurers they had used in the go-go years (Chapter 1) are themselves at the edge of the precipice. At end of July 2008 Merrill said it settled a dispute with XL Capital over CDO hedges it had taken with the troubled bond insurer. XL will pay Merrill $500 million for canceling $3.7 billion worth of policies it wrote but had difficulties honoring. What is $500 million when these $3.7 billion are worth 5.5 cents to the dollar?

2. The mechanics of collateralized debt obligations

In terms of mechanics, CDOs may be single-tranche or multi-tranche. In the latter case, the first-loss tranche (lower tranche) is known as *equity*. Higher-up tranches are rated by not always independent agencies with the objective of selling to investors who may be insurance companies, pension funds, or high-net-worth individuals. Because many CDO upper tranches are sold to other banks, their wrong rating as AAA has brought the banking industry to its knees.

Theoretically, single-tranche CDOs have given investors greater control over the characteristics of the transaction, enabling them to select some or all of the underlying credit. They are also easier to restructure if a credit event takes place, as contrasted to multi-tranche CDOs. Practically, they bring along a greater concentration in exposure than multi-tranche CDOs, which are organized so that:

- The *first-loss* (equity) tranche absorbs the risk of payment defaults or delays.
- *Mezzanine*, the next (more senior) tranche, will incur losses if the equity tranche is exhausted.
- The top *senior tranche* is protected by both the mezzanine and equity tranches – but as the subprime events demonstrated, this "protection" is smoke and mirrors.

Bankers on Wall Street, in the City of London, and in continental European and Asian financial centers thought they had protected themselves from harm by holding only the "safest tranches" of collateralized debt obligations, incorrectly called "super senior," while selling the riskier bits to other misinformed investors. The meltdown of subprimes and Alt-As has shown that losses in these top tranches can be immense.

Even if the senior tranche is (incorrectly) given a high grade by independent rating agencies, this credit-enhancing technique turns to ashes and ends in a disservice to all sorts of investors and the rating agencies themselves. Senior tranches of subprimes should not have been given AAA rating in the first place. As the debacle of July/August 2007 has documented, this sort of fake AAA has discredited both:

- Those who assign it, and
- Those who used it in their investment decisions.

Paul Tucker, a member of the Bank of England's Monetary Policy Committee, likened the system of slicing and dicing credit risk to a set of Russian dolls.[2] Leveraged business loans or house mortgages are packed and sold as CDOs to investors who are unaware of the risk they assume; or, they are integrated into different kinds of complex collateralized debt obligations, conduits, and structured investment vehicles of the most opaque nature.

In mid 2007, JPMorgan Chase, the investment bank, estimated there were some $18 billion worth of US leveraged loan CDOs in the pipeline, and about $15 billion worth of European deals with a great deal of leverage outstanding. (The real figures are much higher.) The moment some elements of this pyramid of leveraged debt hit the rocks, the demand for all other CDOs disappears. Such investments were the most unwarranted, as pseudo-high-rated tranches had much lower income than the riskiest tranches. Moreover:

- Pricing contagion has prolonged consequences for CDOs' viability in financial transactions, and
- The market's response saw to it that if a CDO manager cannot sell the equity tranche then he or she cannot sell the overall deal.

Three months after the debacle, in the first week of December 2007, JP Morgan Chase radically revised its mid 2007 figures. It said that banks alone held around $216 billion worth of super senior tranches of CDOs (another underestimate), backed by assets such as mortgages and issued over the preceding two years. Theoretically, these supersenior tranches protected investors from initial losses on the mortgages backing the CDOs. Practically, as an executive of the Securities and Exchange Commision pointed out in a speech on 28 November 2007 other forces were at work too.

- While banks offloaded the junior CDO tranches and kept the safer ones, the risks they were exposed to became less obvious and, unwisely, they fell off the radar screen.
- Exposures inherent in super senior tranches of CDOs were similar to those in put options. But while options are widely traded on exchanges, CDOs are highly illiquid.

Another negative from the issuer's and trader's perspective is that a CDO dealer is unable to hedge the position perfectly by engaging in an offsetting transaction. Yet, he or she needs to use protection on each underlying credit according to the instrument's *delta*. With delta being the first derivative of the underlying, money-at-risk changes as the levels of *credit spread* change.

3. Synergy between debt market and equity market

The CDOs debacle which started in July/August 2007 had wide repercussions. Already in the week of 14 May 2007, Anthony Bolton, generally considered one of the better British fund managers, warned that the four-year bull market in shares might be near its end. He also complained of a relaxation of standards in lending to private equity firms.[3]

Other senior financial executives, assets managers, and investors have also been privately echoing these concerns but, in spite of that, the:

- Standards used to lend money to private equity firms were becoming weaker, and
- Different "innovations," like covenant-lite loans, have been gaining further ground.

Critics said that this was irresponsible because the market was finding it difficult to digest instruments on which the normal covenants protecting bankers and investors had been stripped away. But the fact banks were running after borrowers, rather than vice versa, saw to it that all sort of borrowers convinced the management of credit institutions to relax the terms on loans. Many banks lowered their defenses even if they knew very well that *covenants* represent the checks and balances put by the lender to be in charge at the first sign of a borrower's distress.

(Classically, contracts governing debt include covenants, which are safeguards for creditors in case a company defaults or goes bankrupt. To the contrary, most of the debt issued in recent years, whether for mortgages, personal loans, company loans or buyouts, has looser terms. This has given banks and bondholders fewer rights.)

The policy of no covenants or light covenants has backfired because it led to much cheaper prices for all sorts of loans. For instance a bond that could probably trade at 85 cents on the dollar with a covenant is going to trade at 65 cents on the dollar or less without covenants since investors are demanding greater safety and they get it in larger haircuts.

Precisely because covenant-lite loans give borrowers greater latitude when the market sours, equity investors started to look at signs of malaise. The irony of this big relaxation of normal lending standards has been that while several economists argued that credit conditions looked over-exuberant, the credit cycle refused to readjust itself since:

- Most bankers were afraid of refusing deals, and
- Paid little attention to the fact that the equity market took notice and speculated the banks' balance sheets would suffer.

In the wake of the US mortgage crisis, the heightened nervousness of market participants could be seen in the implied volatility of options on bond futures. The level of uncertainty increased in all major financial centers, and this mirrored the market players' concern about future development of capital market yields, ultimately leading to a general reappraisal of risk.

For example, in July 2007 the yield spread of BB-rated corporate bonds (non-investment-grade) over euroland government bonds increased by one-quarter to 138 basis points, after it had fallen a month earlier to its lowest level for two years. Analysts considered this development consistent with substantial rises in premiums in the credit risk transfer market of CDSs – with the corrections of the spreads seen as a normalization.

Attention was also aroused by two corporate takeovers in the making that found difficulties in raising needed loans. Some analysts said that this change in market sentiment in connection with private equity reflected the problems in the securitization market, which placed strains on highly leveraged mergers and acquisitions (M&A). Reasons for worry were provided by the fact that:

• Adjustments occurred abruptly in an environment of increased uncertainty, and
• They were accompanied by a drying-up of liquidity in various market segments, which evidently caused problems for market players.

Within this rather gloomy scenario, a piece of good news for investors came from the fact that they could exercise foresight as bond prices and yields helped in providing directional clues about stocks. During one of my interviews, a senior banker commented that, prior to commitment, investors should ask whether an entity's bonds are trading in line with those of companies with similar credit ratings; if not, they should keep away from its equity. The principle is that:

• Disconnects can be signs of trouble, and
• Downgrades in creditworthiness of a company's debt are likely to hit its equity price.

Indeed in July/August 2007 bonds were telling a lot about the stock of the companies issuing them. The fact that the issuer was still able to raise funds gave confidence. The opposite was true if the issuer approached the capital market only through junk bonds. The message to retain from this bond-to-equity linkage is that equity investors need to pay attention to debt. Today, this is true more than ever because:

• Corporate debt levels are at record highs, and

- In mid to late 2007 credit downgrades outnumbered upgrades at US corporations by a margin.

A historical reference helps in providing perspective. Following the stock market bubble of 2000, Chapter 11 bankruptcy filings by publicly quoted corporations rose sharply, to a record 143 companies in 2001. More filings followed as the economy tried to pull out of recession, because of the time it takes for troubled firms to exhaust their financing options with creditors.

The case for more careful consideration of corporate debt is not purely defensive. In the first five years of the twenty-first century, just as individuals were reducing their mortgage payments by refinancing, companies were taking advantage of low interest rates to lighten their debt. This, however, was followed by new leverage, which eventually led to the downturn whose milestones have been:

- The crisis of subprimes, which started mid July, and
- The stock market crisis, which began about ten weeks later, then gave way to a few weeks of equity market euphoria, but led to still another market crisis in November 2007.

From late September to end October 2007, in America and Europe, stock market indices went up, propelled by technology stocks. By contrast, the equity of banks and other financial institutions, particularly those with huge losses in subprimes, descended to the abyss. By January 2008 the equity market sentiment became definitely negative, while equity markets and debt markets have not rediscovered their synergy.

4. Credit rating the subprimes

Credit rating is essentially the grading of risk of loss as a result of failure to meet contractual obligations. Counterparties may default; and even if it does not default a bond issuer may be unwilling or unable to meet assumed financial obligations in a timely manner. Knowing about the likelihood of this happening is important inasmuch as credit risk is an integral part of many business activities, and it is inherent in all traditional banking products:

- Loans,
- Commitments to lend,
- Contingent liabilities, and more.

Credit risk is also present in traded financial products – like derivative contracts (forwards, swaps, options),[4] securitized instruments, structured instruments like CDOs, default swaps, repurchase agreements, securities borrowing/lending and so on. All market players are interested to know about their counterparty's credit risk – provided this information is reliable.

The better-known independent credit rating agencies find their lineage in the late nineteenth century, but the credit rating system as we know it is a product of the 1970s, when the Securities and Exchange Commission (SEC) looked for a way to assure that brokers it regulated had enough capital. It was much better for the SEC to accept the opinions of a small group of dependable rating agencies than to research every single broker or bond itself. Besides, this also saved money for the brokers.

The SEC acted as a kind of commissioning authority, giving credit evaluation status to a few entities known as Nationally Recognized Statistical Rating Organizations (NRSROs). In fact, not only the SEC but also the Federal Reserve and the Basel Committee on Banking Supervision have made credit ratings a formal part of financial system regulation, particularly in regard to capital adequacy of commercial banks under the watch of supervisory authorities.

Critics say that while this system worked well for two and a half decades, it is now falling apart because independent credit rating agencies have been handed a lucrative oligopoly, and they have misused their rights. Claiming that they are acting as a neutral evaluator of credit risk, hence immune to legal challenge on the basis of their "free speech" rights, they have assumed a status much higher than the one originally intended. As Charlie McCreevy, the European Commissioner, points out:

- The rating agencies have a conflict of interest,
- They are paid by the issuers whose securities they rate, and this does away with their independence of opinion.

Even worse, critics suggest, the credit rating agencies have many opprtunitiesto shop around. Making them legally liable, however, is not as easy, as it will expose the rating agencies to huge penalties (which is why, so far, they have escaped the aftereffect of their wrong rating of subprimes). Additionally, in the opinion of some supervisors, increasing the rating agencies' transparency will only then be meaningful *if* a regulatory authority looks over their shoulder while currently:

- Only in the US ratings agencies are being regulated, and

• Even this is done in a very mild way.

Additionally, ratings are not forever. They change over time. An example of expected default rate for corporate bonds with AAA, AA, A, and BBB rating (which are of investment grade), spanning over a 10-year time-frame, is given in Figure 6.2.

Because the inputs impacting on the probability of default change, banks and rating agencies must regularly validate grades given to counterparties, as well as the performance of their rating tools – reassessing their predictive power with regard to default events. Where statistical analysis suggests that the parameters of a model require adjustment, such changes must be given full weight in instrument recalibration.

Where all these references lead is that credit ratings should be realistic and well documented. A special challenge comes from the fact that designing a novel, not-so-well-understood instrument, like a complex securitization, can make small game of the rules of creditworthiness.

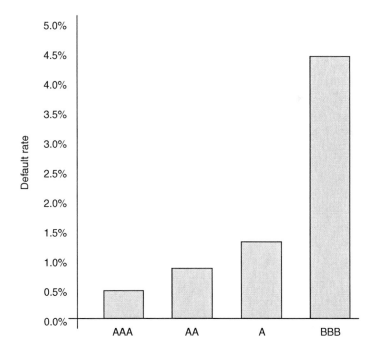

Figure 6.2   Probability of default of AAA, AA, A, and BBB corporate bonds over a 10-year timeframe

Stamped "AAA" by helpful rating agencies, the senior tranches of CDO subprimes were:

- Freely sold to investors,
- Used as collateral by their buyers when raising new loans, and
- Included by banks in their Tier-1 capital, which made a mockery of capital adequacy rules.

When times were good, in the 2005 to 2006 timeframe, the highest credit rating was assigned most superficially to the senior tranches of securitized subprimes. Then, with credit deterioration in certain subprime and Alt-A loans, ratings agencies downgraded an unprecedented amount of asset-backed securities collateralized by subprime mortgages – but it was too late. It also led market participants to expect further downgrades as:

- The underlying loans continued to age,
- Resets started taking effect, and
- Delinquencies were converting to foreclosures.

The independent credit ratings agencies have advanced various reasons that contributed to weaker-than-expected performance by mortgage loans – for example, the impact of risk layering, poor data quality, and aggressive lending practices like offering short-term, below-market interest rates in order to catch borrowers. Critics say that these reasons are thinly veiled excuses, because practically all of them were known when AAAs were assigned to poor credits. Critics also add that the whole rating system has gone out of control, as evidenced by the fact that after the subprimes debacle rating agencies have been revising their ABS rating methodologies to include:

- Assumptions of higher loss severity,
- More severe stress tests, and
- Increased monitoring of fraud prevention by lenders.

As the light credit rating structure started to unravel, in mid October 2007 Moody's cut the ratings of 131 securities backed by subprime mortgages, and said it was reviewing the grades of 136 others. On 27 October 2007, it was announced that Standard & Poor's, Moody's, and Fitch rating agencies were being investigated by the State of Connecticut for their credit rating practices.

Meeting in Amsterdam in the week of 4 February 2008, financial regulators said they would review a code of conduct for independent rating agencies, intended to improve the disclosure and control of agencies that enter into conflicts of interest by giving advice on the creation of securities they rate. The agencies themselves felt that criticism of their role in the misrating of subprimes as AAAs was a result of misunderstanding, as their ratings are based:

- On risk of default, and
- Not on market swings.

This argument is a non-starter, since the risk of default changes with market psychology, over and above the fact that AAA ratings awarded to many mortgage-linked structured products were flimsy, particularly those of collateralized debt obligations. It comes as no surprise, therefore, that in an effort to stem off draconian rating control measures the agencies are ready to make some reforms.

For instance, Standard & Poor's unveiled two dozen reforms, including committees that will oversee modeling and governance; and a response to the request by user organizations that information on non-default factors, including liquidity, be satisfied by attaching it to ratings. And like Moody's, S&P will analyze the effects of unexpected events and "may" introduce separate tags for securitized products. On 13 March 2008 the US Treasury secretary said in a conference that rating agencies *must* differentiate between structured products and the others being rated.

5. Spread of the credit risk crisis: a snapshot

In the opinion of a surprisingly large number of bankers, the securitization of subprimes and other non-investment-grade debt instruments had, till heaven broke loose, "helped the market" and its participants. This is plain misinformation. The CDO tsunami has severely damaged the market, though it might have "helped" some banks over a short period of time, particularly those that forgot that financial failures have often been at the heart of most crises. In the end, mortgage-backed CDOs have:

- Cost billions to the banking industry,
- Given a return which is a small fraction of the losses, and
- Obliged many big banks to go hat-in-hand to Asian and Middle Eastern Sovereign Wealth Funds (Chapter 2).

In many credit institutions, senior management incorrectly thought that, instead of banks taking the first hit from mortgage and other loans' defaults, the sufferers will be insurance companies, pension funds, hedge funds, and individual investors – because of credit risk transfer. Instead, the pain has spread all round the financial system, and one of the key problems is that nobody knows how much toxic waste now lies in each banking book and trading book.

- Many of the collateralized debt obligations are illiquid, hence regular prices are not available, and
- According to widespread opinion, highly rated but low-creditworthiness CDO tranches are still owned by banks that have avoided putting a value on these securities.

Highly paid individuals in credit institutions, insurance firms, and pension funds, as well as other entities, have failed to understand the CDO credit problems until it was too late. Banks were forced to do so by external auditors, supervisory authorities, and for reputational reasons. In terms of market confidence, failure to admit the size of big subprime losses, as Barclays did on 9 November 2007, has been worse than a frank admission.

It comes therefore as no surprise that against a background of rising delinquencies in the American subprime mortgage market, and of increasing uncertainty about the macroeconomic outlook of the US economy, credit spreads widened and market volatility rose across a range of asset classes. Concerns were also raised about other vulnerabilities such as the possibility that the crisis in the American subprime mortgage market could:

- Deepen, spreading over Europe (which it did) and Asia (which so far has been lightly touched), and
- Negatively affect higher-quality structured mortgages and other receivables.

Already in the first semester of 2007 there were profit warnings, but this was not what rocked the market. Still, corporate treasurers were worried about the fallout. In late June 2007, US Foodservice, a wholesaler, delayed plans to raise $2 billion in loans. In Asia, a sizable bond sale from MISC, the world's largest owner of liquefied natural gas tankers, was postponed. In Europe, ArcelorMittal, the world's largest steelmaker, put back a bond sale.

These are only three examples out of an estimated $250 billion of corporate paper supply that was expected to be floated in mid 2007, to finance company treasuries as well as massive M&As and other deals. The market went into reverse gear as the subprime crisis called into doubt the wisdom of throwing debt paper to nervous investors, suggesting that as market confidence waned the buyout boom might be over.

In mid July 2007, investors reacted negatively to more bad news stemming from the slowdown in America's housing market. Both Standard & Poor's and Moody's disclosed that they were downgrading, or considering downgrading, credit ratings on more than $17 billion worth of bonds backed by subprime mortgages – because they had underestimated the level of defaults. The way a Merrill Lynch economic analysis had it, the subprime fiasco was a much bigger issue than the price of corn, milk, tuna, or wheat, which (at the time) zoomed:

- In the US people consume $1.3 trillion worth of food annually,
- But residential real estate is a huge $23 trillion market on household balance sheets.

By mid 2007, in America alone the combined credit market obligations across the household, business, and government sectors represented a record 340 percent of GDP. That ratio had surged by almost 60 percentage points during the late 2002 to early 2007 economic expansion. This had been nearly double what the American economy took on as leverage during the 10-year business cycle that ended in 2000 with the stock market bubble.

The way investigative analysts looked at these statistics and the subprimes aftereffect, the housing market's deflationary impact on the aggregate demand curve was likely to far outweigh the supply-side agricultural inflation (agflation).[5] Several experts suggested that the on-and-off 2007 stock market crisis might well reflect the knock-on effects from the subprime mess, adding up to a critical issue for the Fed:

- Would it try to avert turmoil ahead of time as the subprime situation eroded further, or
- Would it wait to give time to events to unfold, on the expectation that the damage would be contained?

Neither alternative offered only advantages. Investors, homeowners, and the Fed risked falling over the cliff because Alan "Two-Bubbles" Greenspan's expansion in the 2002 to 2005 timeframe was built on a mountain of leverage, promoted by rock-bottom interest rates. In the US and in Western Europe debt rose at a rapid rate in relation to the economy's debt-servicing capacity, creating serious reasons for concern.

On Wall Street some analysts suggested that Greenspan was not paying attention to a good rule of thumb, namely that *if* things cannot get any better then they can only get worse. So it has turned out. To the grim news about the debacle of the subprimes in America has been added grimmer news about the huge losses that hit the balance sheets of big European banks. As far as their exposure was concerned, they could only advance, but had no knowledge of withdrawal.

6. Concentration risk and assets valuations

On 11 July 2007, Anthony Ryan, assistant secretary for financial markets at the US Treasury, stated that hedge funds play major part in perpetuating dangers embedded in leveraged debt. Addressing the Managed Funds Association's Forum 2007, in Chicago, he warned about *concentration risk* in certain financial industries.[6] A few days later, at a hearing of the House Financial Services Committee, chairman Barney Frank pressed Treasury Secretary Henry Paulson on whether Ryan's speech had meant that the Treasury was now waiting for a systemic shock to hit the financial markets.

A month prior to these events, on 17 June 2007, in its quarterly review the Bank of England had already concentrated on leveraged corporate buyouts (LBOs), which had zoomed globally. In the first quarter of 2007, LBOs had grown exponentially in the United States, leading to a bubble of corporate debt. In OECD nations – often considered to be the rich men's club – corporate debt had exploded from 55 percent of GDP in the late 1980s to nearly 85 percent in 2007 – a 54.5 percent increase.

A thesis supported by the Bank of England, in mid 2007, was that the collapse of a single major equity deal could trigger a general economic crisis. Its quarterly review warned further that the rising wave of LBOs meant that the underlying value of a bought-out firm could be allowed to deteriorate before its creditors could intervene, with the result that:

- A large and pervasive shock might cause asset markets to adjust quite sharply, as risk premiums increased, and
- One of the likely triggers for this crunch could be the failure of a large leveraged loan deal to go through.

Experts gave this event a relatively high probability, as with the sub-prime crisis banks became thrifty. A growing market opinion has been that *if* it happened it would be leaving the lending banks with unexpectedly large commitments – causing the value of existing debt to fall suddenly across the entire junk bond market and putting the credit institutions themselves at edge of the abyss.

As for concentrations in low-grade mortgages, which were at the eye of the storm, *the Wall Street Journal* characterized them as a potentially troubling sign for the broader mortgage-backed bond market. The more clear-eyed central bankers have been particularly worried about concentrated exposure to collateralized debt obligations, especially those filled with securities such as US subprime mortgages. In mid 2007 the total US mortgage market stood at $10 trillion, with:

- Subprimes at $1.3 trillion, and
- Alt-As at another $1 trillion.

One of the studies done at the end of July 2007 demonstrated that while CDOs with subprime exposure bear high risk, European CDOs were less exposed than the American – if for no reason other than because CDOs created in Europe were less about mortgages and their total value was less than that in the US. The amount of CDOs issued from 2004 to 2007 was:

- $335 billion in Europe, and
- $786 billion in the United States.[7]

But while some analysts believed that the composition of European CDOs involved less risk, others disagreed, pointing out that while Europe's exposure is indeed less about asset-backed securities (ABS) which are largely mortgages, it does involve *concentration risk* because of lending to corporates and to smaller and medium enterprises (SMEs). Such loans constitute the bulk of European collateralized loan obligations (CLOs); and any concentration is a negative.

To support their thesis, these analysts made reference to a UBS-managed hedge fund closed down in April 2007, which according to certain opinions has been the reason for change in the bank's CEO. Also fingerpointed in early August 2007 was IKB Deutsche Industriebank, a mid-sized German lender who had built a €12.7 billion ($17.5 billion) portfolio of ABS with many CDOs approaching bankruptcy. A couple of weeks later, three hedge funds managed by BNP Paribas suspended withdrawals in securities backed by mortgages after suffering a torrent of red ink due to securitized mortgages.

In other countries, too, concentration risk took its toll. On 15 August 2007, Basis Capital, an Australian hedge fund manager, said losses at one of its funds might top 80 percent. A day later, shares in RAMS, one of Australia's mortgage lenders, tumbled 60 percent after it sought emergency funding. In late August 2007, the Bank of China revealed that it had invested $9.7 billion in subprimes, and part of these funds had gone down the drain.

As these references show, the crisis of the subprimes and of other concentrations in debt instruments has not been confined to America. Apart from individual banks' and hedge funds' losses, concentration risk in subprimes has hit not only a horde of portfolios with plenty of CDOs, but also bank shares and stockmarkets around the globe – while volatility has been rising, as often happens in this case.

Margin calls have forced hedge funds to raise cash, but loans have been hard to come by. The squeeze has often meant purging their most liquid assets, such as oil contracts. In Britain, the Financial Services Authority (FSA) has complained that investment banks and hedge funds are prone to conflicts of interest. In a panic, this could cause the whole system to collapse amid disputes about who owes what to whom, as:

- Firms have wildly different estimates for the risks embedded in similar portfolios, and
- The valuation of portfolios of investments is often based on flawed assumptions.

One subject where everybody seemed to agree is that valuing complex and esoteric securities is far from being child's play. Realistic estimates have to be made because of regulatory fair-value accounting, with assets and liabilities marked regularly to the market price. The challenge is that over-the-counter instruments don't really have a market. Besides, regulators fear that a marking to market approach might turn a liquidity crisis into a solvency one.

With derivatives and other geared and dynamically priced financial instruments, accruals accounting is meaningless. At the same time, in a market crisis holders of products in free fall, like mortgage-backed securities, are likely to revalue their assets at fire-sale prices – and with the result that they may be running short of capital, which can lead to further fire sales.

There are no magic solutions. To mark to market when there is barely any market, some banks rely on credit derivative indices, which are far from being perfect proxies. Others use computer models, but their accuracy is questionable, as most are to subject model risk. "All models are wrong," said a Barclays Bank executive, "but some are useful."[8]

With memories of their ordeal which followed the dotcom bust still fresh, certified public accountants question the validity of models and of their output. This definitely has a positive influence on asset valuation, with many banks asked by their auditors to put more assets into the fair-value regime's lowest bucket (where can be found the most illiquid assets); and to pay greater attention to concentrations. Both requests end up with a higher capital charge.

Another practice adopted by several banks is the use of different indices to help themselves calculate writedowns, as well as to hedge their exposure. Examples are ABX for subprime mortgages, CMBX for commercial mortgages, and LCDX for leveraged mortgages. ABX has proved popular with hedge funds when they take a view on housing-market-related valuations.

The use of indices for valuation reasons is not flawless, and in banking meetings one hears that institutions marking assets far from where the indices trade incur the ire of their auditors. Critics also say that putting too much emphasis on indices alone gives a one-sided estimate of exposure. Also, indices don't help with concentrations which are best expressed through correlations, but many banks have the bad habit of using low correlations – which is open to a Pandora's box of headwinds.

7. A horde of unjustifiable bonuses

On 17 January 2008, Wall Street's five biggest investment banks publicly announced that they were paying a record $39 billion in bonuses for 2007. This had been a year of hefty financial losses, when three of these banks suffered the worst quarterly losses in their history – and their shareholders lost more than $80 billion as the wounded banks' capitalization shrank (see also the case of unjustified jumbo bonuses in section 1 of this chapter).

If compensation and bonuses are added together, *then* Goldman Sachs, Morgan Stanley, Merrill Lynch, Lehman Brothers, and Bear Stearns together awarded $65.6 billion in 2007 to their 186,000 employees. (Two months later Bear Stearns went under.) At 60 percent of the total, year-end bonuses alone exceeded the $36 billion distributed in 2006, when the investment banking industry reported all-time high profits.

Experts said that such huge bonuses were larger than the gross domestic products of Sri Lanka, Lebanon, or Bulgaria. Though averages may be misleading, the average bonus of over $219 thousand has been more than four times higher than the median household income in the United States, while the often touted shareholder value had been left in the backburner.

At least one senior banker said he was surprised that none of the big banks was really willing to call the bluff of its employees, especially when they know the company had lost money and there were going to be significant layoffs. The pros answered that by paying more than they made in revenue, investment banks signaled to employees and the competition that they were still in business and that they would compete aggressively in 2008.

Not everybody is sure however that 2008 is going to be a bumper crop year, and some experts ventured the thought that 2007 bonuses will probably mark a high point as revenue declines stretch into 2008. One of them was quoted at Bloomberg news as having said that "The gilded age just ended. Ferrari dealers are going to be selling Tata cars. I think this is going to be the worst year we've had in a very long time."

According to Wall Street analysts, this flood of bonuses in a dismal business year was not really surprising, as investment banks have always been run, and likely always will be run, for:

- The CEO,
- Senior management,
- The traders and investment bankers.

Huge salaries totally unstuck from business morality and individual performance have become current currency in other industries as well. Patrick Cescau, Unilever's chief executive, earned a big pay rise in 2007, even though the group's net profit fell 18 percent in that year and its shares have continued to reflect the market's disappointment with its performance.

Not to be left behind, in March 2008 Barclays' Bob Diamond, the CEO, received a major salary increase while the bank's profits and share price tanked. In no time this extravagance was followed by another – that of the CEO of Lloyds TSB whose take-home pay zoomed even if the shareholders were confronted with dismal results.

Business morality is at an all-time low and public opinion is appalled. As a letter to the *Financial Times* had it, it is time for executive remuneration to receive long-overdue attention, including the decision to dismantle the pay-for-poor-performance incentives and other exotic rewards. Developed during the 1990s following an American (supposedly) "pay-for-performance" model, nonsensical payments are made to chief executives and other senior executives for no obvious improvement in results, said Ian Dunlop in a letter.[9]

Extravagant salaries and oversized bonuses can also be found in the roost of financial scandals, starting with Enron, Adelphia, WorldCom, Tyco, and Parmalat, and continuing with the banking hecatomb. People still able to think in an independent way express dismay that in the corporate and regulatory worlds there seems to be minimal acknowledgement that:

- Perverse "incentives" create a vicious cycle, and
- Greed feeds on greed all the way to the boardroom.

We have come into a situation where while clients still count for a great deal, shareholders, employees, and other stakeholders in a public enterprise are not the favored people of CEOs and board members. Neither will this salaries and bonuses bonanza be a passing phenomenon, unless and until:

- Parliament passes laws forbidding it, and
- Government as well as regulatory authorities apply the laws.

What critics have found difficult to swallow is that the New York firms that were so liberal with bonuses had at the same time shed over 25 percent of their equity value during 2007 amid mounting losses from the collapse of the subprime mortgage market. They also said that they were eliminating at least 6,200 jobs, yet they spent money lavishly at a time when:

- The US economy was slowing,
- Unemployment was rising,
- Retail sales were declining, and
- New home foreclosures were surging to a record.

The lion's share in bonuses was paid out by Goldman Sachs, closely followed by Morgan Stanley (who lost big money in 2007 and had to sell equity to Sovereign Wealth Funds in order to survive); Merrill Lynch (who also lost billions in 2007 and got billions in loans from SWFs); and Lehman Brothers. Bear Stearns followed at a smaller amount.

Nobody seems to have bothered to match the huge bonuses that so many people got with the profits and losses that the bank made because of the actions of each, individually and as a group. Essentially these fat bonuses seem to have been handed out as retainer fees, for fear of losing traders and investment bankers to competitors – rather than as compensation for significant contributions to the bank's profitability.

The future of traders specializing in structured finance seemed to be mixed. Professionally, they have been responsible for designing and selling instruments connected to asset-based lending, residential real estate lending, servicing and securitizations related to these transactions, asset/liability management portfolios, and principal and equity investments in other secured assets, as well as other instruments connected to:

- Interest rates, including sales and trading activities for interest rate derivatives, obligations of sovereigns, municipals, repurchase and resale financing, and debt financing.
- Foreign exchange, including sales and trading activities for currency, exotic options, forwards, and local currency trading.
- Commodities, including marketing and trading of natural gas, power, coal, crude oil, refined products, emissions, base metals, commodity indices, and new instruments like weather risk.

From these and other domains, equity-linked derivatives, convertible securities, and financial futures, structured products specialists have harvested great bonuses. Some have also developed qualitative and quantitative strategies across multiple asset classes, for which they were lavishly rewarded. But as structured instruments tanked and banks lost billions, their attitude towards traders specializing in structured finance changed. Merrill Lynch fired a bunch out of its London-based operations.

The bet is that for the coming couple of years the major participants recipients of lavish bonuses will be investment bankers responsible for origination and advisory activities on behalf of issuer clients across countries and sectors; also specialists in capital-related activities for issuer clients generated in the equity markets and/or in junk debt markets (including private placements); leveraged finance experts associated with non-investment-grade issuer clients; and versatile bankers able to elaborate strategic alternatives, divestitures, and restructuring activities.

It would be more rational to give top grades to the rarer species of people truly knowledgeable in risk control policies, procedures, and formal risk governance structures; as well as to high-tech specialists in communication and coordination systems among business units and executive management – with the emphasis on exposure and proactive damage control; also to experts well versed in analyzing and implementing limits and risk tolerance levels consistent with the bank's business strategy and capital structure.

8. Golden parachutes[10] for failed CEOs

Among the more interesting (and revolting) issues revealed by the subprime crisis of 2007 has been the racket at stockholders' expense by failed CEOs, CFOs, and other senior managers who brought to bankruptcy or near-bankruptcy the company they were supposed to lead. A typical example is Stanley O'Neil's "retirement package" – which seems completely out of line with the blood-letting of Merrill Lynch while he was the CEO.

The way a letter to *Financial Times* (2 November 2007) had it, it is outrageous, though not surprising, that an investment banker who oversaw the destruction of more than just his shareholders' wealth should be handed a cool $160 million in failure pay. The letter's writer looked at it as evidence that the financial world and its participants:

- Are shielded from any downside risk in their wild speculations with other people's money, and
- When they fail are rewarded with seven-digit-number bonuses, even if the company they have led has lost billions.

Compensation packages for executives have changed dramatically since 1992, when SEC last addressed this topic. Most particularly what has changed in the corporate world in the past decade is the transparency of huge pay packages and golden parachutes. Dependable information about them has become available thanks largely to the seamy scandals that engulfed Enron, WorldCom, Parmalat, and several other high-flying firms in the early years of the twenty-first century.[11] For a couple of years following those scandals:

- Prosecutors and regulators were emboldened,
- Directors were awakened to their responsibilities, and
- According to hearsay, chief executives were humbled.

But in no time all this became a thing of the past, as CEOs restored their ability to award to themselves a big chunk of shareholders' money. As power in the executive suite became more diffuse, it also became easier to control descent through alliances and contractual clauses, stipulating huge payments for self-gratification whether the company prospers or sinks.

To paraphrase Winston Churchill, "Never have so many people been paid so much to do so little." This is true all over industry these days, and most particularly among financial institutions which performed badly in the market or sold themselves to somebody else to avoid oblivion. Liquidation bonuses paid to fired or departing chief executives are a shame to:

- Those who authorize them, and
- Those who take the money and run.

Down to basics, there is no excuse for poor executive judgment that ruins the bank – or any other entity – for which the CEO works. Beyond this, reward for mismanagement is *unethical*, and when it happens it provides a very bad precedent, giving to others the worst possible example.

One of the high-profile cases in 2007 has been Warren Spector, president of Bear Stearns, who was forced out after the embarrassing collapse of two mortgage hedge funds managed by the investment bank that he headed. Another case of an outrageous retirement package has been that of Chuck Prince, Citigroup's chairman and chief executive, as disgruntled investors wanted a change in management in the aftermath of losses on mortgage-backed securities which exceeded all precedence in the bank's history.

Other heads had already rolled at Citigroup prior to Prince's own. On 30 October 2007 Michael Raynes, head of structured credit, and Nestor Dominguez, co-head of collateralized debt obligations, joined on the way out Randy Barker, co-head of fixed income, and his boss Tom Maheras, head of all Citi's capital markets operations. In an earlier October 2007 shake-up the whole bunch left, opening their golden parachutes.

Neither was the cost of these payments the only one that Citigroup incurred because of failures that happened under their watch. As the careful reader will remember, the bank had to accept tough terms from Abu Dhabi, as a condition for the $7.5 billion it needed to raise to avoid having to ask the US government to take it over. (In the late twentieth century a precedent was set by Chicago's Continental Bank.)

Some time earlier, in July 2007, Peter Wuffli was abruptly ousted as chief executive officer of UBS after subprime-related losses at the in-house hedge fund Dillon Read Capital Management (DRCM). Then Huw Jenkins, who led a drive to push UBS into the top investment banking league, left in October 2007 as the bank revealed a $3.7 billion write-down, allegedly by opening his golden parachute.

Blood-letting did not stop there. Clive Standish retired as the chief financial officer at UBS amid the October 2007 shake-up in which 1,500 jobs were axed. Eventually after resisting his ouster tooth and nail, Marcel Ospel also, the chairman, former CEO, and chief architect of UBS's downfall, lost his head (in early 2008). Even so, the cleaning up touched only the surface, as the majority of those responsible for destroying the great Swiss bank's franchise are still at senior management jobs.

We all make mistakes, but this is not supposed to happen every day. *If* it takes place on a massive scale, as has been the case with subprimes, CDOs, CDSs, and other risky instruments, *then* something is wrong with the system and with the people running it. Both in America and in Europe the prestige associated with big banks has gone from Stalin's authority to that of Mr Bean. But those who exercised poor judgment took home tens and hundreds of millions, which Bean has never done.

The question regarding what is enough in ethical compensation does not concern only those executives who have failed. What has unwisely become a feudal status quo of extravagant pay, options, and bonuses engulfs all CEOs and their underlings. As a US representative put it in recent Congressional hearings: "I am waiting for the first executive to come up with a trillion dollar income."

7
Northern Rock: a Case Study

1. Lender of last resort

According to financial history books, the concept of lender of last resort dates back to 1797, when Francis Baring so described the Bank of England. A century later, the Bank of England (BoE) obliged by saving his institution from bankruptcy, but it did not repeat the gesture a second time in 1995, and the venerable Barings Bank went bankrupt; several economists applauded the decision not to intervene.

In 2007 Northern Rock's ill-planned rescue showed:

- Regulatory weakness, and
- Poor judgment under fire.[1]

The Northern Rock story has many ironies, starting with the taxpayers' money spent lavishly for a lost cause. Up to the mortgage bank's nationalization in February 2008, public financial banking amounted to £55 billion ($110 billion). Of this sum, £25 billion has been direct lending by the Bank of England, and another £30 billion was given in British Treasury guarantees.

As the subprimes fiasco unfolded, not only Britain's Northern Rock (and to a lesser extent Barclays[2]), but also the "Who Is Who" in American banking have become damaged goods. With bankers not trusting each other to give loans, the likes of Citigroup, Bear Stearns, Merrill Lynch, and plenty of other institutions like HSBC, Fortis, Deutsche Bank, and UBS, rushed to the Sovereign Wealth Funds (SWFs; Chapter 2) of Asia and the Middle East to get cash, which they did under draconian conditions (Chapter 2). With this turn of events,

- The good money running after bad money at Northern Rock, a small mortgage bank, has been 160 percent of what the big banks had to borrow from SWFs (an estimated $69 billion up to February 2008), and
- Had Britain played white knight to the wounded global big banks, it would have gained 10 percent of their equity at bargain basement price, then could have parceled Northern Rock out to them with the request to take care of it.

This, of course, would have required imagination and plenty of system thinking, which is not characteristic of parties with diverging goals. The British Treasury wanted by all means to avoid political and social upheaval; the Bank of England was caught by surprise; and the hands-off Financial Services Authority (FSA), which was supposed to regulate banks, lost its bearings and started searching for a new chairman through a headhunter.[3]

Critics say that the second half of 2007 was the wrong time for the Labour government to face another public outcry. In the middle of falling house prices and with the Northern Rock still an open wound, came the David Abrahams scandal. He donated more than £660,000 ($1.32 million) to the Labor Party, allegedly using illegitimate intermediaries. The way an article in *The Economist* had it:

> In the case of Mr Abrahams's donations, there have been unsubstantiated hints that he was hoping for a more tangible payback, such as a peerage or favouritism for his businesses. Even he may nor know precisely why he gave so much and in the manner that he did.[4]

Things were different from the central bank's viewpoint. If nothing else, since central bankers use taxpayers' money in saving a mismanaged credit institution from failure, their decisions should be guided by the least-cost approach. But on the other hand, wholesale salvage operations, as well as other legacy initiatives like deposit insurance, create a moral hazard.

Neither was the show of a Treasury becoming first a wounded bank's salesman then its owner giving confidence to the market at a time the primary concern of credit institutions was to deleverage. The more time passed by without a sale materializing, the thinner on the ground private sector saviors proved to be, while Northern Rock's equity descended to the bargain basement:

- In February 2007 Northern Rock's share price touched £12.58, valuing the mortgage bank at more than £5 billion ($10 billion).
- In January 2008 the price fell to 69 pence (£0.69), about 4.4 percent of its 2007 peak, reducing capitalization to £275 billion ($550 billion), *as if* the market thought the bank was walking dead.

Several former suitors, like Cerberus, a hedge fund, and JC Flowers, an American private equity firm experienced in sorting out ailing financial institutions, dropped their initially expressed interest. This left only two contenders in the ring: a consortium led by Sir Richard Branson's Virgin Group (which intended to take a controlling interest in the bank), and Olivant Advisers, a private investment firm which proposed taking a minority stake in Northern Rock hoping that "better management" would do the trick.

To make their offer credible, both would-be rescuers promised swift repayment to the Bank of England, though at a level below 50 percent of the direct loan made to keep Northern Rock afloat. But capital had to be borrowed to fulfill that pledge, and the financial crisis of the subprimes left banks and other borrowers both short of capital and leery of credit risk.

Additionally, in spite of lavish money spent by the British Treasury and the Bank of England on a mortgage bank in distress, there was no assurance at all that this salvage would help avoid potential contagion, because failing banks were not the only negative factor of the economy. Other factors counted a lot.

A few years ago, a Deutsche Bundesbank report stated that the problem is indeed much broader:

> Today there is much evidence to suggest that critical developments in individual countries were ultimately caused by deficiencies in national economic policies, often in conjunction with an inadequate or inappropriate regulatory framework. In many cases, however, these developments were aggravated by herd behavior, which is not untypical of the financial markets.[5]

The Deutsche Bundesbank also brought in perspective that the role of the lender of last resort, which the IMF played *de facto* during the 1997 financial crisis in Southeast Asia, could not prevent stress conditions from spreading throughout the region. As this experience documented, monetary instruments alone cannot correct economic policy deficiencies – for instance, the absence of effective banking supervision, or misjudgments by the private sector and/or by governments.

2. Northern rock and the FSA

During the credit inflation of 2004–2007, Northern Rock had been considered by many analysts (as well as by speculators) as a go-go bank. It was a most aggressive British lender and, through smoke and mirrors, its equity was reaching for the stars. Nobody – including the regulators – seems to have paid attention to the risks inherent in its strategy of short-term borrowing, using the credit markets to raise funds to finance its rapid growth.

Yet there were plenty of reasons for being careful. In the short period of eight years, from 1999 to mid 2007, Northern Rock issued £46 billion ($92 billion) in securitizations, having found the practice of dicing up credit risk, by securitizing and selling mortgages, a very rewarding channel in gaining liquidity for future lending.

Northern Rock's near bankruptcy did not come overnight. It built up over the years of this highly risky borrowing and lending policy, as well as (most likely) of gambling with derivatives. According to information revealed in late September 2007 to the House of Commons Treasury Select Committee, the supervisory authorities were asleep at the wheel. They got the message that Northern Rock was in trouble only on 9 August, after the subprimes crisis was in full swing. This says volumes about the inadequacy of bank supervision, since:

- Up to 2005, securitizations and similar instruments had already made up 54 percent of Northern Rock's typical lending, and
- This share, already too high, mushroomed to 75 percent in 2007 without the regulators bothering to investigate and take measures to right the balances.

Only in the first week of December 2007, more than four months after the July/August subprimes debacle, did the Financial Services Authority issue a severe weather warning about the mortgage market. Clive Briault, the FSA's managing director for retail financial business, told a conference of mortgage lenders on 4 December 2007 that there was "the very real prospect that conditions will worsen further into next year, in terms of both liquidity and credit risks."

At the FSA, as among the bankers themselves, foresight had taken a holiday and along with it went responsibility. For many of the 1.4 million British mortgage borrowers whose short-term fixed-rate loans taken out in more clement times were due to end in 2008, higher refinancing costs might prove more than they could afford. Household savings as a percentage of disposal income, which act as a buffer in times of stress:

* First had fallen to an all-time low of 2.5 percent, and
* Then they turned to negative, if net savings in occupational pension funds were excluded.

Sure enough, the job of banking regulators is not to fill the management gap in supervised institutions. Their duty is to see to it that management safeguards the bank's assets, and curb its excesses. A regulatory body is also required to have a learned opinion about whether a default or bailout is likely. There is no evidence that the FSA was alert to the oncoming danger, in spite of Northern Rock's:

* High leverage, and
* Risk appetite.

Having forgotten the lesson of the August 1998 Russian bankruptcy because of short-term funding of long-term liabilities, Northern Rock management specialized in short-term funding for more than 50 percent of its mortgages – a high ratio. The bank's conduits were issuing short-term paper, with an average maturity of 45 days. As mortgage-backed products were downgraded, illiquidity spread, sending interbank rates soaring and forcing the Bank of England and the British government to step in.

Northern Rock was not alone in tapping the capital markets for funds in this risky way. Bradford & Bingley relied on securitization to write 35 percent of its mortgages, while Barclays did so for a more reasonable 9 percent, which, however, represented a huge 58 percent of Barclays' market value. Still, this 58 percent was small change compared with:

* 1.725 percent for Northern Rock(!!!),
* 566 percent for Bradford & Bingley(!!), and
* 218 percent for HBOS(!).

The good news for the reader is that other British banks have been well in charge of the exposure they assume with securitizations. Two examples are:

- 9 percent for HSBC, and
- 9 percent for Standard Chartered.[6]

The Financial Services Authority, supposedly the watchdog of British banking and insurance, was also insensitive to other worrisome statistics that required investigation. Relative to loans, securitizations represented 54 percent for Northern Rock, 35 percent for Bradford & Bingley, and 19 percent for HBOS. By contrast, these figures stood at 3 percent for Standard Chartered, and 2 percent for HSBC.

It would have been only reasonable to expect that such discrepancies in statistics characterizing the behavior of credit institutions should have triggered a down-to-basics investigation by regulatory authorities: was it that HSBC and Standard Chartered were too timid in taking business initiatives? Or had the reason been that Northern Rock and its pals were digging their own graves, as well as those of their depositors?

This failure to investigate and take action by the Financial Services Authority and (to a lesser extent) by the British Treasury the and Bank of England, cost the British taxpayers dearly but it also has a silver lining. It demonstrated that the share of securitizations to loans is an excellent metric which should definitely be introduced by the Basel Committee into the supervisory rules of Basel II.

- A bank's securitizations must be a low single-digit number relative to its loans, as HSBC has shown.
- A low two-digit number means danger for the credit institution, and
- With a mid two-digit number the bank goes to the dogs, just like Northern Rock.

There is an irony attached to these limits. So far securitization – including securitization without bounds – has been looked at as a relatively stable source of funding because money can be locked in for periods of up to five years. Bankers and their supervisors, however, have missed the major problem that emerged owing to *step-up* dates, when part of the issue matures and has to be refinanced. As the events of 2007 have shown:

- Refinancing can create serious problems, and

- When other institutions and investors stop short-term funding to the banks – the so-called *buyers' strike* – this leads to a crisis.

The lesson is that refinancing has to be planned in the medium to longer term, under worst-case scenarios. This is not being done today, and the results of such failure have been dramatized not only by Northern Rock but also by the whole banking industry, whose equity has dived. The vexing thing is that as of late January 2008, a great risk is deleveraging in the banking industry because it may bring down many other markets.

3. Failure of prudential supervision

Until it hit the rocks and sank in early August 2007, Northern Rock was revered by some analysts as Britain's fastest-growing mortgage bank. Little attention was paid however to the fact that, as we saw in section 2 of this chapter, its secret of success was the unorthodox policy of funding its loan book short-term from the wholesale markets, rather than the secure classical way of funding loans from retail deposits – which after all is the very essence of intermediation in banking.

After the descent into Dante's inferno, rather than recognizing its policy's failure and its own shortcomings, the bank's top brass maintained that this business model had been prudence itself, and had been derailed only by the subprimes crash in America. That position was bigheaded and awfully wrong:

- Mortgage lending is a long-term commitment.
- Buying money has a short-term horizon, and
- Financing the long term through the short term is the worst business model possible.

The bank's top management either had failed to learn the lessons from other credit institutions that crashed for the same reasons, or else did not care about the mortgage institution's future as long as the going was good. An aftermath of this policy is that in Britain Northern Rock is now such a tarnished name that none of the suitors who talked of buying it at a knockdown price wanted to keep that label. With so much money going down the drain,

- A question frequently heard in the City of London has been why the supervisors proved to be so lax.

- The answer came from a committee of the British Parliament, which said that the absence of a careful watch by the supervisory authorities was responsible for the mess.[7]

Critics also point to the fact that after Northern Rock's profit warnings had led to a slip in the share price, to compensate for this its management announced an increased dividend even though it expected profits to fall. This was an alarm signal that should have definitely alerted regulators, particularly in the midst of a general market uneasiness expressed through higher volatility in 2007.

According to information which came to the public eye, the Financial Services Authority not only did not act to straighten the balances; also, when at end June 2007 Northern Rock set aside less capital against its loans, it gave the bank its stamp of approval because it found that it somehow fitted under new international banking rules. In retrospect,

- This has been a major regulatory failure, and
- The capital reduction cast doubt on the dependability of calculating capital adequacy under Basel II.

The way an article in *The Economist* put it,

> The FSA's apparent insouciance was even stranger given Northern Rock's specific history. In 2004, after short-term interest rates shot up, the bank was caught off-guard and profits suffered. It promised investors that half its loans would be matched by retail deposits, a pledge it promptly ignored once rates moderated.[8]

It has also been revealed through testimonies that the wider failure in the functioning of financial markets – and most particularly short-term funding sources, upon which Northern Rock had become reliant – was not foreseen by the Financial Services Authority (let alone by the failed bank). This inability or unwillingness to forecast amounted to an abrogation of duties for a major financial regulatory authority.

"I didn't see this coming. I have yet to find someone who did," said the wounded bank's CEO. And in parliamentary testimony on 9 October 2007, Sir Callum McCarthy, the FSA chairman, insisted that the seizing-up of the money markets was unprecedented. A straight answer to this argument is that it is a basic duty of regulators to project oncoming events through worst-case scenarios, because forecasts are key to:

- Sizing up the risks, and

- Tightening the banks' inspection in a way commensurate with the seriousness of projected events.

Opinions heard after the bank's demise suggested that neither the FSA nor Northern Rock had incorporated stress tests into a scenario analysis of the bank's resilience. Yet in the City of London one hears that simulations are carried out jointly by the FSA, the Bank of England, and the Treasury to gauge the financial system's ability to withstand potential upsets. Some analysts pointed out, however, that the regulators had:

- Failed to involve the banks themselves as players, and
- Therefore they were unable to predict their likely behavior in a major crisis.

This left the financial system overexposed to falling liquidity, as markets dried up globally and investors shunned anything to do with mortgages. With worst-case forecasts non-existent, and with regulation reduced rather than tightened, the inevitable did happen. On 13 August 2007, just two working days after its liquidity dried up, Northern Rock told the Financial Services Authority it was in trouble. Next day the Bank of England and the British Treasury were informed while:

- Northern Rock put itself up for sale, and
- Feelers were put out in every direction where a potential buyer might be found.

In conclusion, for want of bank supervision the Northern Rock crisis had landed squarely on the doorstep of the taxpayer. Reportedly, the Bank of England would have preferred to rescue the mortgage lender behind the scenes, as happened with other cases in the early 1990s. But a covert operation was excluded because of a European Union law, the Market Abuse Directive, applied in Britain in 2005.

There was as well the failure of the so-called "tripartite" system of bank regulation. No single government authority – FSA, BoE, or Treasury – has been in overall charge of financial stability in Britain. Events proved that the unification of regulatory function under the FSA harbored new troubles. On 20 October 2007, two and a half months after Northern Rock, Paragon, a Birmingham-based mortgage bank, announced that it too was in financial trouble. In one day its share price dropped by 51 percent.

4. The many forms of bailouts

The fifty-five billion pounds sterling spent on Northern Rock, ending with a nationalization, raises the question: is it better to let a self-wounded financial institution fail, or to intervene to salvage it with a lot of taxpayer's money? Only the study of what has happened with various types of bailouts can help in answering this query in a factual manner.

In Britain, one of the better-known central bank interventions came in the early 1970s in the course of the secondary banking crisis, when fringe banks struggled to find ways of making money, and took a lot of exposure to the property sector. In a way, what happened then was not dissimilar from events in 2007, though the exposure was taken with traditional loans and not only by gearing through securitizations and collateralized debt obligations.

Then as now, commercial property proved to be much riskier than the banks had thought. When at the end of 1972 business rents were frozen by the Conservative government, while there was a sharp rise in interest rates, both commercial and private property prices fell like a stone and plenty of mortgagee homeowners turned belly-up.

- Depositors took fright, and
- Some of the fringe banks suffered serious runs.

As London and County Securities as well as several other institutions found to their expense, they could no longer obtain funds from the money market. Over Christmas 1973 and New Year 1974, the Bank of England held crisis meetings with the big banks, resulting in a £1.2 billion *lifeboat*, roughly equivalent to about £10 billion under today's prices, to provide liquidity for the secondary banks. (Compare this with the £55 billion advanced to just one bank, Northern Rock, by the Bank of England and the British Treasury in 2007.)

A decade later, in the early 1980s, British banks faced pressure over ill-conceived and risky Latin American loans. In 1984, the Bank of England rescued Johnson Matthey Bankers, buying it for just £1. Then, in 1992, the BoE fought, and lost, when currency speculators forced sterling out of the European exchange rate mechanism (ERM).

But in 1995 the Bank of England decided that Barings should not be saved, after it had gambled and lost a fortune with derivatives at the Osaka stock exchange. Barings presented no systemic risk; this, however, was not the case three years later, in September 1998, with money-market turmoil during the hedge fund crisis which started in the US with the Long Term Capital Management (LTCM) meltdown. In this particular case, the Federal Reserve of New York found itself in the frontline. Like the British *lifeboat*, LTCM's salvage operation:

- Did not use taxpayers' money, and
- The adopted solution, to co-involve LTCM's big investors, did not create any risk of inflation.

A couple of years down the line, on 19 November 2002, addressing the Council of Foreign Relations (CFR) in Washington, DC, Alan Greenspan said that in the event of a financial implosion the Fed stood ready to use its "unlimited power to create money" and to "provide what essentially amounts to catastrophic financial insurance coverage." Critics said that he probably meant a central bank's unlimited power to create inflation.

A similar statement was delivered by then Federal Reserve governor Ben Bernanke to a 21 November 2002 meeting of the National Economics Club, also in the nation's capital. Bernanke promised that the Fed would do whatever was necessary to prevent the deflation of a bubble, including producing "as many US-dollars as it wishes, at essentially no cost." This is, of course, inaccurate, as the history of Germany's hyperinflation demonstrates. Would Bernanke like to be in the shoes of Rudolf Hilferding, the German finance minister in 1923, who presided over the explosion of hyperinflation?

Experts suggested that, since central bankers don't normally say such things publicly, such words raised the suspicion that these statements were intended to uplift spirits when confronted by an economic crisis that might be deep. In the early years of the twenty-first century, that suspicion was furthered by the shift in the Bush Administration's economics team, and by a spreading rumor that:

- Blacklists were circulating in the global derivatives market, and
- They were enumerating financial institutions considered too shaky to trade with.

Rumor had it that JP Morgan Chase, the world's largest trader and holder of financial derivatives, was at the top of that list. Some analysts suggested that it is not unlikely that the aforementioned statements were intended as public confirmation of private promises; that the Fed stood behind Morgan Chase and its derivatives exposure; and that it was ready to support other banks that might face similar woes.

If oral pledges are worth anything, in his aforementioned speech on 19 November 2002, Greenspan tried to be even-handed with derivative financial instruments and their risks. He stated that "Derivatives, by construction, are highly leveraged, a condition that is both a large benefit and an Achilles heel."[9] Then he added that the Achilles heel of derivatives was *excess speculation*, against which one should guard oneself.

On Wall Street, the analysts' opinion was that what transpired from these different statements by Fed executives was that the central bank's policy was that it was prepared to intervene if necessary to save the (then) $300 trillion to $400 trillion global derivatives market from collapse. Some experts even said the Fed and European central banks had already done so, and that the public statements were part of that effort. As evidence they provided:

- The November 2002, $114 billion spike in money supply, a broad measure of monetary liquidity, and
- The fact that JP Morgan Chase's equity recovered from its October 2002 low.

Most market players looked at this switch as the effect of an invisible hand, rather than as a direct central bank intervention. The play was one of market resilience, a short two years after the burst of the equity bubble. By contrast, the housing bubble of 2007 was about high consumer leverage perpetrated by:

- A lowering of credit standards which opened up the huge market of subprimes,
- The householders' propensity to spend much more than they earn, and
- New financial instruments creating the illusion that the party could continue forever.

As a Merrill Lynch report stated, easy money fostered the housing boom; higher income prices begat more leverage on behalf of home buyers and investors; mortgage loans were massively securitized and sold; rating agencies awarded AAA to the upper tranche of junk bonds; home prices and securitized products prices rose, rewarding the "brave"; home price appreciation stalled owing to declining affordability; credit strains emerged; tightening credit and excess housing capacity precipitated housing recession.[10] Then the "brave" fell on their swords – among them Northern Rock.

5. A scandal too far?

Expert opinions at the City of London suggested that the Northern Rock saga still held many surprises. *If* 9 August 2007 was Day One, *then* Day Two came nearly four months later, on 25 November, when the market heard that Sir Richard Branson's Virgin Group was chosen as the preferred bidder for the mortgage bank, which was kept alive only by injections of taxpayers' money.

This seems to have been a Sunday decision, which caught many by surprise. Some market observers wondered whether something might have happened in the margins of acceptability. Critics said that even if one's amazement in favoring out of hand one of the bidders was left aside, this case was serious because haste was unlikely to serve the interest of taxpayers. Contrarians commented that Alistair Darling, the chancellor of the exchequer, should have moved faster to sort out the mess.

Ironically, the Treasury's indecision and delay had strengthened the hand of investors, particularly that of hedge funds that were busily extending their stakes. By late November 2007, the two hedge funds which owned 18 percent of the bank had been threatening to veto any takeover that they reckoned undervalued it – while according to others this was an audacious proposition because Northern Rock would have folded without the open line of credit from the Bank of England.

At the end of November 2007, Bryan Sanderson, the newly appointed chairman of Northern Rock, said that Virgin was chosen because it offered something to all stakeholders[11] – which according to critics was a questionable statement. For his part, Richard Branson proposed putting £200 million ($400 million) of his own money together with Virgin Group's budget for Northern Rock's takeover:

- Half of the budget was supposed to come from current shareholders, through a deeply discounted new rights issue, and
- The promise to pay off £11 billion of the central bank's loan immediately, and the rest within three years, was contingent upon the willingness of money markets to cooperate.

Amid all this, several critics said that taxpayers would be feeling cheated, and for good reason. The government had put into this deal a large sum of public money and whatever went beyond the stated £11 billion would be subject to a significant amount of credit risk. As with all loans, it would not be the first but the last pound, dollar, or euro of the loan that would be hard to get back.

- Northern Rock had failed once;
- Who was to guarantee that it would not fail twice?

In December 2007, critics added that when judged against competing bids the Virgin choice looked even worse. For instance, a rival proposal from JC Flowers, the private equity firm, promised to repay more of the Bank of England's loan to Northern Rock at once. (Shortly thereafter JC Flowers withdrew from the competition.) The general feeling was that shotgun weddings should be avoided, no matter what kind of political will might be behind them.

In the last analysis, a proper auction of the wounded bank was also to the Labour government's best interest. A scandal, if there was one, which came at the heels of multifaced donations by David Abrahams to the Labour Party, and led to the retirement of Peter Watt – the party's secretary general and former head of compliance – might well mean that Gordon Brown, the prime minister, was heading for the exit.

To further complicate matters, government sources let it be known that after all Northern Rock might be nationalized. Nobody bothered however to explain whether nationalizing the bank meant a huge shift in the policy of free enterprise which Labour had adopted. Then on 12 January 2008 it emerged that Ron Sandler, who sorted out the Lloyd's of London insurance market in the 1990s, would take charge of Northern Rock *if* it was nationalized. But it was also said that taking the bank into public hands:

- Would be politically embarrassing for Gordon Brown, who had tried to shed Labour's reputation as the party of state ownership, and
- It would also mean breaking one of the prime minister's self-imposed fiscal rules, as at least half the bank's liabilities would be transferred to the public book.

In an interview with the *Financial Times*, in early January 2008, Alistair Darling had mapped out a wide-ranging response to the Northern Rock debacle, including measures that put the chancellor firmly in charge of dealing with any future banking crisis. Under a proposed new banking insolvency regime, the chancellor of the exchequer intended to intro-duce a series of triggers – including one where a request from a bank for an emergency Bank of England loan would see the FSA step in *if* the institution was in danger.

Critics said that the sweeping powers to intervene in failing banks to be given to the Financial Services Authority, as part of a regulatory shake-up, should have been granted when the FSA was instituted, not just after Northern Rock's failure. For instance, the law should have allowed the FSA to seize and protect depositors' cash when a bank gets into serious difficulty, heading off the risk of a run on the bank. The way *The Economist* put it at end of January 2008,

- The British government was at a loss about what to do with a bank that was the victim of its own recklessness.
- Unable to find a private buyer with access to enough cash to take it off its hands, the government refused to do the politically unpalatable thing and nationalize it.

In some opinions, the inability of the Labour government to make up its mind was proof of its descent into economic miserabilism. Others pointed to conflicts of interest. *If* a suitable deal with a private sector buyer could be negotiated, *and* Northern Rock were to raise the money to pay its debt by issuing some £30 billion in asset-backed bonds, which the government would underwrite, *then* the result would be totally asymmetrical:

- The bank's owners would pocket most of the profits,
- While taxpayers would foot most of the losses, were a lot of these to materialize.

Finally, on 18 February 2008, Gordon Brown's government chose nationalization euphemistically called "common ownership of the means of production." Rumor had it that this decision scared many Labor politicians, not only because it proved that prime minister and chancellor were not market-oriented but also (and mainly) because of the irony of an insolvent bank being "rescued" by a government with a budget deficit of 3.1 percent of GDP.

Critics added that the support for Northern Rock was far larger than any likely call on taxpayers' money, which would have resulted from losses at the bank. They also said that Alistair Darling, who holds the purse of the British government, might have hoped that he was buying time – but he did so by paying a very high price for a job which was:

- Half-baked, and
- Done in a rush.

The abyss of Northern Rock's losses and rescue plans also brought to light that Britain is the only country in the Group of Seven, without a mechanism for dealing with distressed banks. To correct this shortcoming, in addition to a new system of deposit insurance the Bank of England wants an agency that could take control of struggling lenders to protect deposits and then sell their assets. Central bankers, after all, must look for solutions that safeguard taxpayers' money as far as is possible.

When Northern Rock collapsed in 2007, nobody thought that the Labor government would have been caught again (and again ...) unprepared to deal with a severe banking crisis. But this is exactly what has happened in 2008 with the Royal Bank of Scotland, Halifax Bank of Scotland (HBOS), Lloyds TSB, Bradford & Bingley, and Alliance & Leicester.

Executed at the twelfth hour through a fire brigade approach, wide-ranging socialist nationalizations and part-nationalizations of the British banking industry have turned the government into a commercial banker; and this is an expensive business:

- The cost is upwards of $500 billion ($750 billion), which represents for each British citizen (including the newborn) £8,000 ($12,000).
- The result has been to attach the suffix "troubled" to credit institutions which were previously the pride of the banking industry, but have crashed because of superleveraging, excesses, mismanagement and lack of prudential supervision.

In the process, the British pound has lost a quarter of its value against the US dollar and a third of its value against the euro and Swiss franc. And this is not the end of the line. The Bank of England continues pumping billions into the money market to encourage banks to lend again – and the Treasury makes more billions available for banks to guarantee a dubious quality of medium-term debt.

Part III

Bank Supervisors and Their Remit

8
Responsibilities of Financial Regulation

1. Updating the regulation of free markets

The incarnation of the concept of market regulation first saw the day in ancient Athens, when the city-state appointed a regulator of the grain trade. In more recent times, regulatory rules imposed against deception and price manipulation were first put forward in the late seventeenth and early eighteenth centuries. Compared with these efforts, the need for a broader perspective on bank regulation is a relatively recent concept. To operate effectively and within reasonable limits, markets need clear and explicit rules, which include:

- Legally binding and enforced contracts,
- Protection of each party's proprietary and trading rights,
- A system of traffic lights all players must observe, and
- Corrective action for those who get out of line.

Regulation is a long-term investment, not an overnight affair. Today, particular attention is paid to the regulation of banks because they play a central role in the economy. They hold the savings of the public, give loans to enterprises and individuals, provide a means of payment for goods and services, and grease the wheels of industry and trade.

To be effective, the government's financial regulation must follow a grand strategy with biting controls working *by exception*, focusing on cases which fall outside limits for explicit reasons – like a rapid growth in risk appetite in one sector or another or within the whole economy. An example of out-of-control conditions is the three unprecedented risk characteristics of the market in the first years of the twenty-first century:

- A large amount of leverage;
- Growing dependence on derivative financial instruments, and
- In-transit credit risk sold as a commodity to third parties.

Even banking at 8 percent capital adequacy, as required by Basel I for international banks, has a 12.5 leverage factor. That's of course better than the factor of 33 gross by Bear Stearns[1] and typical of hedge funds, or LTCM's 340. The tendency of the financial industry to overleverage itself means that both central banks and regulatory authorities must be watchful because the risk is enormous – apart from the fact that leveraging significantly expands the money supply.

On 15 November 2005, at US Senate hearings on the nomination of Dr Ben Bernanke as chairman of the Fed, one of the senators asked him "Why Basel II?" To this he answered: "Basel I is too elementary for modern banking, which needs a sophisticated risk-sensitive capital adequacy system." The keyword in this statement is *risk-sensitive*; but Basel II has been too much manipulated to be a tool of watchdogs.

During that same hearing, Senator Sarbanes, co-author of the Sarbanes–Oxley Act of 2002 on reliable financial reporting, asked Bernanke if he had seen the results of (the then) recently released Quantitative Impact Study 4 (QIS 4). This had roughly indicated that half the participating big banks – US, British, Japanese, German, French, and others – had *reduced* their capital requirements by 25 percent through the advanced internal-ratings-based (A-IRB) approach of Basel II, and the use of models.

Sarbanes said that Dr Seidelman, former chairman of FDIC and other well-known regulators, gave a deposition to the US Senate, just prior to the 15 November 2005 Bernanke hearing, that this reduction in capital requirements is very, very dangerous. Several senators joined Sarbanes in pointing out that a 25 percent capital reduction leaves the US banking system exposed to worse perils – and not only the US banking system.[2]

Within less than two years, the events of July/August 2007 and subsequent months proved the critics of capital reduction right. *If* they were well capitalized in a risk-weighted way, *then* Citigroup, Merrill Lynch, UBS, and other big names in banking would not have brought themselves to the edge of the abyss – running to the sovereign wealth funds to get badly needed money. Coupled with lack of liquidity (section 2 of this chapter), this highly unwise reduction in capital adequacy happened at a time when the global banking system has been loaded with derivative financial instruments (section 5). To make matters worse,

- Credit risk became a commodity,
- Credit criteria waned, and
- In-transit credit risk has grown to monster level.

In the early 1990s, credit risk transfer was no more than a few billion dollars. In 2008 it stands at 50 trillion (Chapter 1), and it is growing exponentially – while, as we have seen, the overall derivatives exposure is estimated at *1 quadrillion*. As if all this were not enough, the absence of legal and other institutional restraints required for the smooth operation of markets, like a globalized Sarbanes–Oxley Act, leads inevitably to the malfunctioning of the system of checks and balances, and loss of investor confidence. It is *as if* market players, and those supervising them, have forgotten that constraints and restraints are the guardians making sure that the economy remains free of excesses and of fraud.

Until the effects of the mid 2007 credit-risk-and-subprime crisis became felt, the prevailing view had been that central banks should target inflation and that they should not try to influence asset prices because, as Alan "Double-Bubble" Greenspan used to say, they cannot recognize bubbles *ex-ante*. Both with the equity bubble of 2000 and with the housing bubble of 2007, this statement proved wrong. Central banks *can* recognize bubbles *ex-ante*, just as they recognize the need for easing.

It is therefore not surprising that following the subprimes debacle of 2007, the American, German, and French governments are proposing new guidelines that would clamp down on excesses connected to the trading of debt, all the way to mortgage lending practices. Some politicians, too, are concerned that overstretched borrowers had not fully understood the risk involved in subprime mortgage contracts before they signed on.

The more farsighted supervisors are now focusing on the *credit crisis* itself, and on the factors which have promoted it. Indeed, the credit crisis that hit the world economy in July/August 2007 taught many lessons about the workings of the global financial market. It emphasized the changes in responsibilities which have classically characterized supervisory authorities and central banks, and also highlighted issues which warrant attention such as:

- The emphasis to be placed on bank liquidity,
- The need for appropriate limits to leverage,

- The wisdom of funding diversification, and
- New areas of exposure including the aftereffects of *regulatory backlash*, a new term.

In fact, what is currently incorrectly labeled "regulatory backlash" is essentially the pressing requirement for streamlining policies and rules regarding the way central banks and supervisory authorities approach (or should approach) the changing financial environment – in a way promoting corrective action but avoiding overreaction. Concomitant with this is the call for revamping old rules that have become ineffectual, and for establishing new regulatory metrics to replace those obsolete like value at risk (VAR).[3]

2. Liquidity assurance and the regulatory authorities[4]

Prior to the July/August 2007 crisis, the prevailing opinion on regulatory authorities has been that they should content themselves with focusing on the *capital adequacy* of banks under their watch. The *liquidity* of credit institutions was not considered to be part of the regulators' job description. This has changed with the tight liquidity conditions which followed the subprimes crash, leading to huge liquidity injections by central banks as well as the realization of the fact that:

- The banking industry is not insulated from ups and downs in market liquidity, and
- Bubbles in assets markets immediately translate into investor risk aversion, accompanied by drying up of liquidity.

Capital adequacy (therefore solvency) and liquidity correlate with each other, as well as with the quality of inventoried assets and with market psychology. Chapter 9 explains how and why. It also brings to the reader's attention financial products affecting liquidity, such as ABCP and the carry trade:

- Which have escaped prudential supervision, and
- Whose downs make the market nervous as investors fear that banks depending on them for their liquidity may go out of business.

From these two bullets it follows logically that when asset prices experience a bubble and liquidity disappears, this is a matter of concern for both supervisory authorities and central banks, as not only the balance sheet of commercial banks but also their role as providers of credit is seriously affected, with shockwaves felt throughout business and industry.

Based only on its functions as an intermediary, the banking industry is no more the generator of liquidity in the way it used to be. In the course of the last two decades a significant part of liquidity and of credit creation has occurred outside what is classically defined as the *banking system*. Examples of entities that have entered into the liquidity equation are:

- Hedge funds,
- Structured investment vehicles (SIVs), and
- The rapidly growing tribe of off-balance-sheet conduits.

It matters little that SIVs, conduits, and other special-purpose vehicles (SPVs) are outfits connected to banks. Because they are off-balance-sheet they escape prudential supervision; and because they are leveraged they impact on the bank's liquidity – rather than being its source (see the discussion on assets-backed commercial paper in Chapter 9).

At the end of the day central banks found themselves obliged to implicitly extend liquidity to institutions outside the regulatory framework – this being one of the main reasons why the old rules of central banking and supervision are outdated and need thorough revamping. With such references in mind, in an article published in 2007 in the *Financial Times*, Paul de Gauwe[5] proposed two important changes to the current regulatory system:

1. Central banks should recognize that asset bubbles are a source of concern. Therefore, they should act on the emergence of a bubble.

De Gauwe refutes the argument that even if central banks can detect a bubble they are powerless to do something about it, by pointing out that it is inherently no more difficult to stop an asset bubble than it is to stop inflation.

2. Central banks should be involved in the supervision and regulation of *all* institutions that create credit and liquidity (emphasis added).

As the careful reader will recall from the discussion in preceding chapters, commercial and investment banks have in-house hedge funds and a legion of off-balance-sheet conduits and SIVs – while they lend big money to supposedly independent hedge funds. Therefore, the share of the financial sector under present-type prudential supervision gets smaller and smaller every month.

This is a very risky policy, in urgent need of revamping. All institutions that have to do with deposits, borrowing, lending, trading, credit rating, and portfolio management must obey well-established rules, and be under strict supervision. To the two de Gauwe proposals I would like to add a third, also aimed at upgrading regulatory activities:

3. Both central banks and the supervisory authorities themselves should be subject to a higher level of supervision.

The best example is provided by the Federal Reserve System in the US, which regularly audits its twelve Federal Reserve banks. In fact, back in 1998 at the request of the Fed's examiners the Fed of Boston and a couple of other regional Feds were the first to apply the principle of COSO.[6] In euroland, this role can best be played by the European Central Bank (ECB) supervising the fifteen central banks,[7] as well as the regulatory authorities whose countries have adopted the euro. This will be a major step towards:

- A better-governed common currency, and
- A well-functioning banking system.

Beyond these three points, central banks and supervisory authorities should steadily measure the liquidity of each commercial and investment bank (as well as every hedge fund and every other "non-bank bank") under their jurisdiction – not only monitoring but also projecting and experimenting to satisfy themselves that in a market downturn these entities will face no liquidity crisis.

The liquidity crisis launched by the subprimes provides a first class example on what should not happen. Each on their own, the Federal Reserve and the European Central Bank first labored to inject liquidity in the money markets; and they did not succeed. The spread between the cost of borrowing for governments and that for banks widened sharply, suggesting that:

- Investors have been warier than ever of lending to banking companies.

If a company is solvent it can find liquidity (more on this in Chapter 9). The problem with the credit-and-subprimes crisis of 2007 and beyond is that, particularly in the banking industry, nobody believes the other party's assertion that it is solvent. (On 12 March 2008 the CEO of Bear Stearns publicly assured everyone that his bank was solvent; on 14 March it had to be rescued by the Fed.) Everybody is afraid the counterparty's assets are overpriced and its liabilities underreported.

The rush to turn one's money into ashes through subprimes and derivatives has not been limited to banking companies. In mid January 2008, the Technology Research team of Merrill Lynch released a report highlighting that liquidity balances of some technology companies might be at risk because they have invested their cash in short-term debt instruments[8] that are no longer readily marketable.

- The commercial and industrial banks' vows created the fear that they will drag the economy down by starving it of capital.

Hence the December 2007 and mid March 2008 decisions by five central banks – Fed, ECB, Bank of England, Bank of Canada, and Swiss National Bank – to redirect billions of funding to the banking system in order to assure that it would have liquidity. On the other hand, in their anxiety to rescue the banking system from the depth of the abyss to which it had brought itself, central banks have been taking worthless mortgage-backed securities as collateral and endangering their anti-inflationary credentials.

3. Liquidity injection and consumer protection

There are different levels of central bank intervention. One of them is outright salvage and nationalization, as attempted with Northern Rock. More frequent is injecting liquidity into the market, which is also taxpayers' money. Under certain conditions, the shortage of liquidity can freeze the payments system, causing runs on banks which otherwise are solvent. It can also bankrupt businesses that suddenly find themselves unable to raise cash.

To reduce this danger, central banks increase the monetary base, often by an appreciable amount over established targets. Governments also try to calm a panic by providing some form of insurance to depositors. An example is the guarantee given in September 2007 by the British Treasury and Bank of England that Northern Rock depositors would be paid in full (Chapter 7).

The basic instrument for injecting liquidity used by the Federal Reserve, European Central Bank (ECB), and Bank of Japan (BoJ) is *open market operations*. Through this channel they make cash available to the banking industry, at least theoretically on a temporary basis. There are two ways of doing so:

- Outright purchases, and
- Temporary open market operations.

With *outright purchases* assets are bought in the open market and remain on the balance sheet of the central bank. This leads to an increase in banks' holdings of central bank money. By contrast, *temporary open market operations* involve lending central bank money to banks with a fixed and usually short maturity. This approach permits the central bank to manage marginal liquidity conditions in the interbank market for overnight reserves; and, hence, to steer very short-term money market interest rates.

The Fed, ECB, and BoJ also conduct two other types of credit operations: *Lombard facility* and *intraday credit*. Known as the marginal lending facility in the eurosystem, and primary credit facility in the Federal Reserve, Lombard facility aims to provide a safety valve for the interbank market:

- *If* the market cannot offer the needed liquidity,
- *Then* a bank can still obtain it from the reserve institution, preferably at a higher rate.

As these examples demonstrate, a broad interpretation of the function of the classical lender of last resort (but not of the SWFs; see Chapter 2) is that of providing liquidity to the market (via the banks) when there is no alternative. This is not necessarily a gift. Borrowers must provide collateral and pay interest for the cash. Problems arise when (for those central banks which accept securitized assets, like the ECB) the value of this collateral drops in a significant way – as has happened with the subprimes (see Chapter 2).

Traditionally, reserve institutions must have security for advancing cash. Collateralized lending enables the central bank to lend at the same rate to all qualifying parties, which is important for assuring the smooth transmission of monetary policy. The prerequisites are that:

- The collateral can be legally transferred to the central bank, and

- Adequate valuation as well as risk control measures can be provided.

But as Chapter 2 explained, the rule of prime collateral has been bent recently, with central banks becoming buyers of last resort. Another major problem faced by central banks, in July/August 2007 and the following months, has been that Basel II – the new capital adequacy by the Basel Committee on Banking Supervision – relies heavily on credit rating. However, as the subprime mess has documented,

- Credit rating is too easily manipulated, and
- It cannot be trusted to provide evidence on which entities and debt instruments are the riskiest.

Critics say that shortly after their promotion to "semiregulators," because of the importance Basel II has given to credit rating, the independent rating agencies started suffering from skewed incentives and conflicts of interest (Chapter 6). Lured by fat profits, they have helped banks in sugarcoating complex debt products of doubtful creditworthiness. This has raised serious questions about Basel II in regard to:

- The banks' resilience, and
- Their ability to act as financial intermediaries.

The more the market lost confidence in itself and in the banks, the more financial instability worsened. Unable to assess credit risk in complex structured products, investors (and many financial entities) refused to buy any type of mortgage-backed security. A supposedly large and liquid market suddenly dried up:

- Denying credit to institutions, which was their way of financing, and
- Obliging central banks and government to come to the rescue of poorly managed big global banks.

Regaining the market's confidence – and most importantly the confidence of common citizen – is not a matter of salvaging a few mismanaged lenders, or of drawing up new rules. Furthermore, experience suggests that the pace of regulatory change is too slow for an innovative and globalized market. The few new rules that were right, like the supervision of hedge funds, were found to be burdensome, and they have been opposed politically by market players.

Politics usually wins to the benefit of fat cats and the detriment of the common citizen. Still, one thing that continually surprises knowledgeable market watchers is how far central bankers and regulators will bend over to "save" the mismanaged big banks, instead of letting them go bust. This is:

- Creating *moral risk*, and
- Feeding *inflation*, one of the vicious ways to penalize the weaker strata of the population.

Inflation is always higher than that shown in official numbers, as traditionally governments have never failed to underplay its effect. What is relevant is not the core inflation rate, which does not consider energy and food prices, but the actual cost of living of private households shown through *headline inflation,* which in America has hit 4.7 percent, way above the Fed's interest rate, and in Europe 3.4 percent, above the target 2 percent.

Common citizens are not totally unaware of the risks they confront with their hard-won savings. Therefore, they choose to spend and live on credit rather than to save. In 2007, in Japan, once-envied household savings rate dropped to a 10-year low, to 3.2 percent of GDP, as salaries stagnated and retirees cracked their nest eggs. What the financial crisis of July/August 2007 meant for the private individual, and therefore for the reader, can be expressed by two queries everyone should ask himself or herself:

- Am I properly positioned for a Depression?
- Do I have anything in my portfolio that would help me survive under the worst circumstances?

A crucial issue underpinning both queries is whether central bankers and regulators have acted with swift prudence, or ill-judged panic. There is no doubt that the latter will bring frightening moments, because their authority will be greatly diminished when they finally confront the reality of whether or not consumers are able to continue coping with the *quintuple whammy* of rising unemployment, falling house prices, tighter credit, dearer food, and super-expensive oil.

There exist no magic formulas to avoid the negative aftereffects of the crisis that has been created by the big banks. *What if* the issuer of bonds defaults, the market crashes, or inflation takes off in a big way should always underpin risk analysis. *What if* the taxpayer is asked to continue footing the bill of huge losses by mismanaged banks, while CEOs, traders, and investment experts continue to reward themselves lavishly?

4. Derivatives and government policy

In the mid 1990s when the debate about government policy in regard to derivative financial instruments flared up, Richard O'Brien, then chief economist of American Express Bank, expressed the opinion that derivatives reduce the ability of governments to determine exchange rates and interest rates. "The government-versus-the-market battle is not confined to the economic policy arena alone," O'Brien suggested.[9]

The emergence of new generations of increasingly complex and sophisticated derivatives products, and losses being incurred by investors and big banks, rekindled concerns about how well the markets are regulated. After all, as George Soros underlined in one of his books,[10] a main use of derivatives is to circumvent regulations – and Soros has the experience to know what he is talking about.

In his 13 April 1994 testimony to the US House of Representatives Committee on Banking, Finance and Urban Affairs, George Soros made a remark which should be written in capital letters:

> We engage in many different markets. We have a portfolio of stocks, and we also operate in bonds, some fixed interest instruments, and we do it on a world-wide basis. Therefore, we also have significant currency exposure. We use derivative instruments to a much lesser extent than generally believed, very largely because we don't really understand how they work.

Governments, too, lack that knowledge, and in many instances they lack also the will to be in charge. In 1995, the Clinton Administration was not inclined to control derivatives risk through the regulatory agencies of the government. The Bush Administration followed in Clinton's steps by keeping to the same policy, till the 2007 subprime crisis proved the fallacy of that approach. Critics say that the hold of governments over market regulation needs to be rethought and resettled, including the imposition of discipline on:

- Originating banks,
- Traders,
- Borrowers, and
- Issuers of money as lenders of last resort.

In view of these facts, it is pure irony that monetary decisions made by central banks (like the rock-bottom interest rates of 2002–2004) drove pension funds, mutual funds, and other investors who should be conservative, towards highly geared derivatives. It is *as if* not only institutional investors but also central bankers and regulators *don't understand* the risks being assumed by:

- Each of them individually, and
- The economy, as well as the global economy as a whole.

One of the issues raised against derivatives legislation and stricter supervision is that such instruments cannot be regulated as a single product because a transaction may encompass several areas of finance: foreign exchange, equities, debt, and commodities. Professional investors who have been burned by derivatives exposure believe however that derivatives *can* be regulated – and very effectively so – *if* there is the necessary political will.

Invested interests emphasize the contribution of derivatives toward reducing risk, by covering potential currency devaluations when Americans invest in non-US assets. But with the weak dollar this strategy has often unraveled. One of the more classic examples is that of investors who tried to cut their exposure by using forward foreign currency derivatives to protect the value of their Japanese equity investments against the possibility of a sharp fall in the yen. The hedging backfired because the dollar weakened against a strengthening yen.

In other cases, losses mount because investors don't quite understand the instruments in which they deal; or the latter suddenly become the object of speculation. Practically all financial instruments could be manipulated – even those thought to be well established. And there are asymmetries as well. For instance,

- There is a margin requirement for stock transactions.
- But an investor does not need to post a margin for bonds, though bonds too are volatile.

This asymmetry was not lost on speculators who, capitalizing on 1993 low interest rates, rushed into the futures bond market. A meltdown followed when the Fed increased interest rates in February/March 1994 and continued doing so in successive installments. This has been a good example on how derivatives materially change, through their impact, the nature of so far conservative financial instruments.

One of the major subjects confronting national regulators is that banking at large, and most specifically derivative financial instruments, have become global processes propelled by the openness of financial borders. This has significantly reduced territorial and jurisdictional controls. Borders have fallen not only between countries but also between different financial sectors such as banking and insurance; hence the need for a new Glass–Steagall Act (Chapter 2).

Defining a given territory is, to say the least, difficult when markets exist primarily on computer networks and the old way of describing physical locations is valid no more. This has strange effects on the power of international finance, including the power of surprise. Quite often risk, and most specifically systemic risk, shows up in perverse ways. Therefore, bankers who are confident that brand new products can be handled safely in fact deceive themselves:

- To their thinking, complexity does not equal risk.
- But in reality the opposite is true; risk is amplified by complexity.

These are issues that should alert regulators, but many soft-pedal in the exercise of their duties. By 9 August 2007 British supervisory authorities knew that Northern Rock (Chapter 7) was heading rapidly for bankruptcy, but no action was taken. This led to the House of Commons Treasury Select Committee investigation on the reasons for inaction by regulators, which revealed that not only the Financial Services Authority (FSA) but also the Bank of England and the Treasury itself had let things get out of control.

John McFall MP, chairman of the Treasury Select Committee, made a lucid presentation of the dangers of passive regulatory approaches. If lack of coordination and associated inaction happens in one and the same country, think of the challenge of coordinating supervisory activities in the two dozen countries which count in today's globalized economy. Several experts are now suggesting that:

- *If* regulators really want to tighten up their supervision of bank activities, as they should do,
- *Then*, this would evidently require slaughtering some sacred cows of present-day supervision, like looking the other way when banks superleverage themselves.

The expansion of leverage in response to a financial environment of low nominal and often negative real interest rates (as in the US in

2002–2003), as well as of relatively low inflation and fast growth, has generated significant global vulnerabilities. It also weakened the banking system's defenses. Postmortem, it called into question:

- The process of securitization,
- The development of complex products, and
- The practice of arms-length transactions.

Indirectly, the practice of higher and higher gearing also raised the question of whether central banks should continue acting as "borrowers of last resort" (Chapter 2) with the risk of waking up the monster of inflation through the huge sums involved in injecting liquidity into the market. Policymakers should not think that the problems will stay on the desks of bankers, suggests Rodrigo Rato, former managing director of the International Monetary Fund (IMF).

5. Regulating derivatives and hedge funds: a case study

One of the major current problems with derivatives is the lack of clear-cut lines of supervision. Regulated by the Securities and Exchange Commission (SEC), securities firms run their derivatives businesses through subsidiaries that are outside the scope of the regulatory agency's powers. Therefore, as far back as June 1994, the then SEC chairman Arthur Levitt began negotiations with the then six largest derivatives dealers on Wall Street, namely CS First Boston, Goldman Sachs, Lehman Brothers, Merrill Lynch, Morgan Stanley, and Salomon Brothers, to create a set of voluntary standards that would govern activities in the derivatives market.

The idea of voluntary standards caused concern among some legislators because voluntary codes lack teeth. The SEC chairman countered that such arrangements have been effective before, and appeared anxious not to provoke a confrontation with embedded interests over the issue of derivatives. At the same time, however, Levitt warned that:

- The use of exotic financial products was inappropriate for some low-risk mutual funds, and
- Complex financial instruments should not be used without being fully understood by all parties.

On these premises, Arthur Levitt urged mutual funds to sell their holdings of risky derivatives.[11] This concern highlighted an SEC priority of better protection of small investors. But nothing really came out of these efforts because the Clinton Administration failed to stand behind the chairman of the Securities and Exchange Commission.

A few years down the line, the discussion about needed regulation of the derivatives market, particularly of over-the-counter (OTC) trading, got amplified. In 1998, the Commodity Futures Trading Commission (CFTC) issued a concept release suggesting that it might establish some regulation in regard to OTC derivatives. This was a major change from a policy established in early 1993 under then chair Dr Wendy Gramm, when:

- CFTC exempted much of the derivatives market from regulation, and
- Reportedly, did so on the theory that market professionals needed little oversight(!).

Within a year, this hands-off policy of 1993 proved wrong, paving the way for the surge in number and complexity of OTC derivatives trades. In October 1994, Mary Shapiro, the new CFTC chair, promised tougher policing of the derivatives market, but CFTC really moved towards derivatives regulation under Brooksley Born, who took office in August 1996.

During her nomination hearings, Brooksley Born raised the issue of the need to regulate the derivatives markets. In Congressional hearings in April 1997, Born warned that the professional markets exemption issued by Gramm could lead to widespread deregulation, restricting the government's power to protect against fraud, manipulation, financial excesses, and other dangers.

In May 1998 the CFTC issued its concept release about the need for regulation of the OTC derivatives market. This was followed by a wave of protests, not only by banks, brokers, and hedge funds, but also by the other regulators including the Fed, the SEC, and the Treasury Department – which, as critics said, were afraid that some order could be imposed on the bureaucratic chaos that loosely formed the regulatory landscape of the United States.

All sorts of embedded interests got in motion to oppose prudential supervision. One of the funny efforts to sidetrack Brooksley Born's initiative has been a study by the President's Working Group on Financial Markets, created after the 1987 stock market crash. Released in November 1999, this study:

- Concluded that the CFTC had no specific jurisdiction over the OTC derivatives market, and

- Urged Congress to clarify the lack of authority regarding over-the-counter traded derivatives.

In the wake of this report Born resigned and was replaced by William Rainer, formerly of Kidder Peabody, an investment bank. In the aftermath, the whole issue of OTC derivatives regulation was dead in the water, and on Wall Street this was hailed as a good outcome. Slowly however several of the experts started having second thoughts, not only about the need of regulating OTC derivatives but also (if not primarily) of regulating hedge funds – as the derivatives' major conduits.

Well into the twenty-first century, on 14 July 2004, the Securities and Exchange Commission decided that there was a need for hedge funds regulation. This decision was taken through a three-to-two vote by its five commissioners. William Donaldson, a former senior investment banker and SEC chairman, and the two Democratic Party members on SEC's board voted for regulation.

At the beginning of 2003, a year or so before this initiative, during his Senate confirmation hearings Donaldson highlighted potential abuses in the hedge fund industry, as a subject for the SEC to tackle. Intensive lobbying by the industry of highly leveraged financial institutions (HLFIs) had delayed the right decision using the (lightweight) argument that "the SEC should not be concentrating on an area traditionally reserved for 'sophisticated investors' who can look after themselves."

Surprisingly, even the Federal Reserve – one of the key US regulators – moved against the 14 July 2004 SEC vote on hedge funds. In a letter to Congress, Alan Greenspan stated that he saw no reason for regulating hedge funds. Coming from an intelligent, experienced, and well-informed person, also one who had already created a big bubble, this was quite a surprise.

Even more amazing was the fact that when in a subsequent Senate hearing Senator Sarbanes asked Greenspan about "that letter," the Federal Reserve chairman answered he did not recall having signed one. This led Sarbanes to exclaim: "Don't you recall?" (After consultation with his assistants, Greenspan confirmed that, indeed, he had signed such a letter.)

Conflicts of interest are the only way to interpret this wholesome resistance to regulation. William Donaldson did not want to close the hedge funds down. What SEC's ruling said was that hedge fund managers must register with the Securities and Exchange Commission, which any honorable trader should be happy to do. Registration allows financial inspections similar to those to which the banks are subjected – and as everybody knows, many hedge funds are off-balance-sheet outfits of commercial and investment banks.

Probably to ease the occult interests' anxiety, Donaldson said that registration would be used for targeted "sweeps" of the hedge fund industry. This meant small probes of particular types of behavior, which may represent risks for investors. As Harvey Goldschmid, one of the commissioners who backed Donaldson, aptly suggested, more work must be done by the SEC on how it would use the registration data to assess risk, because the hedge fund industry:

- Is vast and growing, and
- Definitely needs to be watched.

"What policy sense would it make for the SEC to turn a blind eye?" Goldschmid asked. But Paul Atkins, another commissioner who voted against the regulatory decision, said: "I will not ask taxpayers to foot the bill for a fishing expedition." In other terms, it is better to have the taxpayer foot the bill for a megacatastrophe like that of the subprimes, than to exercise prudential supervision. Lack of regulation is the best way of driving from one bubble to the next, and that's exactly what Greenspan did.

6. Watch over debt risk

According to the 77th Annual Report of the Bank for International Settlements (BIS), "there are a number of difficult and important questions facing central bankers, to which there are no agreed answers." A good example is the appropriate role of monetary and credit aggregates in the formulation of monetary policy. In the case of credit-driven boom–bust cycles, should central banks:

- Seek to prevent the buildup of imbalances, or
- Spend taxpayers' money to clean up after the bust?

Reading between the lines of these two bullets, the careful reader will detect that, as in 2007 central bankers and market players discovered the hard way, debt is more dangerous than equity because it is a highly leveraged liability. Its securitized form is widely spread, its creditworthiness is uncertain, and this makes it much harder to track and value than classical-type loans.

The difficulty of tracking and valuing securitized debt is increased further by the fact that, as again demonstrated by the July/August 2007 subprime crisis, money markets are more worried than equity markets about how the credit crunch may finish – though in the end equity markets fall like a stone, as they did in the second half of January 2008 and ensuing months. Particularly challenging are the:

- Monitoring of debt risk which is sliced and sold, and
- Repricing of mortgage-backed and other asset-backed securities, under stress conditions

Both are a complex business whose tools are still in their infancy; and the reaction of central banks in righting the balances is far from certain. Major market worries during the last crisis have been the decisions of, and the role played by, the monetary institutions. Will they downplay the risk of inflation, and aggressively lower interest rates? Will they act *as if* gamblers are too big to fail? Or will they hold the line and avoid moral hazard? (See also section 3 of this chapter.)

Since 1980 the majority of Western central banks have justified the notion that monetary policy should be run by independent technicians rather than by politicians, because monetary policy and bank supervision are technical enterprises – and independence of opinion matters. However, July/August 2007 and the following months demonstrated the limitations of the methods and tools central bankers and supervisors of financial institutions use to conduct their business and steer the ship in the right direction. Examples are:

- Targets in money supply which year-after-year overshot,
- Capital adequacy controls which do not account for bank liquidity,
- Mathematical models whose assumptions and inputs are biased, with the result they serve precious little in risk control – or else are altogether misleading.

Not only are past policies and practices unable to meet financial realities in a twenty-first century setting, but even the theoretical foundations of central bankers' monetary policies and intervention practices don't make for unanimity. The huge increase in money supply is disquieting; while the aim of avoiding the boom–bust cycle, which damages the credit system, has not been achieved.

Several economists now maintain that *if* inflation is to remain the monetary policymakers' target, *then* its definition must be recast. The events of 2004 to 2007 demonstrated clearly the need to extent inflation's definition to include:

- All commodities,
- Commercial and household real estate,
- Equity of publicly quoted companies, and
- The relatively novel idea that debt is sliced, diced, and sold as an asset.

Debt is *not* an asset in the etymological sense of the world, even if our economy operates largely through borrowed money, securitizes the receivables, sugarcoats them with high credit ratings, and sells them as assets. This misrepresentation of debt increases the market's exposure, because every new default adds on to previous defaults and together they trigger an avalanche of losses feeding the beast of *stagflation* (combining stagnation in the GDP with inflation). They also cast doubt on:

- How well central bankers have discharged their twin duty of financial stability and price stability, and
- How much they are in charge of the multi-trillion-dollar global markets, which have sprung up through loan conversion into marketable instruments with plenty of default risk.

As the Fed moved to cut interest rates in late 2007 and early 2008, several experts suggested that the bad news for America's economy was not good news for inflation. This judgment was based on the fact that the Fed rode to the rescue of the financial market both by injecting liquidity and by cutting the discount rate and the funds rate. Just like the European Central Bank (ECB) and the Bank of England, the Federal Reserve faced a moral dilemma: "Cut rates now or let investors take more pain?"

The answers given by the ECB and the Fed to this most basic question diverged. The former stuck to its guns, and stated clearly that it was its duty to fight a rising inflation rather than playing with interest rates. By contrast, the Fed cut interest rates in successive installments, well below the prevailing inflation rate.

The market's reaction was mixed. The most aggressive US investment bankers and traders, who had lost a packet by speculating with securitized subprimes, asked for more rate cuts. They also accused the ECB of not playing the low-interest-rates game; which is totally absurd. At the World Economic Forum at Davos in Switzerland, however, several economists were of the opinion that by giving in to the speculators Ben

Bernanke had not run out of bubbles – and that he was preparing the next one.

Years down the line, economists and financial historians will debate whether aggressive interest rate cuts have been the right course. On one side, the Fed could not be insensitive to the fact that the general turmoil has reached beyond the US mortgage market. But on the other hand, with their self-inflicted wounds, banks have raced with devastating speed to hit the heart of the financial system including:

- The concept of creditworthiness,
- The interbank market, and
- The market for central bank reserves.

Globalization, too, contributed to the 2007/2008 credit crisis, by offering a myriad of ways to hide assumed credit risk. All this can be added up in one concept: the inability of all established regulatory agencies to control a highly changed financial environment, which ranged from short-term influences on inflation and money supply to long-term effects which affect market risk, credit risk, liquidity risk, and the promotion of new bubbles.

7. The global need for new financial regulation

Whether it exercises a regulatory function in commodities or in financial markets, a supervisory authority is charged with assuring safety, stability, and the observance of rules aimed to ascertain that participants are adequately and appropriately behaving as well as protected. But since the advent of globalization and the stellar rise of derivatives, there has been a great deal of concern regarding:

- The heterogeneity of financial supervision in global financial markets,
- The too rapid pace of growth in derivative instruments and their unknowns,
- The increasing sophistication and complexity in instrument design and trading, and
- The policy of rewarding bank traders and executives by compensation mechanisms encouraging risk-taking at the expense of financial stability.

In spite of their lavish compensation, or because of it, many senior bank executives are falling behind in their knowledge of how their banks deal, or they are even unaware of the risk involved in structures created by high-powered trading desks that are under their watch. Additionally, few board members appreciate that the bank's clients are being sold financial instruments that they do not understand, and therefore cannot manage.

Evidence that a new regulatory system is required to assure orderly and secure markets, as well as appropriate use of new financial products, has been provided time and again – most of all by the 2007 credit crisis. Ironically, prior to *this* financial debacle, one would often hear the argument that risk had been "diminished" because it was dispersed more widely than ever before across:

- Geographical areas,
- Financial institutions, and
- A growing range of investors.

This ill-defined dispersion system, which sprang, so to speak, out of a blue sky, was seen as able to absorb the stresses of a rapidly growing risk quotient, particularly in credit exposure. The crash of the subprimes and systemic risk it brought along did away with such a silly argument. It also documented that, if anything, the "wide dispersion of risk" has made matters much worse, not better. Economists, as well as central bankers and regulators, are now saying that it is hard to know exactly where the risks are when:

- They have been divided up,
- Structured in a variety of ways,
- Repackaged under unjustifiably high credit ratings, and
- Sold off to all sorts of different *companies and people* in the global market.

The credit crisis precipitated by the subprimes brought into perspective the need for rethinking and revamping important regulatory issues that have been wanting for a number of years. At top of the list is greater transparency by the banking industry and, most particularly, by *nonbanks* such as hedge funds, private equity funds, buyout firms, conduits, SIVs, and more. According to expert opinions, after the debacle, all sorts of financial entities, including most evidently credit institutions, will be asked to provide more information on:

- Capital reserves for incremental default risk.
- How the different exposures they assume are integrated,

- How these exposures are valued and managed, and
- Which action top management will take when the main risks are found to be off-balance-sheet.

But will that really happen? The theme of the first two bullets has been discussed often but has not yet found its way into prudential supervision; valuation, the third bullet, is a sham (see Chapter 6). The 2007 IMF Global Financial Stability report put in the following terms what is needed to confront the challenge posed by the fourth bullet: only by disclosing fully their interrelationships with asset managers, conduits, and special-purpose entities will investors be able to assess the true creditworthiness of the institutions with which they deal.

The IMF is not saying so explicitly, but to be successful such disclosures, and regulatory control over them, have to be set within a *global framework* – with direct authority to see them through and take corrective action. It is not sufficient to have American-only, European-only, or Asian-only regulatory rules. George Soros is right when he asks for a global sheriff (Chapter 3).

Much can also be gained by becoming acquainted with and learning from the great minds of the past. The way Bernard Baruch put it: "What registers in the stock market's fluctuations are not the events themselves but the human reaction to these events, how millions of individual men and women feel these events may affect the future."[12] Any regulatory rules and actions that forget about the people and only reward the fat cats are doomed to failure.

Along with concern for the people comes the need to tighten banking regulation so banks have to hold more capital in respect of off-balance-sheet positions, conduits, special investment vehicles, and other controlled entities that might fail, damaging the banks' reputation and financial condition. To this effect, on 12 October 2007 the Basel Committee on Banking Supervision issued a consultative document, "Guidelines, for Computing Capital for Incremental Default Risk in the Trading Book."

(The issue of an incremental default risk charge (IDRC) to be incorporated into the trading book capital regime had first been raised with the Basel/IOSCO Agreement of July 2005; this had been a revision to the 1996 Market Risk Amendment. The requirement that it posed was that banks show model specific risk to measure and hold capital against default risk that is *incremental* to any default risk captured in the bank's value at risk (VAR) model. But VAR itself is an unreliable measure.)

Banks need the extra capital to confront the risks taken with derivatives, but extra capital by itself does not ensure adequate liquidity. Moreover, as a recent financial publication notes, many regulators are now uneasy about the reliance on rating agencies for risk weightings under Basel II.[13]

Probably reflecting the lessons learned from the disappearance of liquidity in the aftermath of the subprimes crisis, Basel's consultative document reserves an important role to the *liquidity horizon*, accounting for the fact that positions in the trading book tend to be actively traded and more liquid than positions in the banking book. By definition, the liquidity horizon represents the time required to:

* Sell the positions, or
* Hedge all material credit risk factors in a stressed market.

There should as well be clauses and penalties guarding against repetition of the same errors. According to informed sources, in the aftermath of the Société Générale scandal France is preparing to impose punishing fines on banks that fail to monitor trading risks. In Germany, Thomas Mirow, deputy finance minister, said that: "An international approach would be much better [but] if this proves impossible, then we must act at the European level. And if that fails too for political or objective reasons, then we must act nationally."[14]

Additionally, government authorities who care about the proper functioning of the financial system want tougher accounting rules that would prevent banks from shifting certain categories of assets off their balance sheet, and stop other approaches being invented to generate bonuses and hide the risks being assumed. In the background lies the fact that free markets depend on capital and confidence in the counterparty – and the way confidence goes, capital goes.

8. The important role of accounting standards

Even the best intentions of regulators will not bear fruits without close collaboration with accounting standards bodies. It's good news that both the Financial Accounting Standards Board (FASB) in the US and the International Accounting Standards Board (IASB) in Europe (whose standards are also applied in many other parts of the world) are up to the level expected of them.

In September 2006, the more clear-eyed investors paid a lot of attention to the just-released *fair-value* principle, guiding disclosures under

Statement of Financial Accounting Standards 157. SFAS 157 requires that banks sort out their assets and liabilities into three main categories:

- *Level 1* assets and liabilities are those whose prices are readily observable in active markets. An example is exchange-traded equities.
- *Level 2* are quoted prices in markets that are not active. Most OTC derivatives, certain mortgage loans, and infrequently traded corporates are examples.
- *Level 3* are prices or valuations that require inputs both significant to the fair-value measurement and unobservable. Marking to model falls in this class; assets include FX options, CDOs, CDSs, complex derivatives, and more.

Additionally, SFAS 157 prohibits the use of block discounts for large positions of unrestricted financial instruments that trade in an active market, and requires an issuer to incorporate changes in its own credit spreads when determining the fair value of its liabilities.

In February 2007, the FASB issued SFAS 159, providing a fair-value option election. It allows companies to irrevocably elect fair value as the initial and subsequent measurement attribute for certain financial assets and liabilities, with changes in fair value recognized in earnings as they occur. It also permits the fair-value option election on an instrument basis:

- At initial recognition of an asset or liability, or
- Upon an event that gives rise to a new basis of accounting for that instrument.

Several financial analysts see these disclosure procedures as being only a starting point for understanding the banks' activities in complex financial products, as well as for developing the kind of control action that should be associated with them.

In Europe, analysts take heart from the fact that European banks will be using the new IFRS 7 in their 2007 financial accounts. This replaces IAS 30 and 32 and deals with the disclosure requirements in relation to all risks arising from financial instruments. IFRS 7, paragraph 27, encourages European banks to give US GAAP-style disclosure on Level 1, 2, and 3 assets and liabilities. It also goes further than SFAS 157 in requiring banks to provide a sensitivity analysis reflecting reasonably possible changes in the value of unobservable parameters for Level 3 assets.

As the reader can appreciate from these references, the new financial reporting rules represent an improvement over the old, which traditionally required that a bank's accounts record the value of an asset at its historic cost through the accruals method. Even the first versions of fair-value accounting left lots of loopholes for gaming the financial reporting system. Many complex derivatives, such as securitized mortgage-backed instruments, were marked-to-myth.

With the subprimes crisis, banks found out the hard way that gaming the system was not in their favor. When the Bear Stearns hedge funds ran into trouble, their bankers tried to sell their collateral, which was mostly in the form of mortgage-backed derivatives. But entities expected to act as counterparties were worried that:

- There was no way to know the value of these assets, and
- If derivatives were sold into a falling market, their low price would set an ugly precedent for their own portfolios, with fire-sale prices becoming the standard.

Models are supposed to show the price an asset would fetch in a sale. But in an illiquid market, a big sale can itself drive down prices, the more so if investors and bankers supposed to be buyers think that the asset contains lots of toxic waste.

At the eye of the storm lies the fact that the market is finally waking up to the limitations of models, one of the most basic being that they are easy to manipulate. RiskData, a consultancy, studied more than a thousand hedge funds and concluded that nearly a third of funds trading illiquid securities were smoothing the results of their models, so as to iron out too much volatility in their books.[15]

Faced with marking to myth, regulators are tightening their fair-value requirements as well as their rules. Apart from Levels 1, 2, and 3, several start to require that banks examine assumptions and disclose them. Additionally, achieving the right valuation of complex financial instruments calls for a substantial amount of training, and many bank executives have not received extensive instruction in modeling assumptions and results. This, too, is a challenge that needs to be met.

The existence of global accounting standards and supervisory rules will also provide a level field when matters come to an international legal action. There is always the risk of international court proceedings against Wall Street firms and other big banks whose managements failed in their responsibilities. Some experts think it is likely that 2009 will see an alarming number of court proceedings for damages.

Banks have survived the earthquake of 2007/2008 through the use of Scotch Tape, ribbons, and office clips, but in reality there are a horde of hidden, tragic, and difficult to resolve problems. The reasons for court cases revolve around the massive destruction of banks' assets, which belong to their clients and creditors. Ingredients are:

- Large banks which stand at the doorstep of insolvency,
- The relentless coming to the surface of mortgage bonds with massive losses,
- A further falling to pieces of the US real estate market,
- The persistently frozen credit industry, and
- Consumers who lost their houses in the great subprimes scam, and no longer have piggy banks to continue spending.

The US government itself could be subject to claims for damages. Through the fatal low-interest policy of Alan "Double-Bubble" Greenspan, the American financial market expanded much more than the rest of the economy, with the result that the financial industry and the economy got unstuck. According to expert opinions, many big banks would be already in bankruptcy proceedings if their securities were correctly priced.

Furthermore, the steadily depreciating US dollar has fueled a huge rise in oil prices and those of other dollar-denominated commodities. By 2008, the currency exchange problem has become an international political issue not only for Europe but also for Asia and for the global market as well. The discard of financial history by the Fed with the 14 March 2008 Bear Stearns bailout, to the tune of a $30 billion guarantee, did not improve the dollar's prospects but made more likely a new debacle of *stagflation*.

In his article "Warten auf den Dollar Crash" (Waiting for the Crash of the Dollar), Henrik Müller says that a central banker recently told him: "We are confronted with forces which we don't have under control. It could be that we will literally be overrun by investors."[16] The likelihood of this happening is not as remote as some people would like to think, in spite of the dollar's rise to the exchange rate of 1.25 to the euro in mid November 2008; and if it happens its aftereffect on the global economy will be crippling.

9
Solvency, Liquidity, Asset-Backed Paper, and the Carry Trade

1. Capital requirements

Regulators, members of the board of directors, and the public must be confident that the capital requirements of a credit institution are determined in a way that enhances safety and soundness, not only of the company itself but of the banking system as a whole. While capital adequacy regulations should neither penalize banks nor artificially distort the competitive playing field, they should assure the bank's survival in case of crisis – precisely when core capital is the most important. In terms of capital adequacy, banks suffer from two catastrophic risks:

- Insolvency, and
- Illiquidity.

A financial institution is *solvent* when its assets exceed its liabilities. It is *liquid* when it has enough cash, and other short-term assets, to meet legal requirements by its counterparties: depositors, bondholders, lenders, correspondent banks, and tax authorities. Sometimes, illiquidity can turn into insolvency. (More on solvency and liquidity in section 2 of this chapter.)

Whether established by national or by multinational authorities (such as the Basel Committee on Banking Supervision), capital adequacy requirements for credit institutions target resources to be reserved for credit risk and market risk events; therefore, their goal is solvency. Identification of the need for liquidity reserves is more recent, having been brought home dramatically with the 2007 subprimes debacle.

In terms of capital adequacy required by regulatory authorities, commercial bankers have often complained that the standards created in 1988, known as Basel I,[1] keep capital levels too high. Historically speaking, using pre-World-War-I references, this is untrue. But Basel II critics have every reason to say that reducing capital, through the use of an unwarranted dispensation (by regulators and models) makes banks more vulnerable during a crisis or a major economic downturn.

This is by no means a theoretical argument. As a 2006 US study has shown, Basel II capital rules would lead to wide and inconsistent drops in regulatory capital. At thirteen of the twenty-six banks participating to this study, capital fell by 26 percent or more. Subsequently, the crisis of July/August 2007 provided plenty of evidence that, rather than being too high,

- Capital adequacy with Basel I was too low, and
- The concern for funding liquidity (see section 3 of this chapter) was not on the radar screen.

It is interesting to note, at least for the record, that one of the issues on which the aforementioned 2006 US capital adequacy study focused was *how* banks might calculate current risks, and the resulting capital requirements using Basel II rules. On average, the banks thought that Basel II would allow them to decrease their regulatory capital by about 15 percent, reaching that conclusion by means of estimates which gamed the system.

But while American commercial banks have been promoters of value at risk (VAR) and Basel II model-based rules, American regulators did not buy the Basel II package because capital adequately was falling "well short of the level of reliability that will be necessary to allow supervisors to accept those estimates for risk-based capital purposes," said John Dugan, US Comptroller of the Currency, whose job includes bank supervision.[2]

A good deal of evidence behind the unreliability of capital adequacy estimates revolves around the cherry-picking of correlations and other factors that banks are typically choosing in "calculating" *their* capital requirements. Even if banks manage to standardize their calculations, the Basel II rules will still be a cause for concern, according to Donald Powell, former chairman of the Federal Deposit Insurance Corp (FDIC). He told the US Senate that Basel II's formulas for regulatory capital:

- Are inherently calibrated to produce large reductions in risk-based capital requirements, and

- They will be leading to a far lower standard of capital adequacy than the one then in existence (Basel I).

Europeans have discarded Basel II's shortcomings wholesale, so much so that in 2006 the European Union, which has no banking experience, passed legislation to implement the new capital accord. American regulators, by contrast, have been worried on three counts:[3]

- They think the Basel II rules are too slack, allowing banks to reduce capital too far;
- They reckon that banks will not be able to implement the rules reliably without a few more years' practice; and
- They fear that the rules will give the biggest banks too much of an advantage over small banks.

The hypothesis underpinning these concerns has been that big banks, using the internal-ratings-based (IRB) approach and high technology, would be updating their risk calculations second by second, laying off assets that tied up a lot of capital. By contrast, small banks, without the same technology and diversity of assets in which to trade, might end up with a concentration of the worst-priced risks.

We now know that lust and greed saw to it that it did not work at all that way. In the 2004 to 2007 timeframe, because of aggressive policies and fat commissions, big banks accumulated a great deal of toxic waste and finally had to go hat in hand to sovereign wealth funds (SWFs; Chapter 2) because they had depleted their capital resources. Small banks, by contrast, did not enter the big stakes and preserved their capital.

The unprecedented miscalculation of risk that led to the severe credit crunch of July/August 2007 put Basel II under scrutiny before it had even had a chance to be tested in real life. Apart the fact that using supposedly risk-sensitive models to compute capital adequacy proved to be unreliable, the credit rating by independent agencies has become suspect because of too liberally assigned AAA credit. Independent credit rating, another Basel II basic premise, came under the magnifying glass.

A further weakness of Basel II arose from the fact that commercial bankers arm-twisted regulators to allow them to use in a massive way instruments they did not quite understand in terms of further-out exposure, such as credit derivatives. Here again, the events of mid 2007 demonstrated that the complexity of CDOs and CDSs significantly increased the banks' difficulties in knowing where they stood in assumed risk.

Yet, in spite of all these misgivings and loopholes in its implementation, Basel II is an improvement over Basel I; but it is not a holistic solution. A growing body of experts now suggest that Basel II must be seriously upgraded, factoring in not only a dependable, uniform way of computing capital requirements for credit risk but in addition:

- Liquidity risk,
- Model risk,
- Credit rating risk, and
- Management risk.

None of the exposures embedded into these bullets has been taken care of in Basel II, probably on the wrong premise that bankers have got better at banking, turning it into a less risky business. *If* this was the assumption, *then* it has been shattered by the subprimes crisis of 2007, which has underlined the need for the whole system of bank solvency-and-liquidity to undergo a very thorough revamp.

2. Solvency and liquidity

Briefly defined in section 1 of this chapter, *solvency* refers to an entity's ability to meet obligations such as interest cost, repayment schedules, trading commitments, lines of credit, guarantees, and other assumed engagements in the present and in the longer term. Leaving aside hybrids that are a cheat, the most important elements in judging a company's solvency are:

- Equity capital, and
- Debt capital, or gearing.

Equity capital is much less risky for a bank than all other forms of capital, because shareholders receive dividends only at the discretion of the board. Moreover, equity capital is first on the line in case of adversity, if there is a need to cover creditors' claims or face other commitments.

Debt capital is a different name for *liabilities*. Companies leverage themselves with debt capital, often for tax avoidance reasons, but fail to account for risks associated with borrowed money. Unwillingness or inability to meet debt capital requirements usually leads creditors to taking legal action, which may force the entity to bankruptcy.

Another fundamental problem with the solvency of credit institutions is that they make promises they do not expect to have to keep. Many of these come in the form of *contingent liabilities*, which require a bank to come to the support of its clients beyond the level of granted loans. Under certain conditions, a lot of bills associated with contingent liabilities come due at once.

For instance as the July/August 2007 crisis gained momentum, experts estimated that between $380 and $400 billion of loans and bonds linked to pending leveraged buyouts needed to be shifted. The speed of market deterioration surprised many, but did not alter the fact that banks faced bridge loans to private-equity buyers with a typical 1-to-2-month holding period.

- When the markets were buzzing in 2006 and early 2007, banks assumed nothing could go wrong in a short time.
- But with the subprimes debacle and stock market bust, they faced the prospect of having to keep large amounts of debt on their own books indefinitely and at a loss.

Opinions differ on how badly this has damaged the banks' balance sheets. One way to measure the loss has been to rely on the discounted price at which leveraged loans are trading in the secondary market. The problem is that the market price of such loans sank too fast, as investors and fellow bankers tightened their purses.

Moreover, beyond the buyout issue banks faced the conduits and SIVs earthquake. Investors who bought commercial paper by a horde of conduits and structured investment vehicles suddenly decided it was not worth the risk. In the aftermath, many banks have found funding of their commitments, including securitized subprime, either impossible or achievable only at exorbitant levels.

As far as market players were concerned, the failure in *solvency assurance* has been outstanding. Banks are supposed to know the exposure of their peers, but opacity had changed the rules of the game. Worse, none really knew the extent to which it would end up on the credit hook, and therefore all banks were hoarding their capital rather than lending it.

Beyond solvency, in the timeframe in reference, there has been a severe liquidity challenge. As the careful reader will remember from section 1 of this chapter, *liquidity* refers to an entity's ability to meet its current obligations. Therefore, it is a relative concept, having to do with the size and relationships of liabilities due, and with current assets that presumably provide the source of funds to meet such commitments. In the banking industry, a liquidity crisis happens when counterparties such as:

- Depositors,
- Suppliers,
- Creditor banks,
- Other lenders, and
- The central bank (which might have advanced funds)

ask for their money, and such demands cannot be met by the illiquid institution. When depositors get wind of stress facing the bank where they trusted their money, there is a run on the bank's deposits. This is one of the reasons the Great Depression of 1929–1933 was worse than it might have been.

A liquidity crisis and the resulting illiquidity can be defined alternatively as the difficulty of selling assets at a reasonable price. In nearly every financial crisis, a generalized illiquidity is at the heart of fire sales of assets, as well as of market turmoil. To better appreciate the aftereffect of subprimes on illiquidity, it is important to remember that the financial system has been significantly transformed with the emergence of:

- New players like hedge funds, and
- New instruments such as structured products.

Bankers thought that they had solved their liquidity challenges for good because of the freedom to securitize practically everything they held in their books. But what looked like a highly sophisticated strategy turned into a nightmare. Worse yet, banks did what they should have never have done: they borrowed short-term in liquid form and invested the proceeds in longer-term illiquid assets – inviting upon themselves *mismatch risk*.

The market, too, added to the effect of the bankers' miscalculation. With the closing down of commercial paper funding (section 5 of this chapter), as investors abandoned risky deals and ran for cover, big banks, their conduits, and structured investment vehicles confronted a wave of illiquidity. Its effects have been rippling through the banking system:

- Forced liquidations have pushed down the price of assets, and
- As SIVs have gone to the wall, banks have ended on the hook.

The irony associated with the aforementioned events is that, from a risk control viewpoint, the much-touted advantage of the modern financial system that risk is widely dispersed went out of the window. Banks whose management lacked foresight have been saddled with the cost of funding their SIVs and other off-balance-sheet vehicles, as they look desperately around for a savior:

- In the early twentieth century, liquidity crises were solved by the emergence of a confident buyer with deep pockets, like J. Pierpont Morgan in 1907.
- In the early twenty-first century, assets accumulators like pension funds and insurance companies were thought of as having deep pockets – but they don't have sufficient flexibility, while hedge funds are facing tighter funding and the prospect of redemptions.

The market's uncertainty has been further increased by the lack of transparency in the modern financial system. Because of opacity no one is sure who owns what, and hence investors have been treating all counterparties with suspicion.

The banks might have hoped that the liquidity problems would take care of themselves. They did not. SIVs, banks, and hedge funds also bet on forcing the hands of central banks and governments to come to their rescue. Instead, the sovereign wealth funds of Asia and the Middle East took advantage of the Western banking industry's self-inflicted wounds.

3. Liquidity fears

Back in 2002, Dr Tommaso Padoa-Schioppa, then a board member of the European Central Bank (ECB), and subsequently Italy's finance minister, brought attention to the fact that the liquidity of financial markets had grown in importance. With this, he gave the prescient warning that deepening of the markets has improved the ability of banks to access funds in normal times, but liquidity may be more prone to dry up when it is most needed.

At the time, nobody took notice of Padoa-Schioppa's warning, as rock-bottom interest rates created the fantasy that capital will always be readily available and dirt-cheap. Other warnings, too, went unhealed till July/August 2007 when the highly leveraged subprimes bubble blew up.

For instance, in 2006 Moody's Investors Service, the credit rating agency, cautioned that some British banks were exposed to the risk of disruption in wholesale markets because they were increasing their loans faster than they could gather the deposits to back them. This, too, did not raise eyebrows, but in 2007 Northern Rock offered itself as an example on how fallacious this policy of "I see nothing, I hear nothing" can be – as well as underlining that two types of liquidity must be given plenty of attention:

- *Funding liquidity* is linked to the quality of an entity's assets.
- *Market liquidity* shows the ease with which assets can be sold without losing their value.

The problem with funding liquidity is that holding low-yielding liquid assets is not something banks want to do. They would rather leverage themselves and their assets, to earn more money. The problem with market liquidity is that when there is lack of confidence it disappears, making fire sales more likely.

In good times, few regulators and even fewer commercial and investment bankers express liquidity fears, even if everyone knows that the risk appetite of all market players continues to increase and that one day there is going to be a big problem. This happened in August 2007 and the subsequent months, as investors and bankers took fright at their exposure to credit markets and decided to:

- Sell first, and
- Ask questions later.

Liquidity fears were the biggest hurdle in the issuing reappraisal of risk. Those with memories of the 1980s and 1990s recalled that the lack of funding possibilities ultimately drove Drexel Burnham Lambert, the high-flying junk bonds bank, into bankruptcy (in February 1990) and led to the implosion of Long-Term Capital Management (LTCM) in 1988. Market fears over liquidity were exacerbated by the fact that investment banks increasingly stuffed their portfolios with illiquid assets like:

- Bridge loans,
- Private equity investments, and
- Novel, complex, and rarely traded derivative instruments.

The housing bubble also saw to it that the US mortgage giants posed a clear systemic threat. The portfolios of retained mortgages and mortgage-backed securities of Fannie Mae and Freddie Mac (the two government-sponsored enterprises of the mortgage market) added up to over $1.4 trillion concentrated in two institutions. Worse was the fact that both of them lacked discipline because of their implicit mission.

- No matter how much risk they take or how they manage it, they can borrow at rock-bottom interest rates, and
- If they got into trouble, taxpayers and banks would be on the hook because banks may hold as much of Fanny's and Freddie's debt as they like.

Many American credit institutions banks have Fanny Mae and Freddie Mac liabilities that exceed their regulatory capital, which makes the two government-sponsored enterprises the arbiters of whether the US banking industry prospers or sinks. This is evidently ominous, because even with big capital markets banks are still central to the economy's fortunes as:

- Providers of credit, and
- Processors of payments.

Liquidity legislation and regulation of the banking system should definitely account for credit institutions' mismatch between liquid debt and illiquid assets, which makes them susceptible to sudden losses of funding. In a panic, individual depositors have an incentive to withdraw their cash, even if collectively they and the bank might be better off if they held fast – which is, however, contrary to human nature.

Integrally part of liquidity legislation and regulation must also be the knowledge that banks are less than perfect providers of cash (and of several other services for that matter). This is important because the liquidity plans of many banks are flawed, if for no other reason than because:

- Demand for liquidity is unpredictable, and
- Holding liquid assets means forgoing other more profitable investments.

These two issues, as well as coordination difficulties which create sporadic cash shortages, call for regulatory remedies which go beyond capital requirements for solvency reasons. Experts suggest that for liquidity purposes coverage has to be large and repayment swift, which is easier said than done.

Critics suggest that, as commercial banks have discovered, their profitability is founded largely on an excessive reliance on central banks as liquidity providers. Should the current regime continue to prevail then much bigger future shocks would require even larger interventions by central banks.

This leads to the proposal currently under discussion to implement consistent monitoring of banks' liquidity position over the economic cycle by supervisory authorities. A system also be in place for assessing whether banks have enough liquidity "in the future," under a scenario which is based on outliers, extreme events, and stress probability of default (SPD; more on stress testing in section 5 of this chapter).

4. Liquidity management

In 2000, the Basel Committee published a document, "Sound Practices for Managing Liquidity Risk in Banking Organizations." In December 2006, it established a Working Group on Liquidity (WGL) which after the July/August 2007 events found that while the year 2000 guidance remains relevant, there are many areas that warrant updating and strengthening.

One of the several interesting findings of WGL post-subprimes is that the contraction of liquidity in structured product and interbank markets, as well as an increased probability of off-balance-sheet commitments coming onto banks' balance sheets, has led to severe funding liquidity strains, at least for some banks. Moreover, financial innovation and globalizations have transformed the nature of liquidity.

- The product range of the securitization market has been broadened and its growth accelerated as the originate-to-distribute model became widespread, and
- The complexity of financial instruments has increased, making liquidity estimates so much more demanding.

The market crash has been a sad ending to the frenzy of innovation around debt and securitization, which got out of hand. Supposedly to be bought by those best able to manage them, credit risks ended up with those seduced by yields whose exposure they did not understand, and who have been utterly unable to be in charge of their liquidity.

The events which followed the subprimes crisis of July/August 2007 have shattered the theory that financial innovation allows banks and other entities to obtain liquidity from previously illiquid assets, at no extra cost or risk, because at the same time such policies also make them more dependent on the proper functioning and stability of financial markets. Quite to the contrary, as market events documented:

- Innovative instruments are leading banks to building up an inventory of assets that have to be financed, and
- The ability of banks to mobilize other parts of their portfolios is limited, particularly under stress conditions (section 5 of this chapter).

Therefore, both from the perspective of regulators and from that of commercial and investment banks, liquidity must be managed continuously to ensure that the firm can survive a crisis – whether the background reason is an extreme market event, a local disruption affecting the banking industry, or a problem unique to an individual big entity. Generally, though not always, companies unable to meet their liabilities when due:

- Do not have sufficient assets of adequate quality to borrow against, or
- Their liquid assets to be sold for raising immediate cash are inadequate, while a fire sale may severely damage their value.

As these reasons suggest, well-governed institutions know that they must manage their liquidity position with foresight, aim to ride out a crisis without damaging their franchise, and avoid having to go hat in hand to likely lenders, as happened in 2007 with Citigroup, Merrill Lynch, UBS, and many other financial companies. The long-term stability and security of a bank's assets helps in protecting its liquidity position in the event of a crisis.

The practice of proactive liquidity management is relatively new, but not the idea behind it. In his 1872 *Lombard Street*, Walter Bagehot urged the Bank of England to stave off a panic by lending quickly, freely, and readily – but at a penalty rate of interest – to any bank that can offer good securities as collateral. At the time, this was criticized as a mischievous doctrine, but today it has become common practice (save for the penalty rate).

While Bagehot's theory might have become conventional wisdom among central banks, commercial and investment banks running at the twelfth hour for emergency liquidity assistance are typically those poorly governed. The fact not so often discussed is that their liquidity planning has been dismal – and as Aldous Huxley once said, facts do not cease to exist because they are ignored.

A sound approach to liquidity management will be holistic, covering all branches and subsidiaries, to assure that the credit institution always has sufficient liquidity to meet liabilities when due, under both normal and stressed conditions, without incurring unacceptable losses or risking damage to its market standing. This requires a steady assessment of:

- All commitments,
- Expected cash flows, and
- The level of high-grade collateral that could be used to raise additional funding.

Good governance requires that the bank's liquidity position is assessed and managed under a variety of potential scenarios encompassing both normal and stressed market conditions in the short, medium, and longer terms. Intraday, daily, weekly, monthly, quarterly, and annual liquidity positions, representing the net cumulative funding requirement for a specific day, must be projected under conservation assumptions,

- Providing a cumulative cash ladder against assumed commitments, and
- Seeing to it that this is subject to normal tolerances and stress loss limits.

By contrast, bad governance (of which we saw plenty of examples in 2007) forgets about proactive and rigorous liquidity management, depending on the central bank's emergency liquidity assistance (ELA) by injection of liquidity into the market which become a headline event. Classically, this is done by allowing individual banks to borrow from the monetary institution against adequate collateral, but in March 2008 the quality of collateral posted with central banks deteriorated so much that, in the words of an Italian banker, it resembled uncollected garbage piling up in the streets of Naples.

As the 2007/2008 events have tended to suggest, at least theoretically, injecting liquidity in a hurry has been an exceptional and temporary assistance to an illiquid credit institution, but even so it carries with it *moral hazard*. Risk-prone banks can now count on a *deus ex machina* to pull them up from under, so that they don't need to pay attention to liquidity management.

Notice that this is not a critique of liquidity injection as such, but of the way commercial and investment banks manage their liquidity.

"Manage" is of course a misnomer, because what risk-prone banks have done is to exploit a gap in regulations (section 1 of this chapter) and get the wrong investments on their balance sheet – even if they knew that the risks were great and the returns pitiful.

Confronted by the commercial banks' excesses, and wanting regulatory oversight, central banks had to act, and they tried to ensure that the interbank market, which lubricates the financial system by moving cash to where it is most needed, would continue to perform its functions. (Apart from credit, the interbank market defines the price that banks charge each other for short-term lending.) When this failed, they reverted to inflationary policies.

Critics looked at these liquidity injections as being risky moves, because of the precedent they establish, over and above the likelihood of firing up inflation. In July/August 2007, the global economy was still accelerating, with robust growth. Monetary policy was still considered accommodative,[4] outside the US and Britain, and with liquidity growth remaining rapid, central banks had also to look after their other two main functions:

- Assuring financial stability, and
- Promoting price stability in their jurisdiction.

Both of these functions have been suddenly downgraded. The pros say that injecting liquidity had much to do with a market psychology that had turned negative almost overnight. Critics answer that this type of intervention has its limits, feeding the debate on whether it is better to continue increasing the interest rate to stop inflation or to lower the interest rate to please the overleveraged market, and risk sending the value of money to the abyss?

The jury is still out on what might be the better policy. Where there is agreement, more or less, is that the markets will not recover until their players believe the banks have credibly owned up to their losses. At the current pace of the clean-up this is no short-term project.

5. Liquidity stress testing

The banking crisis of the subprimes has shown the need to change directives, methods, and tools for risk management. Future cash flow requirements must be established under both normal and stress conditions, even if dynamic cash flow estimates are a challenge under normal market conditions, as they require to draw information from all types of banking operations. But normal conditions are not enough in assessing the impact of extreme events on the availability of funding liquidity.

- Stress testing is an important part of every liquidity control operation, and
- The stress testing culture must become an integral part of sound governance.

Indeed, the better-managed banks perform regular stress tests covering credit rating downgrades as well as unfavorable market conditions. This is done market-wide, in specific segments and in connection with the institution's portfolio of holdings. Very few institutions, however, apply similar principles to liquidity tests.

Assumptions connected to stress conditions should range from unexpected business interruptions to loss of access to unsecured funding; diminished access to secured financing; runoff in bought money (not only in deposits); and other cash outflows. Experimenters must pay particular attention to loss of funding from off-balance-sheet structured instruments and vehicles; as well as to extra demand for cash because of exposure to such instruments. This experimentation will include:

- Potential funding strategies,
- Steps in funding action,
- Contingency funding plans, and
- Procedures to be implemented in the event of stressed liquidity conditions all over the financial market.

Stress liquidity risk must be evaluated against extreme events, testing the ability to repay short-term borrowings with assets that can be quickly converted into cash – while meeting other obligations and continuing to operate as a going concern. Challenging questions include potential inability to raise funding with appropriate maturity in different currencies, under changes in interest rate(s), and with acceptable contractual clauses.

Attention must be paid as well to the fact that under stress conditions the assumptions underlying funding and market liquidity risk change rapidly: first, as a function of market reaction through changes in counterparty behavior that affect the overall liquidity of financial instruments, and the availability of capital; then, in terms of the entity's portfolio composition and its quality, which impact upon funding liquidity.

Liquidity stress tests include quantitative approaches and scenario analyses aimed at identifying potential weaknesses and vulnerabilities in the ability to meet obligations as they become due under adverse conditions. Tests should be done at 99.9 and 99.99 levels of confidence. Solutions to be elaborated through scenarios must examine the further-out footprint of current commitments, the diversification of funding sources, and changes in contingent liquidity obligations including:

• Off-balance-sheet exposures,
• The impact of extreme events,
• Internal and external pricing, and
• The aftereffect of low probability but high impact factors.

Liquidity stress tests must be undertaken at the long leg of the distribution of risks, and include extending liquidity support to conduits, SIVs, and all sorts of other off-balance-sheet vehicles. They must also take account of contingencies that materialize when banks are compelled to offer capital and liquidity support to affiliated entities or even to competitors, as happened on 14 March 2008 with Morgan Chase pledging capital to Bear Stearns (together with the Fed).

Strong liquidity risk management by banks and well-designed liquidity regimes are evidently the *alter ego* of a sound integrated balance sheet management. This underlines the importance of close coordination between treasury, all business lines, and all business units, to assure appreciation of and account for potential stresses in liquidity, highlighting the effects of:

• New products,
• Evolving business practices, and
• Foreign operations.

Stress tests should compensate for the fact that banks are not rigorous in pricing contingent liquidity internally and externally, which reduces by so much their ability to meet liquidity needs at times of crisis. Senior management is often misinformed on liquidity requirements at future dates and under stress, because reporting frameworks for monitoring liquidity risk are not timely, while the content is inadequate, being deprived of data on extreme conditions.

Additionally, a liquidity stress test should not repeat the failure of current liquidity studies, which have generally been developed along national lines with checks aimed at the preservation of safety, mainly in the country of origin. With globalized financial markets, liquidity problems can be imported and exported, as well as magnified because of transborder reasons.

Indeed, cross-border flows raise the possibility of liquidity disruptions that can pass quickly across different markets and settlement systems. At the same time, ongoing improvements to the design of payment and settlement systems, like the adoption of large-value payment processes with intraday finality, have further promoted liquidity dynamics. Liquidity stress tests must include:

• Challenges associated with transferring currencies and securities across borders, especially on a same-day basis, and
• Risks embedded in operating centralized liquidity management, which depends on foreign exchange swap markets, among other factors.

Stress tests need therefore to factor in the conditions of "other" markets, their prevailing regulations, the time it takes to complete the transfer of funds or collateral across jurisdictions, and the fact that liquidity may not be fully portable across borders. This is particularly true in times of market panics or major political changes.

Along with cross-border money flows and their impact on liquidity, a significant amount of attention must be paid to securitization's after-effects. As the reader is already aware, while theoretically securitization can be used by credit institutions to expand sources of funding and free up additional balance sheet capacity, or create revenue through buying and distributing third-party assets which have not been originated by the bank, practically it presents liquidity risks.

The processes of pooling assets, credit rating them, selling them to a special purpose vehicle, and obtaining and issuing new securities is full of market challenges. Not the least is the fact that the bank has to inventory assets for longer than planned, and provide for them both capital adequacy and liquidity – enough to confront stress conditions during the market's twists.

For its part, asset backed commercial paper (section 6 of this chapter) gives rise to contingent liquidity risk. The subprimes crisis demonstrated the likelihood that the bank will be called upon to provide liquidity unexpectedly, at a time when it is already under stress. Contingent liquidity risk arises also from early amortization provisions incorporated into securitizations of revolving credits, while other liquidity needs are created when banks give support to conduits and other off-balance-sheet vehicles they have sponsored because of reputational reasons.

Additionally, a swarm of changes that during the last decade have taken place in financial institutions also impact on liquidity. The use of collateral is one of them. According to an ISDA margin survey made in 2006, there were an estimated 110,000 collateral agreements that year compared with only 12,000 in 2000 – a 916 percent increase, or 152 percent per year. The underlying reason has been the:

- Changing nature of transactions between financial entities,
- Boom in the use of repos and derivatives in wholesale funding markets,
- Increasing use of collateral as a risk mitigation instrument.

Liquidity stress tests should take full account of the fact that while the employment of collateral mitigates counterparty risk, it impacts upon funding liquidity risk because counterparties have to provide additional collateral at short notice. Examples are margin calls made on a daily and intraday basis, compared with weekly as was the practice a decade ago. Furthermore, bilateral collateral agreement allows both parties to request collateral, making collateralization and its management one of the key factors in liquidity stress testing.

6. Asset-backed commercial paper

Asset-backed commercial paper (ABCP) is an instrument of short-term financing. It is also the nemesis of global banks, which found themselves at the heart of the short-term funding squeeze, as it has been used to finance risky instruments like CDOs and other structured credit products. What happened in July/August 2007 contains a message for financial institutions, big and small, all over the world:

- Under stress the market for ABCP virtually disappeared, and
- Its problems will take months or years to fix, and therefore it is vital for everybody to buy time.

Typically, ABCP consists of short-term debt backed by assets like mortgages, a product that prior to the crisis had been a high flier but after the crisis was rejected by investors. Suddenly the market for ABCF became worried about the falling value of US home loans; risk that structured investment vehicles and bank conduits that use this product as a source of funding might be falling apart; and other weakness. According to the European Central Bank the latter include the:

- Instruments' high level of complexity,
- Valuation difficulties,
- Tendency to over-rely on ratings, and
- Inadequate information on financial institutions' exposure to structured instruments and off-balance-sheet vehicles.

The market crash reversed past perceptions by revealing the fragility of structured credit markets. The way the ECB's *Monthly Bulletin* puts it,

> The weaknesses in the CDO segment, in particular the valuation difficulties, have contributed to the evaporation of liquidity in these instruments since the turmoil began. CDOs need to be valued using sophisticated theoretical models, and the prices the models produce are usually highly sensitive to underlying correlation assumptions and methodologies.[5]

The contrast between the pre- and post-crisis market responses to ABCP could not have been sharper. In the generalized risk appetite of 2005, 2006, and early 2007 a surprising large number of investors were happy to buy that commercial paper because it was theoretically asset-backed, in the form of mortgage debt. Investors' enthusiasm did not waver even if these "assets" were, to say the least, shaky debt obligations with exposure to US subprimes.

Then the picture changed. Because of being worried about the value of the mortgage-backed debt, after the blow-up of the subprimes market, investors have been massively boycotting the commercial paper. This drove the SIVs and banks owing them on an increasingly desperate hunt for funding, with uncertainty about ABCP valuations exacerbated by concerns that structured investment vehicles will be forced to sell their collateral to repay investors.

With the pre-July/August 2007 risk appetite turned to risk aversion, the market for asset-based commercial paper suddenly shrank by about 30 percent, as Figure 9.1 documents. Banks silly enough to depend on short-term financing of huge long-term positions found themselves in a cleft stick; but not everyone suffered.

A good example of how problems could be solved, at least in the earlier days, is provided by the Canadian banks, which had an easier time than most others. Owing to a quirk in ratings in Canada, the banks argued that they did not have to offer backup lending facilities to a

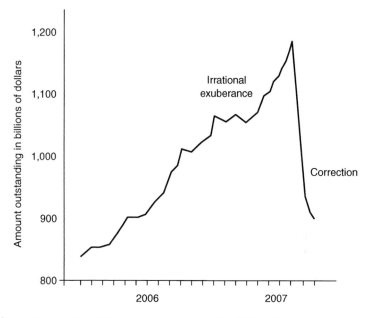

Figure 9.1   Asset-backed commercial paper in the United States

number of ABCP conduits that ran out of funding in August 2007 when confidence collapsed in the American mortgage assets that backed them.[6] In the aftermath:

- Banks and the non-bank conduits got together, and
- They negotiated a 60-day standstill to run up to the end of the reporting period.

Some experts said this approach might work, because in that time every party was supposed to swap commercial paper, which was short-term and hard to refinance, for longer-term funding that matches the maturities of the collateral backing them. Contrarians believed however that it could take much more than two months to sort out parts of the ABCP mess, mostly because of:

- The unique nature of each conduit, and
- The complex opacity of assets within them.

The contrarians were right. Typically, because they are engineered to prop up financially a given long-term investment, conduits differ from one another. Some are very structured and highly leveraged. Others are relatively simple. But at the end, to solve the maze of classes and commitments, conduits will have to be taken apart, and the value of their asset-backed commercial paper put under the magnifying glass.

Other characteristics, too, impact on them. As long as they are going entities, ABCP conduits do not need to mark their assets to market. But if their parent bank was asked (or itself decided) to take over its funding vehicles, *de facto* reconsolidating their assets onto its balance sheet, it would have to make rather significant fair-value adjustments on the portfolio. This has been another factor adversely affecting liquidity.

Additionally, not everyone agrees on what conduits really represent. One approach says that while the conduit is funded by commercial paper, the bank is generally immune to credit risk unless there is a default or the assets get downgraded below investment grade (below BBB–). The bank must then:

• Provide credit enhancement, or
• Take over the underlying problem assets.

Hence the fears regarding the underlying quality of some of the (wrongly rated) AAA and AA junk. Astute investors concluded that it was better to let the banks face losses from negative credit events. As for the banks, whether under IFRS or GAAP they needed to apply fair-value accounting – a fact confirmed by late October 2007, as the contraction of the asset-backed commercial paper market intensified.

Critics said that only then did it filter into the mind of the top brass of financial institutions that the ABCP crisis and the subprimes crisis which underpinned it were there to stay. The withdrawal of liquidity was not a blip on the radar screen. The same critics also suggested that home prices were unlikely to appreciate above their October 2007 valuations over the next 10 years, guaranteeing that 2008 and 2009 would probably be full of horror stories based on the misguided notion, current in the 2004 to 2006 experience, that asset values would appreciate indefinitely.

7. Carry trade

During most of the early years of the twenty-first century, low volatility and large interest rate differentials among First World countries have spurred *carry trades*. Typically, these are contracts by hedge funds and big banks, especially American, through which financial institutions incur enormous levels of debt in low-interest-rate currencies – such as those which have prevailed in Japan and Switzerland. Against them, they are purchasing high-interest securities which carry a large amount of:

- Credit risk, and
- Market risk.

This trade is lucrative up to a point, but if suddenly the financial conditions change it can easily become a disaster. For instance, during the late 1990s, market participants from around the world invested very heavily in the *yen carry trade*. They capitalized on the fact that interest rates in Japan were near zero, while at the same time the yen was tending to lose value. But when the yen suddenly and unexpectedly shot up in October 1998 a global financial panic broke out.

There are two groups of actions and reactions that can rapidly change the scales. The first is exemplified by the behavior of speculators and hedge fund managers, who may exit positions if yield gaps narrow, or return expectations make the trade unattractive. The other is capital flows such as big cross-border loans granted by Japanese banks to non-Japanese banks, which increased significantly throughout 2005, scaled back somewhat in 2006, and then took off again.

Projections about future trends in the carry trade tend to be unreliable. On 24 February 2006, an article run on London's *Daily Telegraph*, titled "Global Credit Ocean Dries Up," identified as the trigger point for a coming financial disaster the collapse of the carry trade. Sizing up the danger, several analysts interviewed by the *Telegraph* warned that:

- If Japan responded to higher interest rates in the US by raising its zero rate, it could shut down the yen carry trade, and
- The entire financial system, which had been fueled by this speculative money machine, would immediately be in jeopardy.

It did not happen that way. Instead, in March 2006, a European country was at the edge of going down the drain. Iceland's currency and stock market fell sharply and its banks struggled to roll over short-term debt. Iceland's massive current-account deficit of 16 percent of GDP made this tiny economy an extreme case, and led to the 2008 virtual bankruptcy of the island nation, but Australia, Hungary, Indonesia, Mexico, New Zealand, and Turkey have also seen their currencies fall.

All these besieged currencies have something in common among themselves and with the United States. Their economies have had big current-account deficits, driven in large part by rapid growth in consumer spending on the back of asset and credit booms. While in the last decades of the twentieth century current account deficits were typically supported by agreements between different authorities and by foreign direct investments (FDIs), in the twenty-first they became the object of speculative currency movements.

The liberalization and expansion of global capital markets was supposed to impose discipline on the different countries' economic policies, but this has not been the case. To the contrary, as many interest rates in Group of Ten countries fell to a record low early in the twenty-first century, cheap money attracted capital into carry trades, targeting high-yield bonds such as those issued by Iceland and New Zealand and greatly leveraging their economies.

• By underpricing risk, investors in effect subsidized extravagant borrowers, and
• They allowed them to run ever bigger deficits, till the next major and painful correction.

One of the interesting and dangerous aspects of the carry trade is that it has proved to be an almost limitless cash machine for banks and hedge funds. They borrowed at near-zero interest rates in Japan, and miniscule interest rates in Switzerland, to re-lend anywhere in the world that offers higher yields, whether Argentine notes (with a huge amount of credit risk), other speculative investments like subprimes, or other pure gambles. Theoretically, profits and losses in the carry trade are influenced by two main factors:

• Direction of monetary policy, and
• Volatility prevailing in the relevant financial markets.

Practically, the commanding criteria are the interpretations given to these events by lust and greed. The topmost challenge of carry traders is to identify when low-yielding currencies can outperform higher-yielding ones, given the direction of monetary policy of Group of Ten countries. The effect of higher global rates and/or a lot of central banks tightening sees to it that carry trades are unwound – as happened, for instance, in January 2008.

Historical references also suggest that higher volatility is typically correlated with the unwinding of carry trades. Critical, however, is the direction of global rates and foreign exchange volatility rather than the magnitude of the change. According to analysts, combining the forex and global interest rate signals enhances the dependability of a prognosis. Just as important are threshold effects for monetary policy. Carry trades are more likely to unwind once interest rates have exceeded a level of so-called neutrality.

The carry trade aftereffects are not necessarily to the central banks' liking. The way a 2007 commentary by Crédit Suisse had it:

> Reduced worries about effects of subprime issues in the USA and overall higher risk appetite have brought back pressure on the Swiss franc... The SNB [Swiss National Bank] is worried about potentially sharp appreciation of the currency if risk aversion were to remerge. It is thus aiming to keep the downside for the Swiss franc limited and, despite low inflation, is likely to follow suit when the ECB continues to raise rates.[7]

Quite similarly, *if* a carry trade crisis hits Japan *then* a mighty player will be the country's central bank when confronted by disorderly unwinding of the carry trade. Japan's monetary authorities could come under international pressure to intervene in the currency markets by selling yen. This would be inflationary, thereby hitting the real value of savings. It is also quite possible that the still weak corporate Japan, as well as the public, would not be able to handle higher interest rates, leading to a collapse of the economy.

8. Liquidity and the carry trade

Cash from the carry trade is widely perceived as an important support for the valuations of other assets. While this perception is an overstatement, it is no less true that markets have worked in this belief, an example being that of equities correlated to shifts in the yen, which has been under downward pressure from the carry trade.

Markets, however, can reverse their trend. At the end of February and in early March 2007, while equity markets were in turmoil, the yen appreciated sharply against a range of currencies, inflicting losses on carry traders. This was followed by a renewed weakening of the yen, with the result that:

- It let the speculators off the hook, and
- Also suggested that there *might* be some subtle correlations.

As the carry trade's funding currencies – Japanese yen and Swiss franc – appreciated across the board, carry traders took fright. The appreciation of the yen was driven both by short covering by foreign investors and by the normal repatriation of funds by Japanese investors ahead of fiscal year-end. Contrarians suggested that, after the start of the Japanese fiscal year (on 1 April 2007) and a global markets calm-down, the negative fundamentals for the yen would reassert themselves.

A worry among carry trade pessimists has been that the apparent nonchalance by the Bank of Japan could provoke a sudden sharp rise in the yen. But at the same time, *if* the central bank failed to raise interest rates, *then* the yen could come under downward pressure, making the potential shock of a subsequent sudden upturn in the currency much greater. Statistics indicated that at the beginning of the second quarter of 2007 just before the credit-and-subprimes crisis in the US:

- The yen carry trade in currency markets was at 97 percent of its highest volume ever,
- While the Swiss franc carry trade, about one-third the size, was at 93 percent of its record volume.

According to one estimate, as much as $250 billion worth of yen annually may be being borrowed out of Bank of Japan currency emissions for speculation worldwide. As one fund manager acknowledged, "If you didn't have a yen carry trade on, you didn't make money last year [2006] in international currency trading."[8]

In a way, the Japanese and Swiss central banks invited this on-and-off disaster upon themselves. The Bank of Japan's discount rate had only been raised from 0.25 percent to 0.50 percent, compared with 5.25 percent for the Federal Reserve and Bank of England (at that time). It was not therefore surprising that the flood of reserves out of yen and Swiss francs had gone into sterling, dollars, and euros (in that order), with due impact on the three currencies' liquidity dynamics.

One of the continuing attractions of the carry trade was that, with very minor reverses, speculation had been a "win–win" situation for several years – even if in early 2007 life for a carry trader was becoming increasingly fraught with risk. On the other hand, *if* the yen or the Swiss franc suddenly rallied, or *if* US interest rates fell, or any number of unpredictable events occurred, somewhere in the world the carry trade could unwind with drastic consequences. According to learned opinions, this:

- Would spark a huge rally in the yen and/or Swiss franc, and

- Leave everyone who borrowed cheaply in these currencies facing hefty losses.

Behind these bullets lies the fact that in 2006 and 2007 carry trades were operating at unprecedented levels, and it is wise to recall that the last time carry trades built up in this way in the financial system was in 1997 and early 1998. At that time, they unwound in a dramatic fashion, after the Russian financial crisis of August 1998; and they contributed to the implosion of Long-Term Capital Management (LTCM), a month later.

In 2007, as in 1997, low-yielding currencies have been used as the global cash machine, pushing more and more liquidity into asset markets till the day of reckoning. Nor surprisingly, regulators are concerned that the very high level of speculation in the yen carry trade has the potential to produce widespread financial market instability all the way to systemic risk.

One of the reasons why the carry trade commands increasing attention is that unlike other elements of global balances the yen has been moving in the wrong direction. Until mid March 2008 when it rose to nearly 100 yen to the dollar, the yen depreciated in spite of Japan's rising current-account surplus, and a slow but steady recovery. Group of Seven finance ministers and central bank governors:

- Have put risks associated with the yen carry trade at par with concerns about global imbalances, and
- Carry trade and imbalances are not all that keeps monetary policy-makers awake at night.

The scale of economic and financial – therefore of social – problems today confronted by the Western nations are enormous, and have the potential to turn on their head the economies of the whole world. Everything in this global market is interlinked as never before, and the fact that leverage has grown beyond recognition propagates the shock waves.

Lehman Brothers, the big investment bank, is geared up 40 times. Subprime delinquencies in the US stand at 18 percent (versus an average of 6 percent for all delinquencies, which itself is quite high). These rotten securitized assets constitute the collateral that central banks find themselves obliged to accept in order to reflate fallen financial institutions, like Bear Stearns, while the CEOs responsible for such king-size failures either continue to head the wounded bank or take the money from their golden parachutes and run.

By far the top reason for the current deep crisis of the capitalist system is not the failure of banks and instruments we are witnessing, but the fact that none of the people responsible for the disaster has been brought to justice. When a bridge collapses, design engineers and contractors find themselves in court. But governments, central banks, and regulators have given indulgences to those who brought the economy to an uncharted downside.

10
Is There a Remedy for the Problems of Bank Supervision?

1. The banks' wounded balance sheets

The first nine chapters of this book should have brought to the reader's attention the impossible situation the banking industry has created for itself, on-balance-sheet and off-balance-sheet. Bad enough though their case is, the subprimes are not the only reason why investment banks, commercial banks, mortgage lenders, non-bank banks, and other financial institutions are in trouble.

The price of $2 per share JP Morgan Chase was ready to pay in March 2008 for Bear Stearns suggested that, even after the 2007/2008 blues, the financial industry's balance sheets remained significantly overvalued and valuations were on their way to drop below book. On-balance-sheet, banks are confronted by past-due loans and other dubious assets; off-balance-sheet, their exposure includes:

- Exotic derivatives,
- All sorts of special-purpose vehicles, and
- Other guarantees like residual value,[1] return on initial principal, letters of credit and more.

Even CEOs, board members, and senior managers have failed to appreciate how deep on-balance-sheet and off-balance-sheet exposures (particularly the latter) cut into their bank's financial staying power. Citigroup provides irrefutable evidence of how easily hundreds of billions of assets go up in smoke, or have to be sold at bargain basement prices, when management decides that the bank has no alternative than to "shrink."

Up to 1 May 2008, while the long list of writedowns from the subprimes drama unfolded, Citigroup had obtained from various sources (including sovereign wealth funds) $42.15 billion in capital infusion. The market thought America's biggest bank was over the cap, but suddenly on 9 May rumor had it that it needed $300 billion (!) to close the gaping holes in its balance sheet.

The level of this unprecedented amount of money changed again on 12 May 2008, when Vikram Pandit, Citigroup's chief executive officer, said that top management planned to shed $400 billion of assets within three years, and also add $40 billion in generated capital. Analysts were flabbergasted, as at the same time the CEO stated that decisions about retained earnings and dividends would be made "sometime in the future."

Commenting on Pandit's plan to prune the bank's balance sheet by $400 billion in so-called "non-core legacy assets" in the next two to three years, some analysts said it was positive for Citi just to shrink. But most analysts and investors were skeptical. It would be an uphill struggle to sell "assets" consisting of real estate, leveraged loans, complex debt, and leveraged instruments, given:

- Tight credit markets, and
- The likelihood of more writedowns in their midst.

Critics also found the CEO's policy for balance sheet restructuring inconsistent. The plan called for expanding investment banking areas in prime brokerage and derivatives where risk devils lay – and at the same time trying to reduce risk; the stated objectives contradicted one another.

All banks caught in the firestorm of CDOs and CDSs are facing Citigroup's dilemmas in cleaning up the mess on their balance sheet. While the credit crisis is going on, decisions on how to sell destressed assets, let alone add internally generated "extra capital," are shaky. The market has become risk-adverse, while the banks have lost control of their intermediation activities and therefore of their loans channel.

The only thing sure is that by being exposed to subprimes, Alt-As and other ill-advised financial operations, credit institutions and other financial entities will continue bleeding. Based on statistics from the International Monetary Fund, Figure 10.1 shows that the chain reaction which started in 2007 can go on for years – up to 2012 or even beyond, according to different estimates.

Throughout the banking industry, management decisions ceased being factual because since 2002/2003 the amount of spoilage (if not of outright looting) has been such that the longer-term perspective is

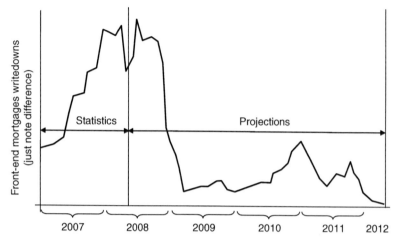

Figure 10.1   Expected American mortgages fallout till early 2012 (statistics and projections by IMF)

awfully clouded. In a 9 April 2008 interview in Bloomberg the chief economist of the IMF said that bank losses from subprimes will rise to nearly $1 trillion.[2] Writedowns of such magnitude have been more than four times the bleeding which had taken place in the 9 months from July/August 2007 to the day this statement was made.

How the different "assets" on- and off-balance-sheet, including the most dubious ones, will be marked in terms of value is a critical question because in extending liquidity, credit, and default facilities banks provide guarantees that they must subsequently honor – for example, guarantees to their special-purpose vehicles (SPVs; Chapter 5) relating primarily to securitizations and structured instruments. They may as well underwrite residual value guarantees related to leasing SPVs where the bank or a third party is the lessee.

Another off-balance-sheet exposure which must be funded originates in standby letters of credit to counterparties or reimbursement agreements issued in conjunction with sales of loans. Still other guarantees are extended in conjunction with certain structured investment funds, an example being the return of initial principal investment at the termination date of the fund. These funds are generally based on a formula that requires the fund to hold a combination of general investments and liquid assets.

Over and above these challenges comes the formidable task of estimating the fair value of credit default swaps, and its balance sheet impact.

Take as an example the case of Icelandic credit institutions. During a liquidity wobble in 2006, CDSs on one of Iceland's bigger banks pushed through 100 basis points, causing all three main Icelandic banks to rein back asset growth and chase deposits. This was bad enough, but at the end of March 2008,

- The Icelandic banks' CDS barometer moved more than 100 bp in a day, and
- It broke 1,000 bp at one of the Icelandic banks, with the other two not far behind.

Do CDS spreads this wide matter? Many experts respond with an affirmative "yes." Others answer "no," using as evidence the fact that the apparent panic was not mirrored in equity markets, where all three banks were on high price/earnings ratios. Additionally, the larger of Iceland's banks said that by tapping private placements it was able to fund itself at prices below the level that derivatives have been indicating.

Technical reasons explain much of the difference between these "yes" and "no" answers. The great unwinding of CDOs and highly leveraged hedge funds has been affecting spreads of Icelandic banks, as many hedge funds have found themselves overweight with CDO junk debt. This has exacerbated price swings in an illiquid market; but at the same time spreads cannot be ignored because in many other cases big CDS spreads are foretelling doom.

Behind this and other cases of worry about the banks' balance sheet stability lies the fact that their balance sheets are badly wounded because the same novel instruments that have turned to junk marketed as AAA tier-1 capital, sold as safe savings products, traded at a high level of leverage, and were subjected to a superficial risk control at best. The laxity of regulators contributed to the notion that modern finance can be turned into a perpetual fat bonuses machine no matter the damage created:

- To the banks, and
- To the economy.

Selling junk and being rewarded for it brought along more selling, cascading as in a nuclear reaction and forcing central banks to accept junk securities and give out treasury bonds. This meant that banks have been virtually nationalized – however, it did not change the fact that their balance sheets remain weak because plenty of financial products have proved to be flawed, house prices are tumbling, and it is harder to secure a loan. The banks brought the crisis on themselves, but are parliaments, governments, and regulators up to the task of averting systemic risk and restructuring the financial industry?

2. Financial Stability Forum

Since the 1980s when financial globalization went into full swing there have been several times when it seemed that the market had outrun itself and the economy, and a healthy correction was on the way. There were the crises of 1987, 1990/91, 1994, 1997/98 and, to a much greater extent, the stock market bubble of 2000. Something similar might have happened in 2007/2008 had it not been for the fact that the subprimes bubble became:

- Ugly, and
- Global.

A global challenge needed a global response, with the Financial Stability Forum (FSF) of the Bank for International Settlements becoming the body coordinating the global response to the financial markets turmoil of 2007/2008. Its meetings, and most particularly that of 28 March 2008, have highlighted the deep concern of policymakers about the financial debacle and their willingness to explore extreme measures such as:

- Temporary suspension of capital requirements, correctly opposed by many central bankers;
- Taxpayer-funded recapitalization of big banks, which most evidently risks igniting inflation; and
- A combination of fire sale and outright public purchase of worthless mortgage-backed securities, the solution the Fed adopted for Bear Stearns.

Some market players, particularly those most hurt by the risks they had unwisely assumed in the go-go years, have been hoping for a relief of capital requirements as well as for the go-ahead to continue to engage in transactions of extraordinary exposure. In other words, capital requirements are good when times are great, but in lean years banks should be allowed to keep on leveraging rather than putting their balance sheets and their houses in order. Total nonsense.

Investment and commercial bankers who in the dismal Greenspan years got into the habit of running wild and disregarding their duty to keep their assets safe wanted to continue doing so. Yet they know very well that the credit crisis is far from over, as evidenced by the fact that:

- The gap between the rate paid by G-7 governments to borrow and that paid by G-7 banks is as wide as ever, and
- By all evidence the Fed's Term Auction Facility introduced in early 2008 (Chapter 2) has not solved the money market squeeze.

The facts surrounding the credit crisis have not changed. A study by Richard Bernstein, chief investment officer at Merrill Lynch, made reference to the economic and financial situation facing the global environment as the "growing global credit pandemic."[3] The Bear Stearns demise, he says, should probably be viewed not as an outlier but as the first of many. In the 1989–1991 cycle, about 25 percent of financial sector companies went away via merger, acquisition, or bankruptcy. By contrast,

- By mid March 2008, as a result of the 2007/2008 events, the financial universe had shrunk by about 7 percent, and
- There may be another 18 percent to go, or more than two-thirds of the road to financial industry consolidation.

The challenges confronting the Financial Forum center around the fact that even if the rout of the financial industry started in 2007 in the US with the subprimes, the torrents of red ink in British, German, Swiss, and other countries' banking prove that this is not simply an American problem but a global credit one. Hence the wisdom of watching the financial industry carefully because its risks are huge, its assets remain overvalued, its earnings momentum keeps on being weak, and the market is starting to appreciate how broad and how deep the credit bubble has been.

With these facts kept under perspective, in March 2007 the Financial Stability Forum prepared an options paper for governments, banks, and regulators. Several steps have been outlined by a team led by Mario Draghi, governor of the Bank of Italy. One of the suggestions that made sense has been that of getting a group of the most important banks to simultaneously disclose their financial positions based on a "common reporting template." This would include information on:

- Prices attributed to different securities,

- Methodologies used to derive them, and
- Standards employed in disclosure of exposure to CDOs.

The further objective is that of establishing an industry-wide standard for disclosing exposure to off-balance-sheet entities, as well as the banks' capital and liquidity resources. As Chapter 9 has explained, in the aftermath of the 2007/2008 banking crisis, liquidity became a focal point of worry for central bankers.

Experts predict that the FSF proposals would be raising plenty of arguments, which are going to take time and a lot of negotiating to resolve. Optimists think that given the gravity of the situation it would not be difficult to find an accord on new supervisory principles. Pessimists answer that the likelihood of a rapid agreement is a pipe dream, even if delays were going to make a bad situation worse. The pessimists are right. What was expected to be a decisive Group of Seven meeting in Washington on 11–13 April 2007 was not decisive at all. In a most vague manner, the ministers of finance and central bankers of the G-7:

- Pledged to purge capitalism of the excesses that caused the latest crisis,
- But failed to agree on, let alone spell out, how to do it.

The Financial Stability Forum asked supervisory bodies to set higher capital requirements and told banks to reveal the full extent of their losses in their first-half 2008 earnings reports. But how was this "full extent" going to be computed? The G-7 stated that the International Accounting Standards Board (IASB) should urgently produce "better ways" to value assets of the kind that have been hammered in the latest crisis – an ill-defined mission.

This is deceptive because policymakers had all the opportunity to act on the proposals of the Financial Stability Forum aimed to rid financial markets of what Mario Draghi called the "perverse incentives" behind the recent credit crisis. "We have to find a better balance between efficiency and innovation and reserves and stability," said Timothy Geithner, president of the New York Federal Reserve Bank. Yes, but how? Where are:

- The concepts,
- The tools, and
- The better method?

Douglas Alexander, Britain's secretary for international development, spoke of a need for coordinated response to the market turbulence and commodity prices. "It will be important for the World Bank, the IMF and the UN to urgently work together to lead the development of an international response to address all the elements of this crisis," he said. Notice that these three bodies rarely agree among themselves.

The only thing decided by G-7 policymakers was "to finish much of the work" within 100 days, and all of it by the end of 2008. But which work? The answer is not at all clear, as generalities and *bon enfant* statements carried the day. World Bank president Robert Zoellick cited the importance of responding in such a way as to make it possible to "seize opportunities" to help developing countries improve health care, reduce malnutrition and infant mortality, care for climate change, and control food prices – the banking crisis was not in the picture.

A similar warning on food prices came from Dominique Straus-Kahn, the IMF's managing director, who predicted dire consequences if food prices remained high in developing countries, especially in Africa.[4] Straus-Kahn added that the problem could create trade imbalances that would impact major advanced economies, "so it is not only a humanitarian question."[5]

Between filling the gas tanks and filling the stomachs, the issue of tough measures needed to avoid a Second Great Depression waned. This is the worst possible way of restoring calm in the markets, because the message to the different players is that governments and central bankers still don't know what to do, and they are far from agreeing on a policy framework or any urgent measures.

3. The shadow banking system destabilizes the economy

Investigation of financial turmoil was the reason for the 3 April 2008 hearing of the Senate Banking Committee, chaired by Chris Dodd, an influential Connecticut Democrat. The testimony was provided by senior officials from the New York Federal Reserve, the Securities and Exchange Commission, and the Treasury, as well as JP Morgan Chase and Bear Stearns. The hearing itself was one of soft questions and self-serving answers for public view, while in all likelihood the real action occurred behind closed doors.

- Implicit in all the answers to committee queries was the idea that the system is undergoing a temporary episode of turmoil from which it will rebound because it is "fundamentally sound."

- But most knowledgeable people considered this to be an outright deception designed to provide cover for a bailout of unprecedented proportions of errant banks, by using taxpayers' money.

Curiously no reference was made to the *shadow banking system* built by all sorts of big banks to allow them to gamble without being bothered by prudential supervision. This shadow system rests on a web of entities that are hidden from central bankers' and regulators' eyes. Its nodes and links are provided by conduits and structured investment vehicles. Once this system faltered, it broke down completely.

In their testimonies the heads of JP Morgan Chase and Bear Stearns followed those of central bankers and supervisors. Tim Geithner, the president of the New York Fed, said that JP Morgan Chase contacted him about taking over the badly wounded Bear Stearns, adding that he was informed only on 13 March 2008 that Bear was broke and would have to file for bankruptcy the next morning. Had that happened, he testified, the result would have been a greater probability of:

- Widespread insolvencies,
- Severe and protracted damage to the financial system, and
- Ultimately a high risk to the economy as a whole.

The Federal Reserve's actions, which involved handing Bear and JP Morgan $30 billion to arrange the takeover, helped reduce the systemic risk, Geithner insisted. In his testimony Treasury Under Secretary Robert Steel followed the same basic line, saying that the failure of Bear would have caused financial disruptions beyond Wall Street.

Chris Cox, the head of the SEC, has his own version of "not my fault." According to his opinion, Bear Stearns had at all times a capital cushion well above what is required to meet supervisory standards. The failure of such "a well-capitalized firm, with its high quality collateral," was said to be an unprecedented event. This contradicted Wall Street's widespread opinion that under the watch of George W. Bush the SEC had failed all the way in its supervisory duties.

Moreover, contrary to Geithner's claim about first contact for Bear Stearns' takeover with a Fed dowry, the CEO of JP Morgan stated that it was the NY Fed who had asked him if he would agree to take Bear over. Chairman Dodd softly demanded a written explanation of this discrepancy, but so far nothing has come to the public eye.

As if his listeners had no memory of recent events, in his testimony, Alan Schwartz, the CEO of Bear Stearns, painted Bear as a victim unfairly destroyed by unfounded rumors and speculation. "You could never get the facts out as fast as the rumors," he complained. "It looked like there were people that wanted to induce panic." As to whether Bear bore responsibility for its demise, Schwartz said "I just simply have not been able to come up with anything, even with the benefit of hindsight." (!)

In contradiction to this generalized "not my fault," on 20 March 2008 (four days after the Fed's endowment of \$30 billion to Bear/JP Morgan) Lyndon LaRouche had said that Congress should conduct an investigation into the "criminality" of the Federal Reserve and Treasury's bailout of the vaporized speculative investment bank Bear Stearns.[6] Passed by Congress on 9 March 1933, The Emergency Banking Act had provided for government assistance to protect vital banking functions , but:

- It restricted such provisions to chartered commercial banks that are a vital part of the economy.
- Brokerage houses and investment banks were not included in this Act, therefore the Fed stepped outside the letter of the law by salvaging Bear.

As if they were unaware that the shadow banking system destabilizes the economy, neither the Bush Administration nor the Federal Reserve paid attention to it while it was still time to break it up. Instead, after the banking and credit crisis they have been concentrating on lowering interest rates at a time when they have had evidence that this aggravates problems in the credit markets while:

- Interest rate reductions did not filter down to the homeowner level, and
- Otherwise sound businesses continued to experience a liquidity problem.

No one really knows how bad this downturn can get because nobody has ever experienced such a headlong slide in the housing market at a time when, at \$20 trillion, it accounts for the vast majority of most families' wealth. In the best of cases, the rest of the economy will be affected by asset deflation. In a worst-case scenario, the entire capital of the US banking system would be wiped out many times over if everyone who is underwater on a mortgage turned the keys over to his or her lender.

As far as the banks themselves are concerned, the spider's web of the shadow banking system has escaped their control because the crisis spread from one asset to the next and nothing can be trusted anymore in terms of valuation. Banks avoided prudential rules requiring them to put aside capital, by warehousing vast sums of dubious off-balance-sheet instruments with disastrous results.

As if to prove that regulators are worried about where the current debacle may lead, in early 2008 the Federal Deposit Insurance Corp (FDIC) began adding staff to its Division of Resolutions and Receiverships in preparation for a wave of bank failures. It also placed job postings on its website for people knowledgeable in duties associated with a financial institution closing – while the number of institutions on the FDIC's "problem" list jumped by 50 percent,

- From 50 in 2006,
- To 76 in 2007.

Whether one looks at the balance sheets of big banks or of smaller banks, one sees an awful mismanagement of assets and plenty of financial resources spoilage. Yet preservation of assets is a basic and integral responsibility of the CEO, board members, and senior management – leading many people to demand that Congress should conduct an investigation into the criminality of decisions which led to the severe banking and credit crisis, and that the wrongdoers must be brought to justice.

4. The error of trying a quick fix

John Paulson, founder of Paulson & Co., a hedge fund, made $3.7 billion in 2007. This was the richest ever one-year take in Wall Street earned by betting against certain mortgages and complex financial instruments resting on them.[7] John Paulson had seen what highly paid chiefs of state, government officials, central bankers, and regulators were unable to perceive: that the house of cards would collapse.

George Soros and James H. Simon each made nearly $3 billion in 2007, according to an annual ranking of top hedge fund earners by Institutional Investor's *Alpha Magazine*. Other names followed in that list, and it is nobody's secret that to break into it a hedge fund manager had to earn at least $360 million in 2007 – nearly 20 times the 2002 figure. This is a dramatic contrast to 2007 earnings of the:

- Average American family, $60,000;
- Average blue-collar worker, $36,000;
- Average non-skilled worker, a little over $18,000.

From the lowest-paid to the highest-paid person the ratio in earnings used to be 1:20, then it rose to 1:40, and at that time many commentators said it was too high. Now it stands at 1:20,000. "There is nothing wrong with it – it is not illegal," said Bill Gross of PIMCO, commenting on some people's three-digit millions earnings in 2007. "But it's ugly."

It is also irrational because it kills the whole sense of free enterprise. Those who interpret freedom as meaning ripoff, promote the revival of twentieth century's *isms*: socialism, communism, fascism, and nazism. The houses of the American middle class as well as of blue-collar workers and non-skilled workers served as cannon-fodder to this 1:20,000 earning ratio; and they were carried away by the bank-generated tornadoes.

Damages are wide, and they cannot be repaired with a quick fix. Proposals made by both Bush Administration dignitaries and the banking industry are looking for easy solutions to the debacle. They revolve around issuing loans by the Federal House Administration (FHA, created during the Great Depression of the 1930s), then having Fannie Mae and Freddie Mac buy them. They have been reportedly instructed to begin purchasing jumbo loans (those over $417,000) despite the fact they already swim in red ink.[8]

- For the fourth quarter of 2007 Freddie Mac reported a loss of $2.5 billion.
- Over the same period, Fannie Mae lost $3.6 billion and on 6 May 2008 it was reported that its balance sheet featured 42 percent in inventoried Alt-As.[9]

Hank Paulson, the Treasury secretary (not to be confused with John Paulson the $3.7 billion 2007 earner) has attacked some of these proposals as bailouts of speculators, even while advancing his own bailout plans. While some bankers are clamoring to be "saved" by taxpayers' money, former investment banker Paulson realizes that his former colleagues will have to eat at least part of their losses. At the same time, as Table 10.1 shows, the capitalization of the big banks themselves has been decimated. The market punished them for their:

- Low quality of governance, and
- Unprecedented amount of writedowns.

To hide their shortcomings some of the banks have tried to change the rules of the game in their own favor. Since marking to market has fed directly into the hurricane of writedowns, they suggested to friendly

Table 10.1   Pre-crisis 2007 and post-crisis capitalization of big banks (in $ billions, in order of magnitude)

Institution	Peak 2007	March 2008
Citigroup	250	120
UBS	152	70
Royal Bank of Scotland	140	74
Barclays	100	64
Credit Suisse	99	65
HBOS	83	42
Deutsche Bank	82	62
Merrill Lynch	80	44
Morgan Stanley	68	53
Lehman Brothers	40	23

regulators that they should be subject no more to objective valuations. Instead, their management should declare what it believes is the value of their (worthless) "assets."

(As a reminder, FASB accounting regulations in the US, IASB accounting rules in Europe, as well as Basel II financial reporting standards are based on *fair-value* accounting. This led to billions in writedowns in the value of financial instruments and triggered a chorus of complaints. The big banks' peculiar argument for being exempt from marking to market is based on the contention that current fair value reflects unusual markets, not the "real" underlying value of their assets.)[10]

Desperately searching for relief, some financial institutions hope that the SEC will allow them not to use market values when it can be proved that sales have been forced or distressed. Little attention is paid to the fact that rules are written for both good times and bad times – and *if* they are changed midstream *then* there exist no rules at all.

There are however senior bankers who don't espouse that thesis, and promote wholesale reform of the banking system. Josef Ackermann, CEO of Deutsche Bank, summed it up in a call for governments to step in: "I no longer believe in the market's self-healing power."[11] The implication is that:

- *If* the market cannot heal the wounds it sustains as a result of its own risky behavior,
- *Then* it must be discouraged from taking such risks in the first place (see also section 6 of this chapter).

Restructuring should definitely lead to proactive bank supervision, not to the *old boys' club* of the British Financial Services Authority (FSA) with its ineffectual "principles-based" approach. The Northern Rock fiasco has tarnished the FSA's image. Besides that, there is need for both a short-term solution and a longer-term restructuring plan. The Swedish example versus the FSA's and the Fed's provides food for thought.

A year after the Japanese economy was brought to its knees because of excesses by the banking industry and in real estate, in 1991 Sweden faced one of the worst financial crises the global economy has seen in the years since World War II. As a way out, Sweden's solution was dia-metrically opposed to Japan's:

- The medicine the Japanese chose was to cut interest rates to nearly zero, like the Fed did in 2001/2002 and 2007/2008.
- In sharp contrast to the Japanese, in a rapid response to the crisis Sweden's monetary policy authority raised interest rates.

Unexpected by speculators, the higher interest rates took the wind out of their sails, helped in containing the damage, and set the country up for more than a decade of strong growth. That proved to be the right solu-tion, and it is regrettable that the Federal Reserve chairman and Treasury secretary copied the failed Japanese response – not the Swedish.

Of course, no solution is free of cost. The Swedish gross domestic product fell by 6% between 1990 and 1993, prompting a tide of bank-ruptcies that threatened to swamp the financial system, though at the same time they pruned it of its excesses. In an effort to halt speculation against the currency in 1992, Bengt Dennis, the Swedish central bank governor, brought the interest rate on loans to banks to 500 percent (which also taught them a lesson).

There is another lesson to be learned from the Swedish experi-ence of 1991/1992 and the years that followed. Contrary to the Bush Administration, Greenspan, the Fed, and US market players, since the aforementioned banking crisis the Swedes have largely managed to keep spending in check, often running budget surpluses. And the cen-tral bank has been a hawk on inflation, even choosing to raise rates by a quarter-point on 20 February 2008, despite the dangers of an American-led economic slowdown.

5. Paulson's restructuring: a call for zero regulation

One thing is clear, stated a feature article in the *Financial Times*: streamlining is nice, but reforms that do not fix the incentives in the financial system will fix nothing. Well said. Examined under this perspective, the proposed new regulatory rules in the US are a non-event because:

- If the perverse incentives feeding lust and greed are left in place, then financial disasters like 2007/2008 will become a regular business.
- If those who brought the US and the world economy to the edge of chaos are not brought to justice, then plenty of others will imitate them.
- If regulators are not autonomous entities endowed with muscles and teeth, then the commercial and investment banks will continue running the show, and we know the results.

Supposedly to take care of these risks, on 31 March 2008, Treasury Secretary Hank Paulson announced his proposals for restructuring the system of bank supervision in the US, including increasing the power of the Federal Reserve to regulate investment banks and supposedly limit the risks they take. Paulson said that his proposals would take many years to implement and the Treasury's priority would be resolving the current market turmoil. But were they really addressing the core problem?

Labelled "Blueprint for a Modernized Financial Regulatory Structure," the Treasury secretary's plan would create for America a "principles only" regulatory system, essentially reducing the control by federal and state governments over the banking industry. At the same time, it would expand the (currently unconstitutional) power of the Federal Reserve to engage in bailouts of:

- Investment banks, and
- Other gambling outfits.

In New York, opinions about these proposals have been divided, ranging from "Paulson's gamble" to "an attempt to make sense of and overhaul the rule book" (they are not). Critics pointed out that they are a bold but unwelcome attempt to legalize the throwing away of public money to cover the huge losses of investment bankers and of their hedge funds.

The pros observed that the Treasury has been working in the proposals since March 2007 in an effort to legally enable the Fed to take action. They looked at Paulson's plan as an initiative to bolster US capital markets amid growing competition from overseas by boosting US competitiveness (This business with subprimes, CDOs, and CDSs has shown the results.)

But Chris Dodd, chairman of the Senate Banking Committee, called the Treasury plan a "wild pitch ... not even close." Other critics point out that Hank Paulson's restructuring plan would increase ineffectiveness by creating another layer of bureaucracy since, for example, regulation of mortgage brokers and many lenders will stay with the states. They looked at it moreover as an attempt to tie bank supervision nearer to the president – opening it up to all sorts of political pressures.

In the background of this criticism lies the fact that the Treasury's plan includes the expansion of the President's Working Group (PWG) on financial markets, a club for only select large regulators dominated by the Treasury and the Fed (whose power would be greatly expanded). This goes against the strong opinion expressed by several experts that political interference has weakened the regulators' hand, and there is no guarantee this will not happen again. Even investment bankers are worried. Dan Alpert, managing partner at Westwood Capital, an investment bank, put it this way: "The present calamity stems not from a lack of regulation, but from a failure to rigorously apply, enforce and maintain many of the regulatory safeguards that developed as a result of past crises."[12]

An article published in *Executive Intelligence Review* on 11 April 2008 expressed the same worries:

> Treasury Secretary Paulson, the President's Working Group, and the bankers know they are bankrupt and cannot survive without a bailout, and the only pockets deep enough belong to the governments. But while they are desperate for government assistance, they do not want governments messing in their affairs; international finance, they insist, must be above mere governments in order to be effective.[13]

In other words, *zero regulation* is the best regulation.

While under Christopher Cox, a Bush Junior appointee, the Securities and Exchange Commission failed in its duties to supervise investment banks, and the result has been the Bear Stearns scandal. In the past the SEC was a most effective supervisor. Therefore, the Paulson restructuring plan:

- Singled it out as an enemy of the hands-off, no-control policy,
- Moved many of its duties to the Fed, and
- Earmarked it for elimination through merger with another agency.

Three former heads of the SEC immediately said that the Bush/ Paulson proposed overhaul of financial regulation threatened to weaken supervision, a process that may already be under way with help from the SEC itself (under Cox). David Ruder, Arthur Levitt, and William Donaldson, all former SEC chairmen, stated that the Treasury's push for the SEC to adopt the regulatory approach of the much smaller Commodity Futures Trading Commission (CFTC) would be a mistake.

- It is "not useful" for the SEC to have "a prudential-based attitude in which regulators solve problems by discussing them informally with market participants and ask them to change," David Ruder, a Republican SEC chairman under Ronald Reagan, said in an interview. "We have to have an enforcement approach."
- Arthur Levitt, who led the SEC from 1993 to 2001 under Bill Clinton, said the terms proposed by Treasury were "wrongheaded" because they would give the trading commission "primacy."
- William Donaldson, who was fired by Bush as SEC chairman (in June 2005) for having dared to propose hedge fund regulation, was also critical of Paulson's approach. "Before you start rearranging the organization of the financial-regulatory agencies you must examine how all of this happened."[14]

Congressmen, too, questioned whether the SEC has eased up in fighting fraud, particularly as it has been moving to transfer some responsibilities for monitoring accounting rules and securities sales to overseas regulators. Chris Dodd and Jack Reed asked government watchdogs to investigate why SEC sanctions against companies and individuals plunged by 51 percent, to $1.6 billion, in the regulator's most recent fiscal year. The agency also opened 15 percent fewer probes over the same period, according to its annual reports.

The drop in fines, Dodd and Reed wrote in a 20 March letter to the Government Accountability Office (GAO, the US government's auditor), raises questions about whether changes have taken place in enforcement philosophy or scope of activity. They therefore asked the GAO to review a policy change implemented last year by Cox that requires agency attorneys to get approval from commissioners before negotiating corporate fines.

6. Nuts and bolts of Paulson's supervisory restructuring

Theoretically, Paulson's "Blueprint for a Modernized Financial Regulatory Structure" calls for widening the banks supervisory net, giving greater powers to a smaller number of regulators. For example, the Securities and Exchange Commission is to merge with the Commodities Futures Trading Commission. Practically, that's like opening Pandora's box.

In no time, CFTC chairman Walt Lukken warned that the action could lead to the "creation of a larger regulatory bureaucracy." Neither is there any question that an SEC/CFTC merger will have great difficulty passing through Congress, because it treads on the toes of two different Congress committees. Even before Paulson's baby is laid on Congress's doorstep lawmakers should ask themselves the prerequisite question: is such a merger making sense?

Commenting on Paulson's plan for restructuring bank supervision in America, Stephen Roach, CEO of Morgan Stanley Asia and a respected expert, said that it is like rearranging armchairs on the deck of the *Titanic*. In his opinion, legislators have to address the mandate of central banks to emphasize their responsibility for financial stability – a basic duty of which Paulson's plan made no mention.

- The core duty of the Fed is not bank supervision but monetary policy and financial stability,
- But under Greenspan and Bernanke, which means for over two decades, the Fed has failed in its core duty.

As for merging the SEC with the CFTC, the issue is not really new; it dates back to the late 1990s. On 16 December 1998, the US Senate Agriculture Committee held a hearing on the over-the-counter derivatives market and the hedge funds. A basic purpose of the hearing was the plan by the Commodity Futures Trading Commission to re-regulate the OTC market.

Some former government officials who appeared at the hearing seemed to suggest that the derivatives markets were sound, and that re-regulation was unnecessary (no kidding). Former Federal Reserve Governor Susan Phillips, who headed the CFTC from 1983 to 1987, claimed not only that "no special oversight facility of Federal protection is necessary" for the OTC derivatives market, but that "exchange-traded futures and options could also be considerably deregulated."

Along the same vein Dr Wendy Gramm, Phillips's successor at the CFTC (1988–1993), cited "the challenge of keeping laws and regulations from stifling innovation or otherwise damaging markets," adding "The regulatory structure seems to be working." Others suggested the CFTC be merged *into* the Securities and Exchange Commission, an issue that soon proved to be a non-starter. (Paulson wants the opposite, which is also nonsense.)

By contrast to these testimonies, however, Brooksley Born who in 1998 chaired FCTC stood her ground, that the lack of reporting requirements for most OTC derivatives by market players "potentially allows them to take positions that may threaten our regulated markets without the knowledge of any Federal regulatory authority." The 2007/2008 hecatomb of the financial industry proved that Brooksley Born was right. (Born was fired by Clinton for her stand.)

Along this same frame of reference, Martin Mayer, another witness, stated that "the law gives CFTC jurisdiction over commoditized financial derivatives – many of which would otherwise be illegal under the gaming and anti-bucket-shop laws of some states, including New York, which provides the governing law for most international swap contracts." Mayer, too, has been right.

- If existing US laws were applied pre-emptively, the financial industry would not have entered a path of self-destruction.
- But both Bill Clinton, who signed the repeal of the Glass–Steagall Act (Chapter 2), and George W. Bush, who fired the SEC chairman when he asked for hedge fund supervision, have bent over to please the financial gamblers.

A curious thing about the Treasury's plan for restructuring bank supervision, and beyond this about the President's Working Group On Financial Markets (FWG), is that neither has addressed, at least publicly, either Brooksley Born's call for reporting requirements on OTC derivatives or William Donaldson's call for the registration and regulation of hedge funds. This raises a most disturbing question:

- Are the people in the FWG and those who drew up Paulson's plan utterly incompetent?
- Or, are they blinded by orders emanating from higher up, and by their own conflicts of interest?

Another nuts and bolts merger protected by the Treasury's plan for restructuring bank regulation is that of its own Office of the Controller of the Currency (OCC) and of the Office of Thrift Supervision (OTS). The OTS is an independent government agency created in 1989 in the wake of the savings and loans (thrifts, building societies) meltdown.

- OTS supervises some 840 banks whose primary market is mortgages.[15]
- By contrast, OCC supervises US big banks and American subsidiaries of foreign banks – a different mission.

In other words, the OCC and the OTS share no common duties in terms of depth, detail, and sophistication – though neither did a commendable job in averting the crisis. The 840 banks the OTS supervises have been among the high stakers in the subprimes, and as of 31 March 2008 (when Paulson's plan was published) they had among themselves $25 billion in red ink. But institutions supervised by the OCC were in much worse shape by almost two orders of magnitude, with admitted and potential losses in the trillions of dollars.

Additionally, as the former boss of Goldman Sachs, Hank Paulson should have known that a merger can only then succeed if it is studied in its every detail, with all problems identified and solved well before it takes place. Investment banks make fortunes because of this important fact in merger activity – yet the principle of thorough study and painstaking analysis which involves all counterparties to a merger has not guided the hand of those who proposed to merge the SEC with the CFTC and the OCC with the OTS, or the insurance industry's regulatory outfits.

Still another of the bolts and nuts in Paulson's proposals is that insurers could opt for federal regulation rather than state regulation. Not mentioned at all in this diatribe is the fact that such options have existed for several decades in the banking industry and the result has been less supervision, not better. Why should things be different with insurers?

Also, most curiously, the plan for restructuring the financial industry's prudential supervision passes in silence whether or not the reserve bank is allowed to take junk bonds and other bad money as collateral for the handout of good money – precisely the new Fed policy that we studied in Chapter 2: offering Treasuries in return, mainly, for worthless CDOs.

By accepting all sorts of past due mortgages in exchange for Treasuries, the Fed is trying to reduce the balance sheet stress at banks and security firms over their badly battered mortgage holdings.[16] But is this really its mission? Nor is the CDO junk limited to subprimes. While still a major challenge, subprimes are yesterday's salient problem. The new and bigger problem today is in other asset categories:

- Prime mortgages,
- Leveraged loans, and
- A swarm of other forms of financial gearing.

What will happen tomorrow if CDSs open a new and bigger financial hecatomb than the CDOs? Will the Fed become an insurer of last resort of highly leveraged credit default swaps? Will it throw good money after bad money while allowing gamblers masquerading as bankers to fill their pockets with hundreds of millions of dollars in bonuses? Will the extended-functions Fed bring money-drunk financial operators to justice? If yes, why has this not been done with the CDOs?

7. The experts' opinion on banks supervision

As the financial and credit crisis deepened and the first quarter 2008 showed a continuing amount of writedowns and other losses in the banking industry, several well-known American financial experts condemned the Federal Reserve's policy of the last 20 years under Greenspan and Bernanke. In their judgment:

- The Fed reacted too quickly with easy money, and
- It rushed to bail out institutions that made bad investments by speculations.

This, critics said, is not the central bank's mission. The job of the Fed is primarily price stability, while the Greenspan and Bernanke policies flooded the market with liquidity with total disregard of its inflationary impact and of the dollar's value. Now the American people must pay through inflation for these wrong policies which have damaged the American economy.

Even investment bankers at Wall Street are now saying that the wrong message to the market by the Fed started with the salvage of Long-Term Capital Management (LTCM) in September 1998. This carried with it the message that bankers and investors could take all the risks they please, because the Fed was ready to pull them out of the hole which they dug for themselves.

Also criticized has been Greenspan's policy, followed as well by Bernanke, to no longer target M3, the broader measurement of money supply, as practically all other Western central banks do. This gave free reign to printing money while both chairmen knew (or at least should have known) that the Fed cannot expand the money supply indefinitely.

At a gathering he addressed on 8 April 2008 Paul Volcker, the respected former chairman of the Federal Reserve (who brought US inflation under control in the early 1980s), said that the 2008 credit crisis is the mother of all credit crises – the most severe one the United States has known since the Great Depression of 1929–1933. Pointedly, Volcker added that the financial system has failed the test of the marketplace.

The former chairman of the Fed also explained that while his biggest concern is the economy of the United States, problems relating to the origin and sequel of the credit crisis are not just American but global. Therefore he sees the need not only for better focused bank supervision through the creation of an independent superagency, but as well for establishing and upholding a global regulatory approach.

Commenting on the reference Volcker had made to the urgent need to redress the value of the dollar, several financial experts have suggested that in effect the dollar crisis is making worse the credit crisis because it puts a limit on the number of dollars foreigners will take. The idea that a cheap dollar is better than a strong one because it promotes exports is utterly wrong, the same critics said. The US imports much more than it exports, as evidenced by its huge current-account deficit.

Investment bankers, too, concurred with the notion that the policies of the Bush Administration are counterproductive, as they make a bad situation worse. In a 5 April 2007 televised interview Stephen Roach said that 78 percent of the US economy is in trouble "right now." Risk problems have built year upon year, leading to the mess in which the economy has landed.

Roach underlined that the party responsible has been the Federal Reserve under Alan Greenspan, with Ben Bernanke acting as second. The Fed's big failure is that it did not intervene to diffuse the piling financial storm, and it waited for the bubble to burst to clean up the mess. Other experts suggested that the real problem with the banks is not that they are short of cash, but that they are carrying in their balance sheets lots of:

- Worthless loans, and
- Underwater level structured securities.

One of the bitter criticism has been that the needed improvements to the banking industry's risk management, generally blamed as substandard, showed nowhere in the Treasury's restructuring plan and the Fed's current preoccupations. By contrast, commercial bankers are worried. In an interview given to Bloomberg on 9 April 2008, Josef Ackermann said that risk management must be both strengthened and extended. Banks should look into elements other than those on which they have been focusing so far:

- Asking questions on the further-out aftermath of assumed exposure,
- Paying attention to their own liquidity, and

- Relying less on external ratings and more on their own evaluation of creditworthiness.

In the background of those comments has been the fact that from July/August 2007 to April 2008 the financial situation has not stabilized; it has even worsened. This made bankers much more careful about new commitments extending the credit squeeze. Responding to a question on why in 2008 banks were reluctant to lend, Ackermann stated as a reason that they didn't know what tomorrow was going to bring.

- Their capital needs were not clear, and
- They had to preserve their cash to meet adversity.

The fact that the supervision of big banks is a ball game totally different from that of medium and small ones has been a top preoccupation of the best economists. In late April 2008, in an interview he gave on Bloomberg TV Dr Henry Kaufman pointed out that there were thirty American institutions in the too-big-to-fail class, and said there is an urgent need to create a special regulatory authority which steadily supervises them. (Not too different a thesis than Volcker's superagency.)

Kaufman is right, and this is not only an American "must." It is reasonable to estimate that there will be another thirty to forty big institutions in Europe plus another forty in the rest of the world including China, Japan, South Korea, India, Brazil and the other countries each of whose economy impacts in global terms and therefore is too big to fail.

These are essentially financial institutions whose bankruptcy or salvage can lead to a wide spectrum of aftereffects ranging from moral hazard to an explosion of inflation and systemic risk; an example of the latter has been the aftereffect of Bear Stearns's bankruptcy. Therefore, these megabanks should not be allowed to gamble – a reason why their supervision must be biting and steady. Moreover, no matter how good a solution may be found on paper, the most crucial issue is how regulators use their power – both in absolute terms and relative to the fact that financial companies continue to innovative.

One day, regulators will again see excesses building up in the system, as has happened with subprimes and structured products under their nose. It will be hard for them to force banks to pull in their horns if politicians are ready to accept (and even encourage) excesses by heeding big banks' complaints about "limits to innovation" or "losing business to overseas rivals." It is better to lose some business than to lose the bank.

*   *   *

This is, first and foremost, a banking crisis. Practically everyone agrees that the fortunes of the banks will decide the length and depth of the dangerous situation we are in. If it is not stopped then the chain reaction set in motion by the worsening economic situation will lead to a breakdown of the financial system, and of the social system as well.

Both the markets and the regulators failed in their duty to keep the economy vibrant and under control. We must now change the regulators and restructure the markets.

Epilog

This is a market driven by fear. In mid 2007 the banking crisis began with *subprime* mortgages given to people who could hardly afford them, and used as raw material for securitizations. The system put in place by the banks was revealed to be complex, expanding all the way from massive usage of collateralized debt obligations (CDOs) to off-balance-sheet conduits and special investment vehicles (SIVs) which served for regulatory arbitrage.

As losses mounted and business confidence waned, the *credit crunch* became the epicenter of a global financial and banking earthquake. The next phase of the crisis has been one of *trust*. Banks no longer trusted one another, because they knew that financial statements were smoke and mirrors – a fear vastly increased by the wide use of credit derivatives and most particularly credit default swaps (CDSs) whose warehoused values reached astronomical levels.

On 17 September 2008, coming on the steps of Lehman Brothers' bankruptcy, Morgan Stanley's CDS spreads of 900 basis points[1] indi-cated a 13 percent probability of default. According to the experts, if AIG had gone bust, Deutsche Bank and Credit Swiss might have fol-lowed it, because the large amount of credit protection they had bought from AIG through CDSs would have turned to ashes.

The lack of trust has been worsened by the fact that bank supervision had taken a holiday not only in the United States but also in the European Union. The regulators did not do their job. The idea that the markets have ever been under strong supervision proved to be a myth. Just ask any firm that had to deal with the Securities and Exchange Commission (SEC) in America or its British equivalent the Financial Services Authority (FSA).

In early October 2008, under intense questioning by Henry Waxman, chairman of the Government Oversight Committee of the House of

Representatives, and, in a separate deposition, by members of the US Senate's Banking Committee, Dick Fuld, CEO of the defunct Lehman Brothers, admitted publicly that his bank had *not* been supervised by the Securities and Exchange Commission.

- *If* the SEC and the Fed had done their job, *then* Lehman, Bear Stearns, and sixteen American commercial banks (so far in 2008) would not have been bankrupt, and
- *If* the FSA had performed its duties, *then* Northern Rock, Alliance & Leicester, Bradford & Bingley, Halifax Bank of Scotland (HBOS), and Royal Bank of Scotland would not have gone to the wall.

Greed, lust, and laxity saw to it that we have now progressed beyond the confines of a global credit crisis, the tons of toxic waste inventoried in the banks' vaults, and regulatory absenteeism. One should not expect the financial markets to perform well until confidence returns, and confidence is a scarce commodity at this moment despite the trillions of dollars, pounds, and euros thrown at the problem.

- The lack of liquidity has spread from loans into commodities, bonds, and equity markets.
- Equities, debt instruments, and vulnerable currencies are falling through key support levels.
- Manufacturing and other companies are shedding jobs and cutting investments that threaten their core business.
- Governments are printing a massive amount of money, shutting stock exchanges. and placing restrictions on the flow of funds,

Equity markets have capsized everywhere around the globe. In just one day, 17 September 2008, Morgan Stanley lost 38 percent of its capitalization and Goldman Sachs 25 percent. A day after, General Electric's stock lost 21.5 percent, on worries about GE Capital – and it recovered somewhat only after the huge injection of liquidity by central banks.

A month later, on 18 October 2008 the Nikkei index saw its biggest decline in 21 years. On that same day, year to date, India's Sensex had fallen by 48.1 percent; Hong Kong's Hang Seng, 46.8 percent; Japan's Nikkei, 45.9 percent; Germany's Dax, 43.7 percent; France's CAC 40, 43.5 percent; and Britain's FTSE 100, 39.1 percent. Russia's equity index had beaten all others, falling by nearly 70 percent.

Through its Troubled Assets Relief Program (TARP) the US Treasury put on the block $700 billion to do "what it takes" to stabilize financial markets – announcing that this could include a wide range of unspecified measures. Britain and the euroland countries (particularly Germany, France, and the Netherlands) more than matched the US amount, with the equivalent of $2,200 billion. But are these three trillions enough to tackle a problem which, at least according to one estimate, may be 20 times greater – at a level of over $60 trillion? This last figure is a guestimate of what the world might have spent over the last four decades:

- By living beyond its means, and
- By accumulating vast amounts of unsecured debt.

One of the unintended consequences of the ongoing ultra-size financial bailouts will be a boost to inflation, with Western and other economies returning to the stagflation of the 1970s, as the global economy goes into severe recession and the crisis deepens. The Chinese economy, which has been the twenty-first century's global dynamo, is expected to retract, and we might all have to pay the unexpected consequences.

Further still, are these three trillion allocated in the best possible way? All we can say at this time is that governments are sacrificing the non-banks to save the banks. But nobody can be sure that the massive bailouts of huge financial institutions serve a purpose. Some of them are too big and too sick to be saved from their self-inflicted wounds. On 17 October 2008, Citigroup and Merrill Lynch reported fresh multibillion-dollar losses, with the total writedowns of $323 billion for the nine largest US banks exceeding all of the combined profits they earned in recent years.

Neither does anybody know the real depth of the abyss – including the banks' own top management. As will be recalled, in August 2008 Merrill Lynch sold to Lone Star, a vulture fund from Texas, at practically 5 cents to the dollar $30 billion of CDOs and other toxic assets.[2] The latest writedowns have shown that what was left was still damaged goods. Such deepening losses raised crucial questions about the Western governments' plans:

- Will lenders deploy their newfound capital quickly, as the politicians have hoped?
- Will they unlock the flow of credit to get the economy moving again?
- Or will they hoard the money to protect themselves and, if so, what will central banks, regulatory authorities, and governments do?

At least some chiefs of state say that they want to revamp regulatory measures and increase their cutting edge. In mid October 2008 the European Commission announced that it intended to propose ways to control risks in the credit derivatives market, which has played a very negative role in the global financial crisis. "Regulators need to have a much better view of where the real risks in these instruments lie," said Charlie McCreevy, the European Union's financial services commissioner.

McCreevy called on national regulators and the financial industry to agree on the real risks posed by credit derivatives and on how they can be limited to prevent further losses. Nicholas Sarkozy, the French president, and chair of the EU from 1 July to 31 December 2008, called for the top 30 global financial institutions to get regulated by a panel of supervisors from the countries they operate in – also bringing in as coordinator the International Monetary Fund (IMF).

The careful reader will recall that one of the proposals this book has made is to have the 30 top American banks, plus another 100 big banks around the globe, supervised and rigorously controlled by the same authority all the way to credit allocation. This is necessary to assure a level field and see to it that the debacle of 2007/2009 is not repeated. But George W. Bush opposes regulation of what he calls "free markets,"[3] and for the time being regulatory duties are being let down rather than being strengthened.

This started with the early October 2008 Troubled Assets Relief Act (TARA), which authorized TARP's $700 billion. To get it passed, standards-setters in the US have been arm-twisted into relaxing rules that force banks to mark assets to market. Moreover, the pending implementation of Financial Accounting Standard (FAS) 140, intended to oblige banks to take back into their book off-balance sheet securitizations, has been delayed till 2010 (for the time being).

Not to be left behind, the European Union too watered down the marking to market accounting rule of International Financial Reporting Standards (IFRS) for the stated reasons that its banks should not be at a disadvantage compared with the American ones. On both sides of the Atlantic, politicians have been busy bending even the few rules that stood upright – a move which would prove to be counterproductive, because:

- It will hurt market confidence in the health of bank balance sheets, not help it, and

- It will push further away the day of a reboot of lending, by reducing transparency and increasing existing suspicions that banks lie about their assets and liabilities.

True enough, on 15 October 2008 Ben Bernanke, the Fed chairman, proposed a macroprudential regulatory system that takes into account the way bubbles are formed. That's good. Analysts interpreted it as a first indication that, through a change of policy, the Fed will be willing to diffuse developing financial bubbles. But this is still an idea, and it only addresses part of the necessary measures.

In conclusion, the scale and speed of downwards market pressure is so intense and unpredictable, that by the time the reader looks at this text conditions may have changed substantially from the time of writing. Unchecked, the current situation could continue into a deeper and deeper nose-dive by both the markets and, even more ominous, the real economy.

There is something of a perfect storm in the financial industry's meltdown, created when arguably the worst president in the history of the United States,[4] a Federal Reserve chairman renowned for hubris and monetary policy mistakes in the 18 long years of his tenure, and Wall Street's unprecedented excesses met at the pinnacle of power.

Notes

1   The Mismanagement of Credit Risk

1. *The Economist*, 23 February 2008.
2. ECB, *Financial Stability Review*, December 2007.
3. *Financial Times*, 4 February 2008.
4. *The Economist*, 16 February 2008.
5. In the US, the economy became a casualty with the Greenspan years because of his policy of attacking one problem at a time, while leaning towards the markets. In contrast, the European Epilog Central Bank has a balanced approach towards economic stability, avoidance of inflation, and economic growth.
6. D.N. Chorafas, *Rocket Scientists in Banking*. Lafferty Publications. London and Dublin, 1995.
7. Borrowed from swaps deals, the notional principal amount is specified by the contractual obligations, and is used as the reference on which profits and losses will be calculated.
8. Over-the-counter transactions are bank-to-bank (more precisely trader-to-trader) commitments, which do not transit through an established exchange. Therefore, they are very difficult to control and mark-to-market; most often the OTC instrument has no market.
9. *The Economist*, 19 April 2008. The same article also stated that at end 2007 CDSs exposure (section 5 of this chapter) stood at $62 trillion.
10. Bernard M. Baruch, *Baruch: My Own Story*. Henry Holt, New York, 1957.
11. Warren Buffett, "Avoiding a Megacatastrophe," *Fortune*, 12 March 2003.
12. Originally invented by Thales, one of the sages of antiquity, an option is an agreement between a buyer and a seller that, when exercised, gives the former the right but not the obligation to require the option writer to perform certain specific financial duties. Futures are current commitments that can be exercised, as th*eir* name implies, in the future. They are traded in exchanges. Forwards are like futures but they are not traded in exchanges. They are essentially customized bilateral agreements that have no active market. A standard swap involves period receipt of a predetermined fixed amount, and corresponding period payment of the spot value of a unit of the reference asset. Swaps usually involve two parties that enter into an agreement that, for a certain period, they will exchange regular payments; for instance, swapping floating-rate interest for fixed-rate interest.
13. D.N. Chorafas, *An Introduction to Derivative Financial Instruments*. McGraw-Hill, New York, 2008.
14. A CDO is a structured financial instrument which, with issuance of rated debt securities (tranches) based on a pool of loans or other debt, funds the purchase of an asset. It is the most complex and opaque instrument to have become mainstream.

15. *The Economist*, 9 August 2008.
16. On 27 February 2008, a Reuters report indicated that Norway's StatoilHydro (the national oil firm) posted a loss of Kr800 million, after tax in derivatives transactions, for 2007.
17. Statistics from *The Economist*, 1 September 2007.
18. D.N. Chorafas, *Alternative Investments and the Mismanagement of Risk*. Palgrave Macmillan, London, 2003.
19. Deutsche Bank insists that all the risks were spelt out in its marketing materials. It is wise to wait for the judge's decision.
20. Exposure to CDSs stood at $50 trillion, according to a late February 2008 report by New York money managers. But on 19 April 2008, *The Economist* estimated it at $62 trillion as of end 2007.
21. Basel Committee, *Liquidity Risk: Management and Supervisory Challenges*. BIS, Basel, February 2008.
22. *Executive Information Report (EIR)*, 25 January 2008.
23. Notice that CDS losses come over and above the subprimes losses, which on 9 April 2008 the chief economist of the IMF estimated at $1 trillion – or, about four times the losses incurred up to that date by the banking industry.
24. Responsible for the stock market bubble in 2000, and hefty buildup of the subprimes bubble.
25. A writedown and a credit loss are not the same. Investment banks and other financial organizations mark-to-market their assets, whether these are loans, securities, CDOs or something else. They write them down when values decline. Credit losses are charge-offs for loans.
26. *Financial Times*, 8 February 2008.
27. In mid April 2008 the Bank of England also made available to the banking industry £50 billion against which they could deposit worthless mortgages and mortgage bonds taking instead valuable British government bonds.
28. *Wall Street Journal*, 1 February 2008.
29. The other side of the coin is that, since the 1990s, complex structured finance deals have been made possible because insurers, who act as third parties, have shouldered some part of the credit risk that others could or would not take.
30. With the help of Citigroup and Dresdner Bank.
31. The bank or other institution that gave a loan, and buys an insurance of sorts that it will get back its money if the borrower defaults, is the protection buyer.
32. A payment which will come into definite exercise only on occurrence of some event, such as bankruptcy, credit downgrading, or other well-established reason, is known as a contingent payment.
33. A bank, insurance company, hedge fund, or other entity providing against a fee a guarantee that the protection buyer will be reimbursed in case of its borrower's default or other specific credit event, is the protection seller.
34. The amount loaned to a borrower is always subject to credit risk (and, depending on the contract also to market risk): credits may be secured (by collateral) or unsecured; the borrower may default; be downgraded; or be subject to a leveraged buyout; or its collateral may turn to ashes (as with subprimes). All these are examples of credit events.

35. Whether we talk of loans, trading, or other financial operations, a counter-party is the other party (usually a client) with which the bank engages into a legally binding transaction.
36. The International Swaps and Derivatives Association (ISDA) has produced standardized documentation for these transactions under the ISDA Master Agreement.
37. A binary payoff is all or nothing.
38. D.N. Chorafas, *Economic Capital Allocation with Basle II: Cost and Benefit Analysis*. Butterworth-Heinemann, London and Boston, 2004.

2   The Fed Has Got It Wrong

1. The fourth function of a central bank, to act as the government's commercial bank, is not part of this discussion.
2. In the 1920s, Carlo Ponzi, an Italian-American operating in Boston, was rewarding old depositors with a hefty interest taken out of the money of new depositors till that money, and his luck, ran out.
3. The measures proposed on 31 March 2008 by Treasury Secretary Hank Paulson for supervisory restructuring in the US are way short of what is necessary (see Chapter 10).
4. Above the Western countries' average.
5. *Financial Times*, 24 January 2008.
6. *Business Week*, 11 February 2008.
7. Merrill Lynch, *Investment Strategy Update*, 22 January 2008.
8. D.N. Chorafas, *Economic Capital Allocation with Basle II: Cost and Benefit Analysis*. Butterworth-Heinemann. London and Boston, 2004.
9. European Central Bank, *Financial Stability Review*, December 2007.
10. A similar list exists for British, American and Japanese LCBDs.
11. The Securities and Exchange Commission is conducting more than twenty investigations, including one into the arrangements banks entered into with hedge funds that may have been designed to delay or actually hide losses from marking-to-market t*heir* positions.
12. *The Economist*, 22 December 2007.
13. *The Economist*, 2 August 2008.
14. *Executive Information Report (EIR)*, 11 January 2008.
15. Critics have said that the very special care the US government and Federal Reserve have shown for self-wounded big banks but not other companies "too big to fail" has been a bias toward certain firms and markets.
16. *The Economist*, 23 February 2008.
17. *Financial Times*, 17/18 May 2008.
18. *The Economist*, 14 June 2008.

3   The Globalization of Credit Risk

1. *Financial Times*, 6 February 2008.
2. *The Economist*, 3 May 2003.
3. They may also be preferred stocks and student loans.
4. The 7, 14, 28, and 35 days are the intervals more frequently used.
5. But by 2008 it fell to $200 billion.

6. *The Economist*, 9 August 2008.
7. *Bloomberg News*, 11 August 2008.
8. *Financial Times*, 27 February 2007.
9. Merrill Lynch, *Investors' Strategic Update*, 19 February 2008.
10. European Central Bank, *Monthly Bulletin*, January 2008. China is in 5th position after the US, South Korea, Japan, and Germany. India, by contrast, is in 24th position behind Mexico, Argentina, and Turkey

4 Earthquake in the Subprime Mortgage Market

1. D.N. Chorafas, *Reliable Financial Reporting and Internal Control: A Global Implementation Guide*. Wiley, New York, 2000; D.N. Chorafas, Implementing and Auditing the Internal Control System. Macmillan, London, 2001.
2. In lending jargon, a prime borrower is one of high creditworthiness justifying a reasonably low interest rate. Practice has seen to it that this term has been extended to cover nearly all qualifying borrowers. Subprime refers to borrowers who do not qualify under proper credit terms.
3. *Executive Information Report* (*EIR*), 9 November 2007.
4. *Executive Information Report* (*EIR*), 23 November 2007.
5. On 1 March 2008, Goldman Sachs said banks may face an additional $60 billion in writedowns.
6. People, and most particularly bureaucrats, never learn. In 1994, Orange County had lost a *fortune* with "inverse floaters" – another derivative instrument whose risks were unknown territory to its treasurer. In the aftermath, the county had no money to pay its teachers and other civil servants.
7. A borrower's credit rating is an assessment of his ability to pay his obligations.
8. Alt-As stands for "alternative As," meaning A credit rating. The term is a cheat because contrary to a correct credit analysis, the "Alt-A" is based only on usually fake borrowers' declarations about their income.
9. *Financial Times*, 17 October 2007.
10. *Financial Times*, 21 March 2007.
11. *Financial Times*, 17 October 2007.
12. The large Dutch banking and insurance conglomerate.
13. An unsecured loan made to a customer with no job.
14. D.N. Chorafas, *The Management of Bond Investments and Trading of Debt*. Butterworth-Heinemann, London, 2005.
15. William D. Cohan, *The Last Tycoons*. Doubleday, New York, 2007.
16. *Bloomberg News*, 2 April 2007.
17. *The Economist*, 24 March 2007.
18. *Bloomberg News*, 2 April 2007.
19. Bad car loans in the US increased 30 percent in 2007. An article in the French Le Figaro (31 January 2008) suggested the average debt of American car owners is $4,221 above the value of their cars

5 The Industrialization of Credit Risk

1. D.N. Chorafas, *Stress Testing for Risk Control Under Basel II*. Elsevier, Oxford and Boston, 2007.

2. *Executive Information Report (EIR)*, 14 September 2007.
3. Quotation from a personal interview.
4. Sterling Seagrave, *The Soong Dynasty*. Corgi, London, 1996.
5. In fact there is a structured instrument named "airbag" by its designers and vendors; D.N. Chorafas, *Wealth Management: Private Banking, Investment Decisions and Structured Financial Products*. Butterworth-Heinemann, London and Boston, 2005.
6. William D. Cohan, *The Last Tycoons*. Doubleday, New York, 2007.
7. D.N. Chorafas, *After Basel II: Assuring Compliance and Smoothing the Rough Edges*. Lafferty/VRL Publishing, London, 2005.
8. *The Economist*, 30 June 2007.
9. A variable-interest entity (VIE) is a term used by the US Financial Accounting Standards Board in FIN 46 to refer to an entity (the investee) in which the investor holds a controlling interest but is not based on majority of voting rights. This is closely related to the more popular concept of special purpose vehicle (SPV), discussed in section 5 of this chapter, the one practically being a different term for the other.
10. According to bond research firm CreditSights.
11. From here on will be used the more commonly employed SPV rather than VIE.
12. *The Economist*, 18 August 2007.
13. Merrill-Lynch, *Economic Commentary*, 19 November 2007.
14. According to some experts, the danger associated with adjustable rate sub-primes and Alt-As will continue till late 2010.
15. *The Economist*, 1 December 2007.
16. European Central Bank, *Monthly Bulletin*, June 2008.
17. *Executive Information Report (EIR)*, 25 January 2008.
18. *Financial Times*, 6 February 2008.
19. In December 2007 the US trade deficit hit $64 billion, the highest in 14 months and 5 percent over forecast. This cancels the argument that the reason for keeping the dollar at an all-time low is to cut the current account gap.

6   Leveraged Instruments, Their Credit Ratings and Other Unorthodox Practices

1. *The Economist*, 2 August 2008.
2. *Financial Times*, 3 July 2007.
3. *Financial Times*, 19/20 May 2007.
4. D.N. Chorafas, *An Introduction to Derivative Financial Instruments*. McGraw-Hill, New York, 2008.
5. Merrill Lynch, *Global Research Highlights*, 29 June 2007.
6. Ryan cited the fact that hedge funds account for 30 to 60 percent of all trading activity, depending on asset class and instrument. He also pointed out that the surge in liquidity has brought down lending standards, which is a generally held opinion.
7. Merrill Lynch, *European Equity Strategy*, 14 August 2007.
8. Reference made in a personal interview.

9. *Financial Times*, 1 April 2008.
10. In Greek slang, "para" means money. This fits well with the allegory of parachutes, because what the failed CEOs and their underlings are really doing is self-gratification with big money.
11. D.N. Chorafas, *Management Risk: The Bottleneck is at the Top of the Bottle*. Palgrave Macmillan, London, 2004.

7 Northern Rock: a Case Study

1. *The Economist*, 1 December 2007.
2. Which sold 5 percent of its equity to Sovereign Wealth Funds to get cash (this volume, Chapter 4).
3. Advertising the chairman's vacancy in *The Economist*, 19 January 2008, page 19.
4. *The Economist*, 8 December 2008.
5. Deutsche Bundesbank, *Monthly Report*, September 2000.
6. Statistics as of 13 September 2007 by Collins Stuart.
7. The British public will doubtless want to know why the authorities took their eye off the ball.
8. *The Economist*, 20 October 2007.
9. *Executive Information Report (EIR)*, 20 December 2002.
10. Merrill Lynch, *Interest Rate Committee Forecast*, 19 November 2007.
11. *The Economist*, 1 December 2007.

8 Responsibilities of Financial Regulation

1. Merrill Lynch, *Bear Stearns*, January 2008.
2. This happens because banks manipulate the correlation coefficients relating to their exposure. Correlation coefficients used in Basel II are unstable, uncontrollable, and unreliable.
3. In early 2008, Bloomberg television said that using VAR Merrill Lynch calculated its maximum exposure equal to $65 million. Instead, it was $8 billion.
4. The theme of liquidity, its importance and impact on individual banks and the banking industry as a whole, is treated in Chapter 10 – in conjunction with solvency, assets-backed commercial paper (ABCP), and the carry trade. This section addresses itself to liquidity assurance in the banking industry as a new regulatory function.
5. Professor of economics at the University of Leuven; *Financial Times*, 2 November 2007.
6. D.N. Chorafas *Reliable Financial Reporting and Internal Control: A Global Implementation Guide*. Wiley, New York, 2000.
7. The original twelve plus Slovenia, Cyprus, and Malta.
8. Merrill Lynch, *Investment Strategy Update*, 22 January 2008.
9. *Private Banker International*, June 1995.
10. George Soros, *Soros on Soros: Staying Ahead of the Curve*. Wiley, New York, 1995.
11. *Financial Times*, 1 August 1994.
12. Bernard M. Baruch, *Baruch: My Own Story*. Holt, New York, 1957.
13. Merrill Lynch, *European Banks*, 29 October 2007.

14. *Financial Times*, 6 February 2008.
15. *The Economist*, 21 July 2007.
16. http://www.manager-magazin.de/unternehmen/artikel/0,2828,druck
532124,00.html

9   Solvency, Liquidity, Asset-Backed Paper, and the Carry Trade

1. The result of international cooperation among Group of ten banking regulators.
2. *The Economist*, 20 May 2006.
3. American regulators imposed strict capital requirements for all banks in 1984, after Continental Illinois, the country's seventh-biggest bank, lost half its funds overnight. Until then, US big banks had not been subject to minimum capital requirements, in the belief that they could be trusted to manage th*eir* own balance sheets.
4. A monetary policy is "accomodative" when the central bank keeps its rate low, either because of government pressure in order to reduce unemployment and increase consumption or else to give a hand to the banking industry and capital markets, as was done by the Fed in 2007 and 2008.
5. European Central Bank, *Monthly Bulletin*, February 2008.
6. As of mid 2007 there has been a C$115 billion ($110 billion) ABCP market in Canada.
7. Credit Suisse, *Economics/Research Monthly*, 24 April 2007.
8. *Executive Information Report (EIR)*, 2 March 2007.

10   Is There a Remedy for the Problems of Bank Supervision?

1. For instance, relating to controlled leasing entities where the bank itself is the lessee.
2. The exact figure the IMF has projected is $945 billion, and even this is a guestimate.
3. Merrill Lynch, *Investment Strategy*, 17 March 2008.
4. Strauss-Kahn did not forget to add flavor to the banking crisis, declaring himself in favor of bailouts. Issued 8 and 9 April 2008, the IMF's Global Financial Stability Report and its World Economic Outlook support the lie that the global financial crisis was caused by a combination of a US housing crisis and "profound errors in risk management among its leading financial institutions." Of "errors" there was a horde, but they were made willingly – not accidentally. Dominique Strauss-Kahn also suggested that France bails out its banks along the model of the 1990s bailout of Crédit Lyonnais, which is preposterous because as a nationalized bank Crédit Lyonnais was abused by all sorts of politicians during the Mitterand years and finally the French taxpayer paid the bill.
5. *International Herald Tribune*, 14 April 2008.
6. *Executive Information Report (EIR)*, 28 March 2008.
7. *New York Times*, 16 April 2008.
8. *Executive Information Report (EIR)*, 7 March 2008.

9. *Bloomberg News*, 6 May 2008.
10. Another of the crazy suggestions is that the housing deflation should be counted to counterbalance inflation in energy and commodity prices. But if house prices rise, then this should not be counted as inflation.
11. *The Economist*, 5 April 2008.
12. *Financial Times*, 1 April 2008.
13. *Executive Information Report (EIR)*, 11 April 2008.
14. http:www.bloomberg.com/apps/news 08/04/2008
15. In 1998 when I made a study in which OTS participated there were 1100 thrifts. Their number has shrunk significantly in 10 years.
16. And the loans will be for 28 days instead of just overnight.

Epilog

1. Which means a 9 percent cost of insuring the bank's debt against default.
2. The announced price was 21 cents to the dollar, but Lone Star asked and obtained from Merrill a loan for 75 percent of the amount due, which practically replaced one credit risk with another.
3. Which are certainly not "free," since governments are hand-feeding them with lavish amounts of money and take positions in big banks, effectively nationalizing them.
4. Whose 8-year watch over the *fortunes* of America Maureen Dowd, of the *New York Times*, has named "The Reign of Error."

Index